The Reader's D

GOOD
BEACH
GUIDE
1995

with Ordnance Survey Maps

COMPILED BY THE
MARINE
CONSERVATION SOCIETY

with a foreword by
Jonathon Porritt

David & Charles
A Reader's Digest company

Acknowledgements
The information from which this guide has been compiled was supplied by the National
Rivers Authorities of England and Wales, the River Purification Boards of Scotland, the
Department of the Environment for Northern Ireland, the Governments of Jersey, Guernsey
and the Isle of Man, the private water service companies, the Water and Sewerage sections of
the Regional Councils of Scotland, Environmental Health Offices, Tourism Offices, the
National Trust, and data from the Reader's Digest Beachwatch survey which was co-ordinated
by the Marine Conservation Society.

All information received up until 1 January 1995 has been included in this guide. The Marine
Conservation Society and David & Charles take no responsibility for changes occurring after
compilation of the work.

The Editors would like to thank all those who provided information, Reader's Digest for
sponsoring the publication and the staff and volunteers of the Marine Conservation Society
for support and assistance.
Cait Loretto, Maggie Dowle, Marine Conservation Society

Picture Credits
Paul Glendell p6, 14, 38, 39, 40, 44: Chris Warren p9, 186, 188, 191, 192, 196, 198: Paul Watts
p16, 20, 22, 24, 26, 28, 34: Kerrier District Council p30, 32 (David Hastilow): Restormel
Borough Council p36: South Hams District Council p42, 46: Tim Cuff/Apex p48: English
Riviera Tourist Board p50: Bob Croxford p52, 54: Bill Foster/MCS p56: Poole Tourism p58:
Tourism Services, Poole p60: Bournemouth Tourism p62, 65: Sarah Wellon/MCS p67: Roland
Kemp p87, 88: Tim Badman p80: Havant Borough Council p78, 82: Ian McGowan p84: Swale
Council p90: Tendring District Council p92: Alan Blair p94, 98, 108, 116: Dawn Runnals p97:
Countryside Commission p106: East Lindsey District Council p110: Northumberland District
Council p112: Alnwick District Council p114: Sue Gubbay/MCS p125: Cait Loretto/MCS p129:
R Jarman p130: East Lothian District Council p133, 134, 137: STB/Still Moving Picture Co
p138, 154: Abbeyford Caravans p140: St Andrews and NE Fife Tourist Board p142: Robert
Walker/Still Moving Picture Co p146: Wade Cooper/Still Moving Picture Co p148: Balmedie
Country Park p150: Banff and Buchan District Council p152: Duncan I McEwan p156: Wales
Tourist Board p166, 168, 180, 182, 185: Turtle/Cyngor Dosbarth Dwyfor p170, 172, 174: Celtic
Picture Library p176, 179: Mike Williams p206: Northern Ireland Tourist Board p208, 210, 212,
214, 217, 218: Peter McMahon p223, 225, 230, 232, 234: Guernsey Tourist Board p226, 229:
Jersey Tourism p236, 238, 240, 241, 242, 244: Ethel Davies p243.

A David & Charles Book
Copyright text © Marine Conservation Society, 1995
Maps reproduced from Ordnance Survey Landranger 1:50,000 series with the permission of
Her Majesty's Stationery Office © Crown Copyright, Permit No 768 – Northern Ireland
First published 1995

The Marine Conservation Society has asserted its right to be identified as author of this work
in accordance with the Copyright, Designs and Patents Act 1988.

A catalogue record for this book is available from the British Library.

ISBN 0 7153 0341 4 Paperback
ISBN 0 7153 0362 7 Hardback

Printed by Butler & Tanner Ltd, Frome
for David & Charles
Brunel House, Newton Abbot, Devon

FOREWORD

BEFORE YOU GO TO THE BEACH, THINK. WHAT ARE YOU GOING TO FIND THERE? SUN, SEA AND SAND? OR SOMETHING ELSE?

•

It is an unfortunate fact of life that for many of us the average trip to the seaside involves unpleasant encounters with sewage, sewage-related debris and sometimes sickness – not the best ingredients for a nice day at the beach.

This is the second year that I have written the foreword for *The Reader's Digest Good Beach Guide*, compiled by the Marine Conservation Society, and since the first edition I'm happy to report that there has been a great deal of action on the beaches front. Legislation is being amended, the water companies are acting (if slowly) to treat sewage, and the pressure to clean up our dirty coast is increasing all the time. The issues surrounding water quality and beaches are controversial and confusing. It is not uncommon to hear conflicting statements in the same news item, so it is hardly surprising that a lot of people have ended up either confused or resigned. And that's where *The Good Beach Guide* comes in: it is still the best source of clear, impartial information about the beaches around England, Northern Ireland, Scotland, Wales, the Channel Islands and the Isle of Man. It tells you everything you need to know about water quality and sewage discharge, giving you the ability to choose where to go and whether to bathe when you get there. For once you know what a beach and its bathing water is like, you can take steps to avoid the sewage that is still such a huge problem around our coast.

Consumer pressure has the power to change things. And change is still absolutely crucial. We have had to put up with sewage in the water and sanitary towels and condoms on our beaches for far too long. We do have good beaches in this country and we should sing their praises. But we also have some appalling stretches of coast that desperately need cleaning up. A pretty looking beach can have a dark side to its nature, with raw sewage lurking at the water line. It is difficult to believe, but sadly true, that in the UK around 300 million gallons of raw and practically raw sewage is pumped into the sea each day.

Using the information given here we can vote with our feet, go to the good beaches and shun the bad. Year by year, people are wising up to these things. Directors of tourism know they are in trouble if their beach gets a lousy write-up, and in clover if it is given the all-clear. Hoteliers depend in part on having a clean and safe beach to direct people to. A dirty beach is a drain on the local economy.

The Marine Conservation Society has compiled the *Guide* to make sure that you, the consumer, have better, happier and, hopefully, healthier holidays than you might otherwise have had. Please help them too by telling them about the beaches you visit and supporting them in their campaigns to increase the pressure on the water companies and politicians. This is no time to be dragging our feet on cleaning up a disgraceful legacy of neglect and dereliction. We must do everything we can to ensure that improvements already underway are pushed through as fast as possible to protect the interests of future generations.

Jonathan Porritt

1:50 000 Landranger Series Map
CONVENTIONAL SIGNS

Ordnance Survey

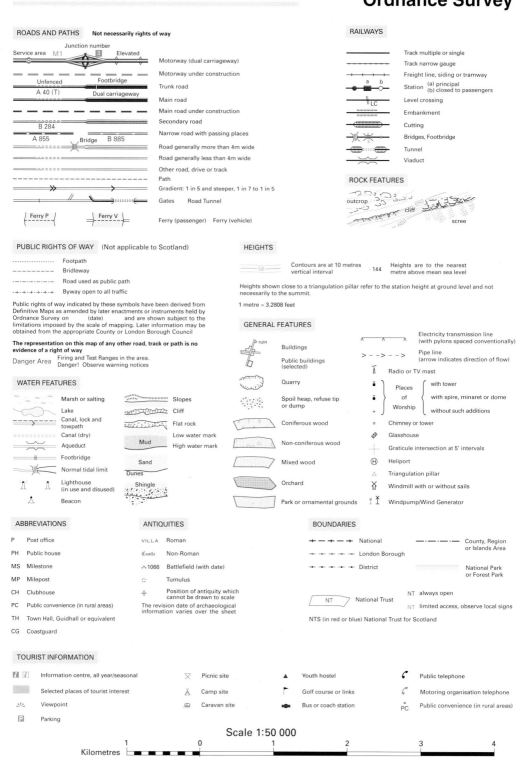

ROADS AND PATHS — Not necessarily rights of way

	Motorway (dual carriageway)
	Motorway under construction
	Trunk road
	Main road
	Main road under construction
	Secondary road
	Narrow road with passing places
	Road generally more than 4m wide
	Road generally less than 4m wide
	Other road, drive or track
	Path
	Gradient: 1 in 5 and steeper, 1 in 7 to 1 in 5
	Gates Road Tunnel
	Ferry (passenger) Ferry (vehicle)

Service area   M1   Junction number   3   Elevated
Unfenced   Footbridge
A 40 (T)   Dual carriageway
B 284
A 855   Bridge   B 885
Ferry P   Ferry V

PUBLIC RIGHTS OF WAY   (Not applicable to Scotland)

....	Footpath
– – – – –	Bridleway
–·–·–·–	Road used as public path
–+–+–+–	Byway open to all traffic

Public rights of way indicated by these symbols have been derived from Definitive Maps as amended by later enactments or instruments held by Ordnance Survey on   (date)   and are shown subject to the limitations imposed by the scale of mapping. Later information may be obtained from the appropriate County or London Borough Council

The representation on this map of any other road, track or path is no evidence of a right of way

Danger Area   Firing and Test Ranges in the area. Danger! Observe warning notices

WATER FEATURES

	Marsh or salting		Slopes
	Lake		Cliff
	Canal, lock and towpath		Flat rock
	Canal (dry)		Low water mark
	Aqueduct	Mud	High water mark
	Footbridge	Sand	
	Normal tidal limit	Dunes	
	Lighthouse (in use and disused)	Shingle	
	Beacon		

RAILWAYS

	Track multiple or single
	Track narrow gauge
	Freight line, siding or tramway
a b	Station (a) principal (b) closed to passengers
LC	Level crossing
	Embankment
	Cutting
	Bridges, Footbridge
	Tunnel
	Viaduct

ROCK FEATURES

outcrop   cliff   scree
600   650

HEIGHTS

——50——	Contours are at 10 metres vertical interval
·144	Heights are to the nearest metre above mean sea level

Heights shown close to a triangulation pillar refer to the station height at ground level and not necessarily to the summit.

1 metre = 3.2808 feet

GENERAL FEATURES

ruin	Buildings		Electricity transmission line (with pylons spaced conventionally)
	Public buildings (selected)	> – –> – –>	Pipe line (arrow indicates direction of flow)
	Quarry		Radio or TV mast
	Spoil heap, refuse tip or dump		Places of Worship { with tower / with spire, minaret or dome / without such additions }
	Coniferous wood	○	Chimney or tower
	Non-coniferous wood		Glasshouse
	Mixed wood		Graticule intersection at 5' intervals
	Orchard	Ⓗ	Heliport
	Park or ornamental grounds	△	Triangulation pillar
			Windmill with or without sails
			Windpump/Wind Generator

ABBREVIATIONS

P	Post office
PH	Public house
MS	Milestone
MP	Milepost
CH	Clubhouse
PC	Public convenience (in rural areas)
TH	Town Hall, Guildhall or equivalent
CG	Coastguard

ANTIQUITIES

VILLA	Roman
Castle	Non-Roman
⚔1066	Battlefield (with date)
⁘	Tumulus
+	Position of antiquity which cannot be drawn to scale

The revision date of archaeological information varies over the sheet

BOUNDARIES

–+– – +– +	National
–·+·–·+·–	London Borough
–+– +– +–	District
	County, Region or Islands Area
	National Park or Forest Park

NT   National Trust   NT always open
NT limited access, observe local signs
NTS (in red or blue) National Trust for Scotland

TOURIST INFORMATION

	Information centre, all year/seasonal		Picnic site
	Selected places of tourist interest		Camp site
	Viewpoint		Caravan site
	Parking		

▲	Youth hostel		Public telephone
	Golf course or links		Motoring organisation telephone
	Bus or coach station	PC	Public convenience (in rural areas)

Scale 1:50 000

Kilometres   1   0   1   2   3   4

Statute miles   1   0   1   2

CONTENTS

INTRODUCTION

Britain is an island nation with a strong maritime tradition. With around 15,000 kilometres of coastline to choose from, ranging from dramatic granite cliffs to seemingly endless salt marshes, and relatively easy access – nowhere in the country is more than 200 kilometres from the sea – most of us have visited the coast at one time or another. All too often we imagine the seas around Britain as lifeless and forbidding, when the reality is very different. Our coastal waters contain as rich and diverse an array of marine life as one could wish to find; although cold, they are highly productive, supporting populations of everything from jewel anemones to basking sharks and dolphins. Beyond the indigenous wildlife, the seabirds and grey seals, the British coast is of international importance for overwintering and migrating birds. It is our responsibility to treat our coast and coastal waters with the respect they deserve, and to ensure we keep the marine environment fit for wildlife and for our own use.

And yet the seas around our coasts are under constant pressure. Each day hundreds of millions of gallons of raw or partially treated sewage are pumped into the sea, wreaking havoc on marine life, causing us to fall ill and reducing some of our finest stretches of coast to an aesthetically revolting mess. Much of this sewage – which includes not just human waste but everything else that gets flushed down the toilet: sanitary protection, condoms and all manner of bathroom junk – ends up on our beaches. As a result, the shores around Britain are increasingly littered with sewage-derived rubbish. A survey conducted by the National Rivers Authority in the south-west of England showed that out of 202 beaches only eight were judged to be free of sewage-related debris and many were found to be objectionable. In 1993 in Rossall the Reader's Digest Beachwatch found 1,389 separate items of sewage-derived rubbish along a 300-metre stretch of beach. Littering of this sort on such a huge scale is visually repulsive but it is more than just an aesthetic problem. Plastic is often harmful to wildlife: many seabirds are known to ingest it, mistaking it for food. The scale of the problem is graphically demonstrated by the fact that 80 per cent of the nests on Grassholm, the third largest gannet colony in the world, contain plastic in one form or another.

The quality of the beaches and bathing waters around our coasts has been the subject of controversy and heated debate for the past four decades. An initial problem was the lack of an independent and impartial source of information on water purity. This was addressed by the publication of the first Golden List of Beaches, compiled by Tony and Daphne Wakefield following the death of their daughter, Caroline, from polio which they believe she contracted from swimming in sewage-contaminated water. The Wakefields established the Coastal Anti-Pollution League (CAPL) to campaign against the disposal of raw sewage near bathing waters. In the 1980s CAPL merged with the Marine Conservation Society, an environmental organisation working exclusively to safeguard the marine environment. Over the years MCS has continued and expanded the work of CAPL and has campaigned for improvements in the treatment of our coast and coastal waters, particularly with regard to sewage pollution. This guide is the eighth produced by the Marine Conservation Society and is directly descended from the very first Golden List of Beaches.

Thurlestone North beach (p. 40) was a favourite haunt of the artist JMW Turner.

There is much conflicting information about the state of British beaches. Their eligibility for a whole range of different awards and accolades, many of which mean different things, only adds to the confusion. Two of these, the European Blue Flag and the Seaside Award (a yellow and blue flag), are regularly given to beaches with widely differing water quality. Beaches flying the European Blue Flag and the Premier Seaside Award will have met the higher Guideline standards of the EC Bathing Water Directive for the previous bathing season (see page 11 for an explanation of the standards) and should therefore have reasonable quality bathing water. But the Standard Seaside Award can be awarded to areas with far lower water quality, in some cases the bare legal minimum allowed by the EC Bathing Water Directive. A beach flying the Standard Seaside Award may be well managed and have good facilities; the water quality, however, is very likely to be sub-standard. MCS would like to see a mandatory water-quality factor introduced into the award of flags of every colour, for as long as beaches whose water quality is below par are awarded flags there will be continuing confusion about their meaning. After all, is not the cleanliness of the water the most important consideration when visiting a beach?

Precisely because there is so much conflicting and ambiguous information around, it is essential to have an independent and impartial source of information about the state of the water at our beaches. That is what this book aims to provide. It was compiled by the Marine Conservation Society, who for the past eight years have produced the definitive guide to the quality of bathing water in Britain, to give a clear guide to the state of our beaches and to allow you, the reader, to make an informed choice about where – and whether – to bathe. Britain has thousands of beaches and over 900 of them are included and summarized here. The very best are recommended and featured in detail with photographs and maps of the area.

We all have our own ideas about what makes a 'good' beach; the prime criterion for a beach to be featured here, however, is water quality. If you are wondering why your favourite beach is not included in the *Guide*, the answer may be that the water quality is not monitored, or that monitoring has shown that the quality of the sea-water is not satisfactory. Remember: even a beach that looks superficially immaculate may have dangerously high levels of bacteria and viruses in the water due to sewage contamination.

Although it is the prime reason this book was written, sewage is not the only problem to plague our coastline. It is also under pressure from construction, industry and fishing. Fortunately, some areas do enjoy a degree of protection. Britain has around 40 stretches of Heritage Coast, unspoilt areas with a high scenic value. Although this is a definition rather than a statutory designation, specific management plans and policies exist for these sites to ensure their survival. There are many Areas of Outstanding Natural Beauty in coastal locations; these too are protected through management plans or through special policies in local planning. In addition there are the statutory designations; numerous coastal areas have been identified as Sites of Special Scientific Interest because of their flora, fauna or landscape features. These are managed through agreements with the nature conservation agencies of England, Scotland and Wales which permit the restriction of potentially damaging operations.

Many nature reserves have coastal sections and through management to protect the environment the coast, too, is shielded. The National Trust, through a project called Enterprise Neptune, owns nearly one thousand kilometres of coastline in England and Wales. Many of the beaches featured in the *Guide* are in the care or under direct management of the Trust; at others, the land adjoining the beach is owned by the Trust and access for visitors has been improved. The Trust also manages conservation interests such as sand dune restoration or cliff grazing schemes to maintain habitats for coastal birds and other species.

The sites and reserves described are for the protection and management of land and coastal land. There is, in contrast, very little protection for the environment below the surface of the water. Britain has only two statutory Marine Nature Reserves, in the waters around Lundy and Skomer. In both cases the total area of protected marine environment is very small. These reserves were designated because they are in known areas of special interest, but much more of the marine environment deserves the same level of protection. There are moves afoot to shield other marine environments, around the Menai Straits in Wales and at Strangford Lough in Northern Ireland. But considering that the legislation for the establishment of these areas was put forward in 1981 with as yet little tangible result, the future for the underwater environment does not seem very bright. Part of the problem stems from our difficulty in relating to the sea and in understanding that such a vast resource is not infinite. The oceans may be huge but it is the coastal areas and the continental shelves that are the most productive and the most at risk. We can exploit and use the sea, but whether the present scale of exploitation is sustainable is highly doubtful. The marine environment needs management and protection as much as any site on land. Just because we cannot see the effects we are having under the surface doesn't mean that all is well. Current trawling pressure in the North Sea has been likened in its effect to ploughing a field seven times a year.

Not many of us get the chance to explore the sea bed, but wherever we go we should be thoughtful and responsible when exploring the coast. Visitor pressure can disrupt shore life and lead to the erosion of fragile ecosystems. When at the seaside, follow the Marine Conservation Society's Seashore Code: be careful at the coast, always keep an eye on the tide and be aware that the sea can be a very hostile environment. Show respect for the coast: don't drop litter, drive on the roads, not on the beaches and try to avoid disturbing the wildlife.

Take nothing but photos, leave nothing but footprints, waste nothing but time.

The Norman castle at Manorbier has splendid views to the bay and beyond.

HOW TO USE THE GUIDE

This chapter explains exactly how to use *The Reader's Digest Good Beach Guide*. It includes a key to the water quality rating system used in the *Guide* and an explanation of the summary information presented in the tables. It will enable you to sit down and plan your holiday around one of the featured beaches, or possibly one of the listed beaches with top-rated water quality and an adequate level of sewage treatment (a full explanation of sewage treatment and its implications for your health is given on pages 246-8). If you have already chosen your holiday destination, the *Guide* will tell you whether or not it is safe to swim when you get there.

Recommended Beaches and Summary Listings

The *Guide* is divided into eight regional chapters: the South-West, the South-East, the East Coast, the North-West and the Isle of Man, Scotland, Wales, Northern Ireland and the Channel Islands. Each regional chapter lists all the beaches identified under the EC Bathing Water Directive (see below) and many non-identified beaches – nearly 900 in total. All but one of these regions have beaches that we are happy to recommend, with a high standard of water quality and a low probability of being contaminated with sewage, and these beaches are fully featured with photographs, maps and a full dossier of useful information. The summary listings of beaches that do not, for one reason or another, merit recommended status – because of unsatisfactory water quality, a litter problem, or perhaps simply due to lack of adequate information – give a water quality rating for each beach, sewage outfall details and explanatory notes, all of which will enable you to decide for yourself whether you want to visit these beaches or not.

The EC Bathing Water Directive (76/160/EEC)

The *Guide* makes no apology for placing maximum emphasis on water quality: as the most important feature of any beach, it is absolutely essential that the seawater reaches a certain standard. The basic standard is that laid down by the European Commission in the EC Bathing Water Directive (76/160/EEC); since the Directive does not have a scientific base, however, the microbiological standards set are rather arbitrary. For this reason, the Marine Conservation Society insists that beaches must reach a significantly higher standard, based on rigorous scientific research, before they are featured and recommended in the *Guide*.

At present around 450 bathing waters have been identified in the UK under the EC Bathing Water Directive. These include all featured beaches, except where noted, and listed beaches indicated by the letters 'EU'. These sites are regularly monitored from May to September by the National Rivers Authority (NRA) in England and Wales, the River Purification Boards (RPB) in Scotland, and the Department of the Environment in Northern Ireland. Samples of seawater are taken from the identified areas at regular intervals over the official bathing season; these samples are analysed for the presence of coliform bacteria, faecal coliform bacteria and faecal streptococcus bacteria, and the counts are recorded. All of these bacteria are found in the human gut and are therefore useful indicator species for sewage pollution. Some are better indicators than others: coliform bacteria can occur naturally in the environment and may not necessarily originate from a human gut. Faecal streptococcus bacteria, on the other hand, are almost always associated with human sewage, and their presence in a sample is unambiguous. They can also cause illness, especially infections through cuts and wounds. Other disease-causing agents regularly present in sewage include enteric viruses, salmonella and the hepatitis A virus. Although the Directive allows for the monitoring of enteric viruses and salmonella, the Government bases its results only on the coliform and streptococcus counts and we are therefore limited to the use of this data.

The Mandatory Standards and the Guideline Standards

The EC Bathing Water Directive sets out two standards against which water cleanliness is measured: the Mandatory Standards (also known as the Imperative or Minimum Standards) and the Guideline Standards which are twenty times stricter.

The Mandatory Standards are the minimum legal standards that almost all Britain's identified bathing beaches have to reach by the end of 1995, a target that most certainly will not be met. When a beach is declared a pass or fail by the Department of the Environment, it is the Mandatory Standards that are referred to – it should be noted that a pass here is not a claim to be sewage free, merely that the sewage has reached a certain degree of dilution. The Directive stipulates that member states must comply with the Mandatory Standards and should strive to achieve the Guideline Standards.

The European Commission has put forward proposals to amend the Directive and, although they do not go far enough, the amendments represent a considerable tightening of the present standards. The amended Directive is due to come into force at the end of 1995 and is warmly welcomed by the Marine Conservation Society.

The MCS Water Quality Grades

The Marine Conservation Society divides bathing water quality results into five quality grades rather than the rudimentary pass/fail used by the Department of the Environment. A full explanation of the water quality rating system follows. It should be noted that the MCS grade system operates on a cumulative scale: a beach not qualifying for the two dolphins grade cannot qualify for the higher quality three dolphins grade and so on.

---

f - fail
less than 95% pass of the Mandatory Standards

The Department of the Environment regard this as a fail. These beaches are heavily contaminated by sewage. The Marine Conservation Society advises that these waters should not be used for bathing or any other water contact sports.

Vote with your feet – don't swim here. This water is polluted with sewage.

---

one dolphin
95% pass of the Mandatory Standards

The Department of the Environment regard this as a pass of the EC Bathing Water Directive, the minimum legal requirement for bathing beaches. The UK has promised that 95% of bathing beaches will reach at least this 95% level of Mandatory pass by 1995. These waters are, however, almost certainly contaminated by sewage and carry a significant health risk according to recent research carried out by the Water Research Centre.*

Vote with your feet – this water achieves only the bare minimum legal requirements.

---

two dolphins
100% pass of Mandatory Standards

Although consistently passing the Mandatory Standards, research suggests that water of this quality may still place your health at risk. The Marine Conservation Society cannot recommend such beaches.

These standards are not sufficiently high – keep out of the water.

---

three dolphins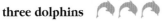
100% pass of Mandatory Standards
80% pass of Guideline Coliform Standards

This is the minimum standard that a beach's bathing water must reach for us to recommend it.

Come on in! The water's lovely.

---

four dolphins
100% pass of Mandatory Standards
80% pass of Guideline Coliform Standards
90% pass of Guideline Faecal Streptococcus Standards

These beaches have the lowest bacterial counts in the country and should be free from sewage.

These should be the cleanest bathing waters in the UK.

Track Record

Most beaches, both featured and those in the summary listings, include a symbol showing their record of pass or failure of the Mandatory Standards over the preceding years. This is particularly useful for pinpointing those that have either failed or passed consistently. A pass is indicated by a tick, a fail by a cross; for example, ☒☑☑ would indicate that the beach had passed in 1994 and 1993, failed in 1992 and that no data was available before then. Featured beaches not identified under the EC Bathing Water Directive are also noted under this heading.

Sewage Discharges and Sewage Treatment

Under the column heading Sewage Outlet, the summary listings give detailed information on the number of sewage outlets in the area, the degree of treatment the sewage has undergone prior to discharge, the number of people served by the out-

---

* It should be noted that some beaches which have met this standard may be placed in the Guideline pass category, since the Department of the Environment accepts 95% compliance with the Mandatory Standards coupled with the requirements for a Guideline pass as adequate for an overall Guideline pass. The Marine Conservation Society believes that 95% compliance with the Mandatory Standards is inadequate, and will not recommend a beach in *The Reader's Digest Good Beach Guide* if it has failed the Mandatory Standards at any time over the bathing season.

let and where the discharge point is relative to low water mean (all distances are given in metres unless otherwise stated). For example, the entry: 1, screened and disinfected, 75,000, 100 below LWM – means one outlet serving 75,000 people discharges screened and disinfected sewage 100 metres below the low water mark. This level of detail is available nowhere else and, taken in conjunction with the water quality grade and the track record, gives you the fullest possible information about a given beach, enabling you to make an informed choice about where and whether to bathe.

Naturist Beaches

There are a growing number of specialist naturist beaches in Britain. Some people may not wish to visit a naturist beach and these areas should be clearly signposted. If you wish to find out more about naturism contact the Central Council for British Naturism (see appendix).

Safety at the Seaside

Please take care at the beach. We have tried as far as possible to note those areas where it is dangerous to bathe, but remember that the sea is a highly variable environment which under certain conditions can be extremely hostile. There are some basic rules to follow when bathing at the seaside to minimise the possibility of getting into trouble in the water. Always listen to lifeguards, follow their advice and make sure that you understand the system of safety flags; do not swim when the sea is rough or where there are known currents or riptides; swim parallel to the shore rather than out to sea; don't swim immediately after a meal and never after drinking alcohol. If you see someone else in trouble, fetch the lifeguards or contact the coastguard (999) – do not attempt to rescue them yourself. Further information on lifesaving and training schemes is available from the Royal Life Saving Society whose address is given in the appendix.

Maps

All mapping in the *Guide* is from the Ordnance Survey Landranger 1:50,000 series and is reproduced at this scale. Each centimetre square represents 2 kilometres.

Abbreviations

The following abbreviations are used throughout the *Guide*:
LWM – low water mark
HWM – high water mark
LSO – long sea outfall (see page 247)
UV – ultraviolet

The South-West is home to many of Britain's cleanest beaches, such as this one at Challaborough.

South-West England

COVERING THE COAST FROM CLEVEDON NEAR BRISTOL TO BOURNEMOUTH IN DORSET, AND INCLUDING THE ISLE OF WIGHT, THIS SECTION ENCOMPASSES SOME OF THE BEST BEACHES IN THE COUNTRY AND SOME OF THE FOREMOST RESORTS. THE COASTAL SCENERY RANGES FROM THE HEAVILY INDUSTRIALISED AREAS AROUND THE SEVERN ESTUARY TO THE RUGGED BEAUTY OF THE NORTH CORNISH COAST.

•

There are hundreds of kilometres of glorious coastline along the south-west peninsula and the south-west coast has a high number of bathing waters identified under the EC Bathing Water Directive. Long sweeping bays and small secluded coves are separated by rugged headlands. Spectacular rocky cliffs contrast with smooth turf slopes where wild flowers abound. Some of Britain's loveliest unspoilt scenery is to be found along this coast and many of the cleanest beaches and bathing waters are located in the West Country.

The area is not free of problems, however, with various forms of pollution affecting several beaches. Untreated sewage is discharged close inshore and is washed back on to the sands at popular resorts. Both South West Water and Wessex Water have considerable investment programmes to deal with the sewage problems of the region, but there is still a very long way to go and in the immediate future it appears that sewage-related debris is going to be an everyday obstacle faced by the surfers at Newquay. In other areas, the china clay industry has covered once pristine sands with a film of white dust and the Cornish tin mining industry has been responsible for chronic and acute pollution by mine waste; the most notorious incident was in 1992 when the Wheal Jane, a disused tin mine, spewed 10 million gallons of heavily contaminated water into the Carnon River which spread in a brightly coloured toxic plume through the river to the sea.

Congestion builds up in the summer as large numbers of tourists flock to the coast. Long queues of traffic develop on the narrow lanes and the picturesque fishing villages heave with cars. The beaches become crowded and this can lead to environmental damage, with the erosion of paths over dunes and beautiful areas despoiled by thoughtless littering. You can help to minimise the damage by using public transport, or by visiting the area in the spring or autumn. Remember that, out of season, you can have huge expanses of golden sand to yourself.

About 40 kilometres to the south-west of Land's End, in the track of the North Atlantic Drift, lie the Isles of Scilly. This most westerly land of Great Britain comprises an archipelago of some 200 granite islands and rocks separated from each other and the mainland by a shallow sea. The climate is mild with little variation in summer and winter temperatures. Many of the islands are small and devoid of vegetation, but the five largest – St Mary's, St Martin's, Bryher, Tresco and St Agnes – are inhabited and support farming, fishing and tourism industries; they are marvellous places to explore. Visitors to the Isles of Scilly are rewarded by beautiful scenery, shallow seas and a fascinating insight into the islands past. Since no bathing water quality information is available to us we have not featured any individual beaches on the islands.

BUDE – SANDY MOUTH
Cornwall
OS Ref: SS202099

Awide sandy beach backed by a pebble ridge and steep cliffs, Sandy Mouth is a paradise for surfers. Care needs to be taken at high tide, however, as the rocks can make surfing dangerous. The National Trust owns this beach and much of the surrounding area.

Water quality

No sewage is discharged in the vicinity of this beach.

Bathing safety

Swimming is safe, but be aware of rip currents particularly at low tide. Lifeguard cover from May to September.

Litter

Sandy Mouth beach is cleaned daily in the summer.

Access

From Bude take the road to Stibb, turn left and first right again. Access is via some steep steps after a steep loose gravel path.

Parking

Good parking is available nearby.

Toilets

Toilets are available including facilities for disabled visitors.

Food

There is a beach café owned by the National Trust.

Seaside activities

Swimming and surfing.

Wet weather alternatives

There are plenty of wet weather facilities in and around Bude.

Sculpted by wind and weather, jagged pinnacles of rock rise above the sands like primitive pyramids.

Wildlife and walks

The North Cornwall Heritage Coast and Countryside Service operates a programme of guided walks throughout the district during the summer. There are specially devised circular walks in the area and a National Trust leaflet on the Duckpool/Sandy Mouth properties is available. Free information leaflets on wildlife habitats, walking, cycling, and activities within the area are available from the Bude Visitor Centre. The Tamar lakes to the north-east of Bude offer fishing and boats for hire.

Track record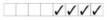

DAYMER BAY
Cornwall
OS Ref: SW928776

This wide sandy beach on the Camel Estuary is backed by sand dunes and a golf course. The water is shallow and ideal for bathing.

Water quality
No sewage is discharged in the vicinity of this beach.

Bathing safety
Swimming is safe.

Litter
The beach is cleaned regularly by the District Council.

Access
Take the Wadebridge to Polzeath road and turn left to Rock, then right for Daymer. Alternatively go to Polzeath and continue up the hill and right for Daymer. Access to the beach is good but does require the use of some steps.

Parking
There is ample parking right next to the beach.

WC Toilets
Toilets available including facilities for disabled visitors.

Food
A beach café opens in season.

Seaside activities
Swimming.

Wet weather alternatives
Information on the many activities can be obtained from the information point at Wadebridge and Polzeath Tourist Information Centre.

Wildlife and walks
There are excellent opportunities for walking and numerous published circular walks. The North Cornwall Heritage Coast and Countryside Service publishes information on wildlife, walking, cycling and other activities, available from Tourist Information Centres throughout the district.

Track record ✓✓✓✓✓✓✓✓

ROCK BEACH
Cornwall
OS Ref: SW927758

Rock lies opposite Padstow on the sandy estuary of the Camel and may be reached from the fishing village by a regular ferry service. A wide expanse of sand at low tide is mostly covered at high water, making this a popular site for launching sailing dinghies and sailboards. The beach is sheltered by Rock Dunes, a Site of Special Scientific Interest.

Water quality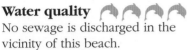
No sewage is discharged in the vicinity of this beach.

Bathing safety
Swimmers should beware of strong river currents. There is no lifeguard cover.

Litter
The beach is cleaned regularly by the District Council.

Access
Take the Wadebridge to Polzeath road, then turn left to Rock. Steps and a ramp lead down to the beach.

Parking
Parking is available in an old quarry, but there are limited spaces and it may be difficult to park in the height of summer.

Public transport
There is a bus service from Wadebridge to Rock.

Toilets
Toilets available including facilities for disabled visitors.

Food
There are a number of shops, pubs and cafés in the area.

Seaside activities
Yachting, windsurfing, boat fishing and water skiing.

Wet weather alternatives
See Daymer Bay opposite.

Wildlife and walks
The Camel Estuary near here is the largest on the north coast of Cornwall and includes tidal mud and grass meadows. This is one of the few sites in the country where white fronted geese winter regularly. The Cornwall Birdwatching and Preservation Society has two hides on the site.

Track record ✗ ✗ ✓ ✓ ✓ ✓ ✓

The old quay at Rock attracts sailing boats and windsurfers throughout the season.

HARLYN BAY
Cornwall
OS Ref: SW877755

Ahorseshoe-shaped, north-facing, sandy beach, half a mile wide and backed by low cliffs, Harlyn is fast becoming a favourite with surfers. The discovery of a large Iron Age cemetery in 1900 made Harlyn Bay famous; the relics unearthed there are now housed in Truro Museum.

Water quality

One outlet serving 4,900 people discharges secondary treated sewage at LWM.

Bathing safety

Generally safe but certain circumstances cause rip currents and it is advisable to be aware of local conditions. Lifeguards cover the beach in summer.

Litter

Cleaned regularly.

Access

On the Padstow to Newquay road, turn right at the signpost for Harlyn just before St Merryn village. There is easy access to the beach.

Parking

Ample space is available in a fee-paying car park.

Public transport

The Western National Bus runs a service here.

Toilets

Toilets are located less than half a kilometre from the beach including facilities for disabled visitors.

Food

There is a shop, café and pub adjacent to the beach.

Seaside activities

Swimming, surfing, with surfboard hire available.

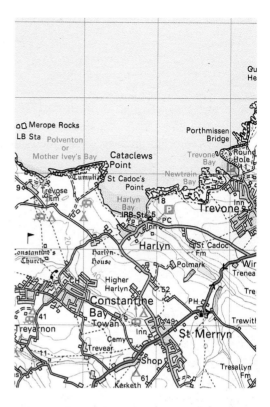

Wet weather alternatives

A museum, a medieval church and other interesting sights can be visited in nearby Padstow.

Wildlife and walks

There are many fine walks on the coastal path, including especially designed circular walks, details of which may be found in 'Coast Lines', a free newspaper for visitors available from all Tourist Information Centres.

Track record ✓✓✓✓✓✓✓✓

A superb sheltered beach with plenty of surf draws summer visitors to Harlyn Bay in their droves.

CONSTANTINE BAY, TREYARNON
Cornwall
OS Ref: SW857746

This wide, sweeping arc of gently shelving soft pale sands, backed by large marram-covered dunes and bounded on either side by low headlands with rocky outcrops stretching seaward, is a breathtaking sight. Few facilities are available at the beach.

Water quality
No sewage is discharged in the vicinity of this beach.

Bathing safety
Bathing is dangerous near the rocks. Lifeguards patrol from Whitsun to August Bank Holiday.

Litter
The beach is cleaned all year round.

Access
Off the B3276 at St Merryn.

Parking
There is space for 200 cars off the B3276 two minutes away from the beach.

Public transport

Nearest rail station is Bodmin Parkway; there are infrequent buses to Constantine Bay.

Toilets

At the entrance to the beach.

Food

There are shops ten minutes' walk from the beach.

Seaside activities

Swimming and surfing.

Wildlife and walks
See Treyarnon Bay opposite.

Track record   ✓✓✓✓✓✓

TREYARNON BAY
Cornwall
OS Ref: SW857740

A wide sandy bay in an Area of Outstanding Natural Beauty, Treyarnon is sometimes overlooked by virtue of its location next to the larger Constantine Bay. Swimming is dangerous near the cliffs and surfing is hazardous at low tide due to exposed rocks.

Water quality

Bathing safety
Swimmers should keep to the centre of the beach where lifeguards patrol from Whitsun to August Bank Holiday. A natural pool in the rocks provides safe swimming at low tide.

Litter
 The beach is cleaned regularly.

Access
Turn off the B3276 through Treyarnon. The Bedruthen steps down to the beach have been restored by the National Trust and open in 1995.

Parking
Car park adjacent to the beach with approximately 150 places.

Toilets
There are toilets near the beach including facilities for disabled visitors.

Food
 Beach shop and hotel.

Seaside activities
 Swimming and surfing. Surf boards are available for hire.

Wildlife and walks
Treyarnon is on the North Cornwall Coast Path which has some spectacular views to Trevose Head in the north and south towards Newquay. Nearer the shoreline many rock pools are exposed at low tide and these provide a fascinating close-up of local marine life.

Track record ✓✓✓✓✓✓✓

A gently shelving sandy beach makes Constantine popular with swimmers; safe areas are marked by flags.

THE TOWANS, HAYLE, ST IVES
Cornwall
OS Ref: SW563395

To the west of St Ives lies a magnificent necklace of golden beaches, backed by high dunes and some rocky outcrops. The approach to the beach at Hayle is uninspiring, as much development has taken place on the landward side of the dunes. The beach, however, is pristine: five kilometres of pale rippled sands fringed with dunes and fingers of rock. Dogs are banned from Easter to 1 October.

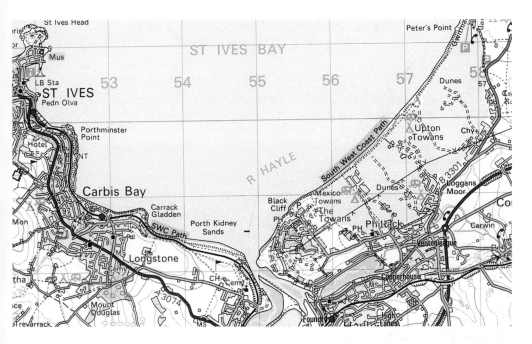

Water quality

No sewage is discharged in the vicinity of this beach.

Bathing safety

Currents around the river mouth mean bathing is dangerous. Lifeguards patrol in summer.

Litter

The beach is cleaned regularly.

Access

The beach is signposted from the A30 through Hayle. Follow the road to the car parks behind the dunes and the sands are no more than five minutes' walk away.

Parking

Car parks behind the dunes have ample spaces.

The River Hayle separates The Towans from Porth Kidney Sands, with St Ives in the background.

Public transport

The nearest rail station is at Hayle; an hourly bus service goes to The Towans in the summer.

Toilets

At the car parks.

Food

There is a beach shop and cafés at the car parks.

Seaside activities

Swimming and surfing; surfboards are available for hire.

Wet weather alternative

Hayle Paradise Park.

Wildlife and walks

Following the beach north brings you to the rocky shore by Godrevy Point from where the coast path leads along the cliffs to Navax Point affording splendid views across St Ives Bay.

Track record ☐☐☐☐ ✓✓✓✓

25

WHITESAND BAY, SENNEN COVE
Cornwall
OS Ref: SW360270

On the rugged Land's End peninsula the splendid sweep of Whitesand Bay is in sharp contrast to the many rocky coves that indent the cliffs. From the picturesque little harbour of Sennen Cove the beach stretches north for more than a kilometre to Aire Point, with steep cliffs ringing the northern section. The southern end of this moderately shelving beach is good for swimming and surfing, being sheltered by offshore reefs. The northern end is open to the full force of the Atlantic and conditions can be wild and dangerous. Dogs are banned between Easter and 1 October.

Water quality
One outfall serving 1,489 people discharges macerated sewage at LWM by the harbour.

Bathing safety
Safe at the southern end of the bay and safest at high water. Lifeguards patrol during summer.

Litter
The beach is cleaned regularly.

Access
A right turn off from the A30 to Land's End leads steeply down to Sennen Cove. There is easy access to the beach.

Renowned for its breakers, Whitesand Bay draws surfers from all over the country.

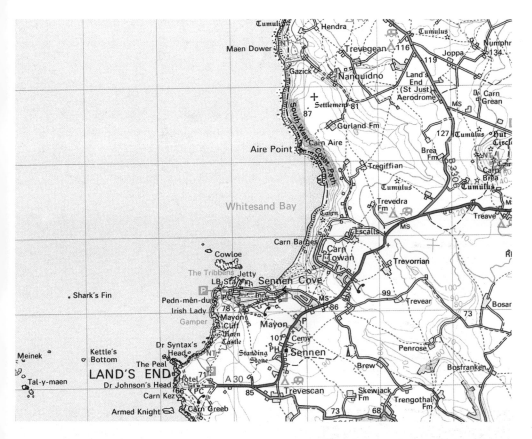

Parking

A car park in Sennen Cove and another on the approach road ensure ample space.

Public transport

The nearest rail station is at Penzance; a regular bus service runs in summer.

Toilets

There are toilets in the village.

Food

There are shops, cafés and a pub in the village.

Seaside activities

Swimming, surfing and angling. Fishing trips are available from the harbour. Surfboards can be hired.

Wildlife and walks

The granite cliffs south from Sennen Cove to Land's End are owned by the National Trust. The coast path along the cliff top, although it can be wild and windswept, is probably the best and certainly the most spectacular way to approach Land's End avoiding the severe summer congestion of the most westerly tip of England. Porthgwarra (SW367216) is an exciting birdwatching area similar to Scilly, a good place to spot migrants after heavy cloud and rain, or to indulge in some seawatching following southwesterly gales.

Track record ✓ ✓ ✓ ✓ ✓ ✓ ✓ ✓

Not EU designated.

PRAA SANDS (EAST AND WEST), ASHTON, HELSTON
Cornwall
OS Ref: SW580279

A particularly attractive sweep of beach between two rocky headlands, Praa Sands is very popular with families. Sheltered by Hoe Point cliffs to the west, edged by high dunes, and stretching east to Lesceave Cliff and the granite Rinsey Headland, around 100 metres of gently sloping sand is exposed at low tide with rockpools at either end of the beach. Caravan parks nearby mean that the beach is often busy.

When the beach gets too crowded, the relative solitude of the coast path is only minutes away.

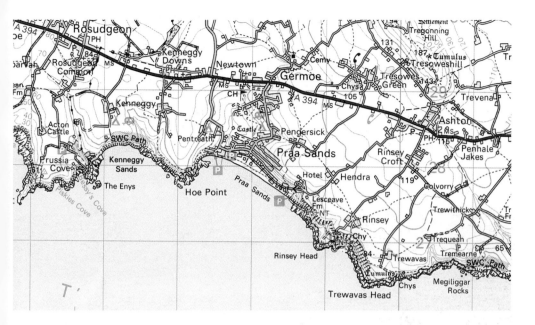

Water quality

Bathing safety
Bathing at low tide is unsafe due to a rip current: observe the warning signs. The beach is patrolled by lifeguards in summer.

Litter
The beach is cleaned by the National Trust but marine litter is frequently washed up.

Access
Praa Sands is signposted from the A394 between Helston and Penzance. From the car park there is a short walk to the beach.

Parking
On the road down to the beach there is a car park with 100 spaces. There is another car park at the bottom of the hill.

Public transport
The nearest rail station is Penzance; an hourly bus service goes to Praa Sands.

Toilets
At the entrance to the beach.

Food
Café and take-aways at the beach entrance.

Seaside activities
Swimming, diving, surfing, windsurfing, sailing, raft racing and fishing.

Wildlife and walks
The coast path from the eastern end of the beach leads away from the often crowded sands up Lesceave Cliff and on to Rinsey Head. Wheal Prosper, the engine house of an old copper mine, stands on the headland; the property and the surrounding land is owned by the National Trust. The mine shaft has been capped and the building restored. A large reedbed five kilometres east of Penzance gives superb viewing of the rare Cetti's warbler.

Track record ✓✓✓✓✓✓✓

GUNWALLOE COVE
Cornwall
OS Ref: SW654225

Gunwalloe is a long, gravelly beach, mainly covered at high tide, with a sandy cove to the north of the main beach. The National Trust owns much of the land in the area and a leaflet with further information is available from them. Dogs are banned from the beach.

Water quality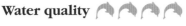

Litter
The beach is cleaned regularly by the National Trust.

Bathing safety
The beach shelves steeply, giving rise to an undertow which makes bathing very dangerous in rough weather.

Access
Signposted from Porthleven; easy access suitable for wheelchairs.

Parking
Available around 150 metres from the beach.

 Public transport
No direct services.

 Toilets
At the beach but no facilities for disabled visitors.

Food
There are cafés in the area.

Seaside activities
Swimming, surfing and fishing.

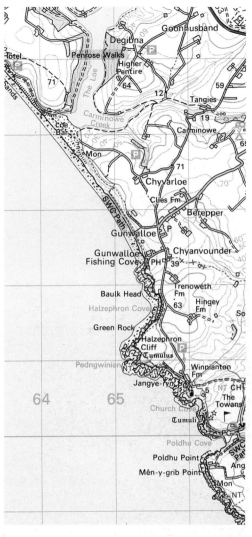

Wildlife and walks
There are many walks in the area. A walks pack is available from Kerrier District Council.

Track record ✓✓✓✓✓✓✓✓

The four kilometre stretch of Gunwalloe Cove is the longest continuous beach in Mount's Bay.

KENNACK SANDS, KUGGAR
Cornwall
OS Ref: SW735166

Probably the best swimming beach on the Lizard, Kennack is famous for its silver sands. Two separate 500-metre beaches merge at low tide to form one wide, gently sloping sandy strand. The pale sands, on the sheltered eastern side of the Lizard Peninsula, are fringed by dunes. At either end of the bay the sand gives way to shingle, bounded landward by cliffs. This is a popular family beach.

Water quality
No sewage is discharged in the vicinity of this beach.

Bathing safety
Bathing is safe.

Litter
The beach is sometimes affected by marine litter.

Access
A road from Kuggar village signposted for Kennack ends behind the beach, after which there is just a short walk through dunes to the sands.

Parking
There is a 250-space car park at the beach entrance.

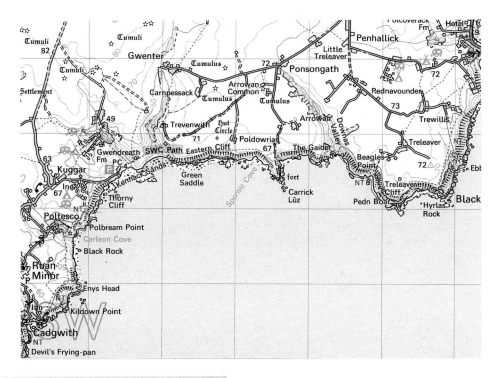

![WC] Toilets
In the car park.

Food
There are cafés at the entrance to the beach.

Seaside activities
Swimming, surfing, diving, windsurfing and fishing. Surfboards may be hired adjacent to the beach.

Wildlife and walks
The Cornwall South Coast Path proceeds east from the beach along the cliff tops with good sea views all the way.

Track record ✓✓✓✓✓✓✓

The clear, sheltered waters offshore make Kennack Sands popular with snorkellers and divers.

ST MAWES
Cornwall
OS Ref: SW849331

St Mawes is a small but popular holiday resort situated on the eastern shore of the Falmouth Estuary, close to the tip of the Roseland Peninsula. It is a popular yachting centre and has every facility for yachtsmen to moor up and take on provisions. Its sandy beach offers safe, sheltered bathing.

Water quality
One outlet serving 1,500 people discharges secondary treated sewage 100 metres below LWM.

The picturesque village of St Mawes is presided over by a 16th-century castle.

Bathing safety
Although there are no lifeguards at this beach, swimming is regarded as safe at all times.

Litter
The beach is cleaned daily by hand throughout the summer.

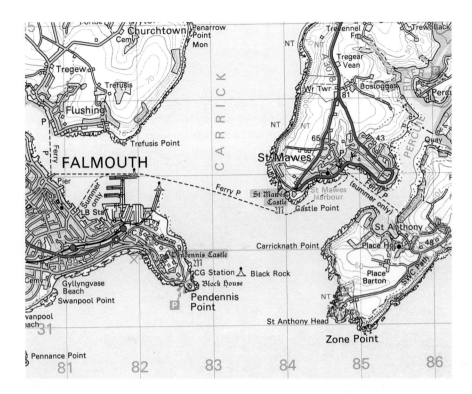

Access

St Mawes is signposted from the A39 on to the A3078 through the Roseland Peninsula. Alternatively visitors may take the car ferry from Falmouth crossing the narrow reach of the River Fal at King Harry's passage, and from there join the B3289 to St Mawes.

Parking

A large car park at the eastern end of the town operated by the Parish Council caters for coaches and cars.

Toilets

These are available in the car park.

Food

The proximity of the beach to the town means that refreshments are within easy reach, ranging from pubs to take-away restaurants.

Seaside activities

Swimming and sailing. There is a five knot speed limit off the beach, thus jet-skiing is not allowed.

Wet weather alternatives

St Mawes Castle, built in the reign of Henry VIII, is situated at the western end of the village. St Just in Roseland, a church described as one of the most beautiful in the country, is only a short drive away. The town of Falmouth is a short (covered) boat ride away.

Wildlife and walks

The coastal footpath stretches to both sides of the town and provides some spectacular scenery. Information on this and other walks is available in the town.

Track record

No track record is available for this beach. Not EU designated.

BOW OR VAULT BEACH, GORRAN HAVEN
Cornwall
OS Ref: SX010408

Sheltered on the eastern side of Dodman Point is the superb Vault Beach, a sweep of sand and shingle below steep, bracken and heather-clad cliffs. From Maenease Point the beach curves for one kilometre to the rock outcrop of Penover Point. The cliffs rise to an impressive 110 metres at Dodman Point, capped by its distinctive granite cross.

Nestling below the cliffs, and reached only by a steep path, the beautiful Vault Beach still draws determined visitors in their hundreds.

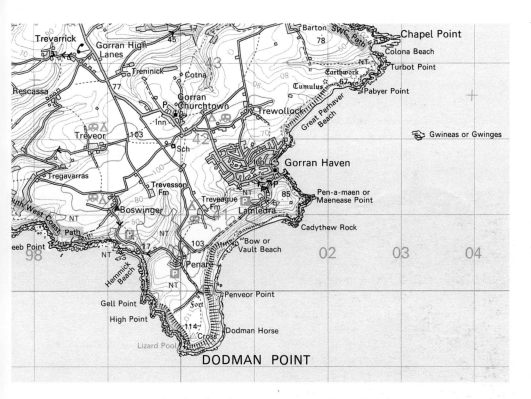

Water quality

Secondary treated effluent is discharged from one improved outfall south of the village towards Maenease Point.

Bathing safety

Bathing is safe, with normal precautions.

Litter

There is occasionally litter on this beach.

Access

Follow the coast path south from Gorran Haven to reach a steep path down the cliffs.

Parking

National Trust car park at Lamledra Farm above the beach.

Toilets

None.

Food

None.

Seaside activities

Swimming.

Wildlife and walks

The coast path along the cliff top leads on to Dodman Point; here there is evidence of an Iron Age fort with a ditch and bank. A granite cross stands as a memorial to the many ships wrecked on the point in the days before radar. There are marvellous views along much of the Cornish coast.

Track record ✓✗✓✓✓✓✓✓

CHALLABOROUGH
Devon
OS Ref: SX648448 (see map on p. 41)

Challaborough is a sheltered horseshoe-shaped cove with fine sand and rocks, and extensive rockpools to explore at low tide. Dogs are banned from the beach between 1 May and 30 September.

Water quality

 Bathing safety
Safe with normal precautions.

 Litter
The beach is cleaned five times a week by hand and twice a week by tractor.

 Access
Take the B3392 off the A379 from Kingsbridge to Plymouth. The beach is off a minor road beyond Ringmore.

 Parking
Adjacent to the beach.

 Public transport
No direct services.

Fine sand makes Challaborough a superb sandcastle beach.

 Toilets
In the car park.

 Food
Fish and chips and bar meals are available nearby.

 Seaside activities
Swimming, surfing and walking.

 Wet weather alternatives
There is a sports and leisure club next to the beach.

 Wildlife and Walks
The beach is on the South West Way. This stretch of the walk starts at Wonwell Beach on the eastern side of the River Erme estuary.

Track record ✓✗✓✓✓✓✓✓

BIGBURY-ON-SEA
Devon
OS Ref: SX649443 (see map on p. 41)

A pretty village with a sandy beach at the mouth of the South Devon Avon, Bigbury-on-Sea is connected to Burgh Island, just off the beach, by a causeway passable at low tide; at high tide a unique sea tractor transports passengers to and from the island. The hotel on Burgh Island was reputedly the inspiration for Agatha Christie's 'Ten Little Indians'.

Water quality
One outfall serving 1,286 people discharges secondary treated sewage 50 metres below LWM.

Bathing safety
Bathing is safe, except near river mouth. Lifeguards patrol between May and September.

Access
From the village and car park.

Parking
There is a car park with space for 900 cars.

Public transport
The beach is not easily reached by public transport.

Toilets
There are toilets in the village and on the island.

Food
There is a kiosk and café in the village, and a pub and hotel on the island.

Seaside activities
Swimming, surfing, windsurfing, fishing, jet-skiing.

Wildlife and walks
Bigbury is on the South Devon Coast Path, between the rivers Avon and Erme. The route follows the undulating cliff-line passing Burgh Island and the beaches of Bigbury and Challaborough, leading on through one of the most strenuous sections of the coast path. After rounding Beacon Point walking becomes easier as the path drops down to Wonwell Beach and the Erme Estuary. The many wild flowers attract numerous butterflies in summer.

Track record ✓✓✓✓✓✓✓✓

Bigbury beach is linked to Burgh Island by a causeway.

THURLESTONE NORTH
and SOUTH MILTON SANDS
Devon
OS Ref: SX674421, SX676417

These two beaches to the south of the village of Thurlestone in an Area of Outstanding Natural Beauty offer coarse sand with rocky outcrops and plenty of rock pools to explore at low tide. The most prominent feature in the area is the famous Thurlestone Rock, painted by Turner and best seen at high tide. Dogs are not banned from these beaches.

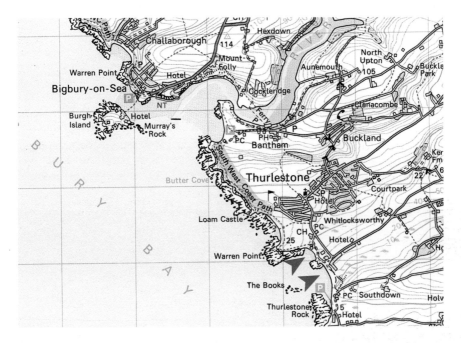

Water quality

North

South

Bathing safety
Bathing is safe but follow the advice given by lifeguards and observe the warning flags.

Litter
The beach is cleaned regularly over the summer.

Access
Thurlestone is off the A379 on minor roads from Kingsbridge to Modbury.

Parking
There is a car park next to the beach.

Thurlestone's best known landmark is the pinnacle of rock holed by the waves. The name Thurlestone comes from the Saxon Torleston meaning pierced stone.

Public transport
It is not possible to get to the beach using public transport.

Toilets
Situated at the car park.

Food
There is a café at the car park.

Seaside activities
Windsurfing, swimming, snorkelling, golf and walking. There is a windsurf school at the beach.

Wet weather alternatives
There are none available at the beach.

Wildlife and walks
Thurlestone is on the South West Coast Path. South Milton Ley is the second largest reedbed in Devon and provides an important habitat for reed and sedge warblers and migrating birds.

Track record ☐ ☐ ☐ ✓ ✓ ✓ ✓ ✓

MILL BAY near SALCOMBE
Devon
OS Ref: SX742383

Aprivately owned beach across the estuary from Salcombe, this fine sandy cove is sheltered and set in a beautiful rural area with gentle slopes down to the beach. The picturesque village of East Portlemouth is about a kilometre away although it is a steep climb to get there by foot. During the Second World War Mill Bay was used as an American base. Air-sea rescue boats were moored in the harbour and an anti-aircraft battery was sited on the cliffs above the beach.

Just far enough off the beaten track to keep the hordes away,
Mill Bay is still popular with visitors in the summer months.

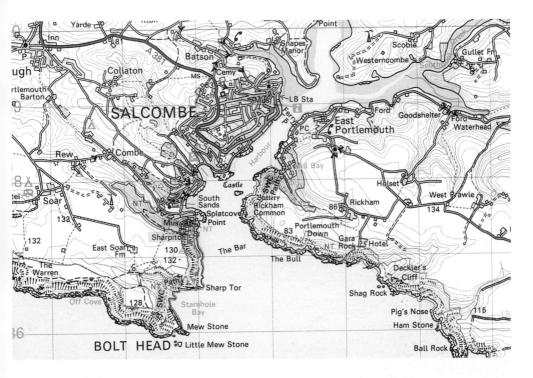

Water quality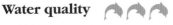

 Bathing safety
There is no lifeguard cover but bathing is generally safe.

Litter
The beach is regularly cleaned.

Access
The easiest approach to the beach is by passenger ferry from Salcombe.

 Parking
It is an easy walk from the car park to the beach.

Public transport
There are bus services to Salcombe and from there take the ferry across the estuary to Mill Bay.

 Toilets
Adjacent to the beach.

Food
The nearest café is about one kilometre away.

Seaside activities
Swimming, windsurfing and walking.

Wet weather alternatives
There are none at the beach.

Wildlife and walks
Walk leaflets are available from the local tourist information centres. Prawle Point – the southernmost tip of Devon – (SX772350) is nearby. This is a rocky coastline with areas of steep scrub and open grassland and farmland, where the cirl bunting (a Mediterranean species in decline in Britain) breeds.

Track record ✓✗✓✓✓✓✓✓

SLAPTON SANDS
Devon
OS Ref: SX828440

Afour-and-a-half kilometre stretch of shingle beach extending from
Pilchard Cove in the north to Torcross in the south, Slapton Sands is
separated by the main road from Dartmouth to Kingsbridge from a large,
reed-rimmed freshwater lake (Slapton Ley) on the other side. The village of
Slapton itself is about one and a half kilometres inland. The beach was
used in 1943-44 as a practice area for the D-day landings and the local
villages were evacuated while the US army took over the area. A Sherman
tank has been salvaged from the sea and is on display in Torcross as a
memorial, and opposite the lane to Slapton a stone obelisk erected by the
US army commemorates the co-operation of the local people. At low tide it
is possible to walk round the headland from Torcross to Beesands, but if
you get cut off there is an arduous walk back on the cliff path.

*The beach is often windy, as might be expected on such a long exposed stretch,
but the views around Start Bay are spectacular.*

Water quality

One outfall serving 889 people discharges secondary treated sewage into Slapton Ley.

Bathing safety

Bathing is generally safe, but the beach shelves steeply – beware of the undertow. Watch out for fragments of wartime debris when swimming. There is a zoned bathing area at Torcross and a beach patrol in the summer.

Litter

Some marine litter, particularly after bad weather, but the beach is cleaned frequently.

Access

The A379 runs along the edge of the beach; access is easy.

Parking

There are car parks at Strete Gate, Torcross and approximately half-way down the length of the beach.

Public transport

By bus from Plymouth to Slapton Sands or by bus from Totnes to Kingsbridge and then from Kingsbridge to Torcross.

Toilets

In Torcross and at the car parks.

Food

There are shops, cafés and pubs in Torcross.

Seaside activities

Swimming, fishing.

Wet weather alternatives

Children's play area at Strete Gate. Slapton Ley Field Study Centre.

Wildlife and walks

The area is rich in differing habitats and the Field Centre organises guided walks throughout the summer. On the edges of the beach itself the rare Yellow Horned Poppy can be found: do not pick the flowers. Slapton Ley is the largest body of fresh water in the south-west of England and attracts many species of wildfowl and other animals. At Torcross a hide (with disabled access) allows panoramic observation across the Ley and there is a corner where children can feed the ducks and swans. The three-kilometre South Devon Circular Walk starts and finishes at Torcross.

Track record   ✓✓✓✓✓✓✓✓

BLACKPOOL SANDS, STOKE FLEMING
Devon
OS Ref: SX855478

Blackpool Sands stands in complete contrast to its Lancashire cousin: the only development on this beach, an unspoilt cove at the northern end of Start Bay, comprises a car park, a shop and an attractive toilet block. A crescent of coarse golden sand around one kilometre long is flanked by steep, wooded cliffs. On the southern side of the cove below Matthew's Point a valley opens to the shore, from which a stream, Blackpool Lake, flows across the moderately shelving sands into a pool, very popular among families with small children. Dogs are banned from the beach between May and September.

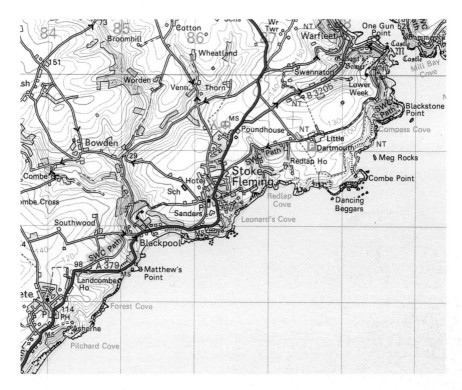

Water quality

No sewage is discharged in the vicinity of the beach.

Bathing safety

Bathing is safe, but care is required because the beach shelves steeply.

Access

Blackpool Sands is signposted from Dartmouth on the A379, south of Stoke Fleming. A side road leads to the car parks.

Parking

Ample car parking adjacent to the beach.

Toilets

At the car park.

Pine-clad cliffs sweep down to a crescent of golden sand – the very picture of unspoilt beauty.

Food

A kiosk sells sandwiches, hot and cold drinks and arranges the occasional beach barbecue.

Seaside activities

Swimming, windsurfing, sailing, fishing and diving. Toppers, windsurfers and surf canoes are available for hire. Sailing and windsurfing school with RYA instructors. Beach shop offers deckchairs and parasols for hire.

Wildlife and walks

North of the beach the South Devon Coast Path can be followed through Stoke Fleming to the entrance to the Dart Estuary. To the south, the footpath leads to Strete Gate and along the eight kilometre sweep of Start Bay, fringed by shingle beaches, to Start Point.

Track record ✓✓✓✓✓✓✓✓

SHOALSTONE BEACH
Devon
OS Ref: SX932566

This shingle beach close to the old fishing port of Brixham affords excellent views across Torbay. Low tide exposes pools between angled tablets of rock. There is an open-air swimming pool at the eastern end of the beach. Dogs are banned between May and September.

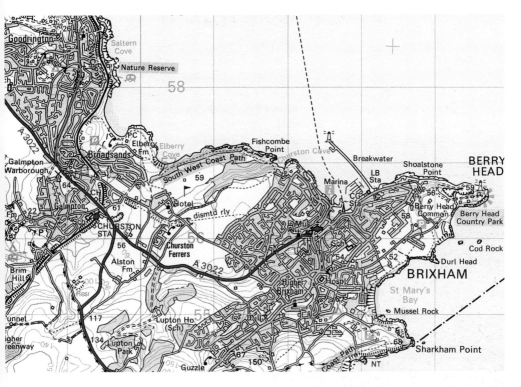

Water quality

No sewage is discharged in the vicinity of this beach.

Bathing safety

Trained beach attendants operate here.

Litter

The beach is cleaned daily.

Access

A left turn off the road from Brixham Harbour to Berry Head.

Parking

Adjacent to the beach.

The bustling harbour of the old fishing port of Brixham is one of the many attractions to be found within a short distance of Shoalstone Beach.

Public transport

A local bus service to Shoalstone.

Toilets

Adjacent to the beach.

Food

There is a café near the beach.

Seaside activities

Sub-aqua diving, fishing and rockpooling.

Wet weather alternatives

Brixham Aquarium and museums, Berry Head Country Park.

Wildlife and walks

Shoalstone is situated close to Berry Head, a Site of Special Scientific Interest. There are numerous walks and trails in the area.

Track record ✓✓✓✓✓✓✓✓

BABBACOMBE BAY, TORQUAY
Devon

Torquay and the surrounding area is one of Britain's most popular seaside destinations; the mild climate, abundant palm trees and other subtropical vegetation along this stretch of coast have earned it the soubriquet 'The English Riviera'. There are numerous beaches, some of which have good water quality and most of which ban dogs between May and the end of September. The coast along Babbacombe Bay to the north of Torquay is particularly clean, with four beaches in one 10-kilometre stretch which meet the highest standards of water purity. These are:

Oddicombe Beach, OS Ref: SX926657
Watcombe Beach, OS Ref: SX926673
Maidencombe, OS Ref: SX928685
Ness Cove, OS Ref: SX937717

Water quality
No sewage is discharged in the vicinity of these beaches.

Bathing safety
Generally safe, with beach attendants at Oddicombe, but swimmers should observe the safety flags at all times.

Litter
Beaches are cleaned daily over the summer season.

Access
All beaches are accessible off the A379 Torquay to Teignmouth road. Steps or paths lead to the beaches, and these are steep at Watcombe and Maidencombe. Oddicombe Beach is served by a cliff railway.

Parking
Car parking is widely available along this stretch of coast, though sometimes in the towns and at a little distance from the beach.

The dark red sandstone cliffs backing Oddicombe Beach stand out starkly against the pale golden sand.

Public transport
Nearest rail stations are Torquay, Torre and Teignmouth. Oddicombe, Watcombe and Maidencombe are served by bus from Torquay. Ness Cove is on the Teignmouth to Shaldon bus route.

 Toilets
All beaches have toilets in the vicinity, some including facilities for disabled visitors.

Food
A wide range of hot and cold food and drinks is available from cafés and kiosks near the beaches and the nearby shops and pubs.

Seaside activities
Swimming, fishing, sailing, windsurfing; boat and pedalo hire.

Wet weather alternatives
The Riviera Centre in Torquay, Paignton Zoo, Torbay Aircraft Museum, Kent's Cavern, Babbacombe Model Village, Berry Pomeroy Castle and the Dart Valley Railway are all within easy reach. There is a good range of shops and amusements in Torquay.

Wildlife and walks
The South Devon Coast Path extends around the bay, offering some of the most glorious views on the south coast. The mild climate encourages unusually luxuriant plant life and the area is favoured by rare butterflies. Leaflets describing Torbay's wildlife are available from the Tourist Information Office in Torquay. From Ness Cove the Teign Estuary can easily be explored and the Wildlife Trust has a centre near the beach.

Track record

WEST BAY (WEST)
Dorset
OS Ref: SY459904

West Bay (West) is separated from West Bay (East) by the twin piers of Bridport Harbour at the mouth of the River Brit. A shingle beach with large pebbles, it is bounded at both ends by towering cliffs dropping steeply to the sea. The village was once an important shipbuilding and sea-trading site; it has buildings that date from the 17th century and can trace its history back to Anglo-Saxon times.

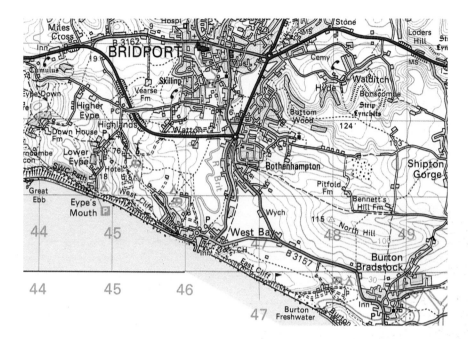

Water quality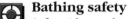

One outlet serving 30,000 people discharges screened sewage 1.5 km out to sea.

Bathing safety

Safe with usual precautions; lifesaving equipment is available.

Access

Signposted off the A35 and also off the B3157 Weymouth to Bridport road.

Parking

Short stay car parks on the esplanade and beside the harbour.

Toilets

Toilets with facilities for disabled visitors are situated beside the harbour.

West Bay has a small harbour providing facilities for fishing boats and pleasure craft.

Food

Harbour-side cafés and pubs.

Seaside activities

Swimming, sailing, diving and fishing. Boats are available for fishing trips. Paddle boats may be hired at the mouth of the River Brit.

Wet weather alternatives

The harbour museum illustrates the history of West Bay, as well as the rope and net trade for which Bridport is famous worldwide. There are also amusement arcades.

Wildlife and walks

The coast path follows the cliffs, leading to Burton Bradstock in the east and Eype in the west. Spectacular views of Lyme Bay can be had from the cliffs: on clear days you can see as far as Portland in the east and Lyme Regis in the west.

Track record ☐ ✓ ✓ ✓ ✓ ✓ ✓ ✓

53

WEYMOUTH CENTRAL
Dorset
OS Ref: SY681794

Approximately one and a half kilometres in length and ranging from 40 to 150 metres in width on mean tides, the beach at Weymouth is of mainly fine sand with shingle and pebbles evident at the north end. Two internationally recognised nature reserves are less than five minutes walk from the beach, Lodmoor Nature Reserve and Radipole Swannery Reserve. The bay is sheltered and renowned for its safety; swimmers, bathers and other water-users benefit from the gradual slope of the seabed which gives shallow inshore waters.

Water quality
No sewage is discharged in the vicinity of this beach.

Bathing safety
The inshore water has a speed limit of eight knots, defined by buoys across the bay. Water sports and bathing areas are segregated from each other and council beach control staff enforce the water safety byelaws assisted by the harbour authority. Beach safety signs are situated at all the access points.

Weymouth's fine Georgian seafront bears witness to its history as a fashionable summer retreat.

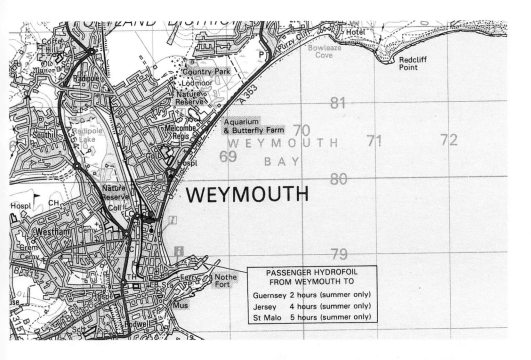

Litter
The beach is cleaned daily by hand and machine. Dogs are banned between May and September.

Access
Weymouth is signposted from junction 25 of the M5.

Parking
There is plenty of parking in car parks and on the road.

Public transport
Weymouth is the nearest rail station; there are frequent buses from Dorchester (number 10), Salisbury (number 184), Portland (number 1), Bridport and Portesham (number 31).

Toilets
There are excellent toilet facilities including those for disabled visitors and mother-and-baby changing rooms.

Food
Several kiosks and cafés are in the area.

Seaside activities
A wide range of activities, from international events to Punch and Judy, beach games, windsurfing, sailing, water-skiing, jet-skiing and children's play areas.

Wet weather alternatives
Sealife Centre, Brewers Quay and Timewalk, Nothe Fort, Deep Sea Adventure, Shire Horse stables, Weymouth Pavilion Theatre, Model World, Tropical Jungle and Wessex Water Museum.

Wildlife and walks
The RSPB organise walks at Lodmoor and Radimore. There are several different wildlife walk booklets currently available for the surrounding area.

Track record ✓✓✓✓✓✓✓✓

DURDLE DOOR (EAST AND WEST)
Dorset
OS Ref: SY805803

Famous for Durdle Door Arch, one of the wonders of the British coastline created by the great erosive power of the sea (and probably the most photographed view along the Dorset coast), the beach is a narrow strand of mixed shingle, gravel and sand. The eastern end (Durdle Door Cove) is protected by the arch while the rest of the beach is partially sheltered by a submerged offshore reef. The beach is bounded at the western end by Bat's Head, a chalk headland. All the cliffs backing the beach are steep and prone to occasional rockfalls, so climbing or sheltering underneath them is not advised.

A testament to the power of wind and waves, the arch at Durdle Door shows the differing hardness of the rock strata along this stretch of coast.

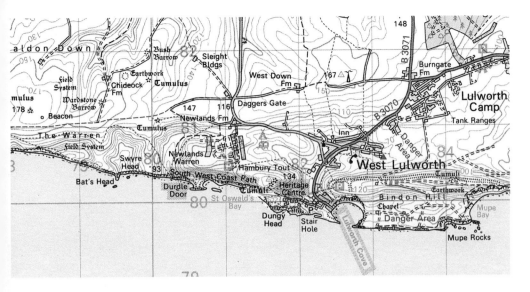

Water quality

No sewage is discharged in the vicinity of this beach.

Bathing safety
As with most shingle and gravel beaches care is required since there can be sudden steep slopes underwater. The western end of the beach may be cut off under certain tide and wave conditions.

Litter
Occasional marine litter, including plastic, rope and wood, is washed up in Durdle Door Cove.

Access
The beach is approached by a steep 800-metre footpath from the cliff-top car park. Access on to the eastern end of the beach down a steep flight of steps cut into the bay cliff can be slippery in wet weather.

Parking
There is a large cliff-top car park at Durdle Door Caravan Camping Park (with excellent views across Weymouth Bay to the Isle of Portland).

Toilets
At the caravan park.

Food
There is a café and store in the caravan park.

Seaside activities
Swimming, diving, snorkelling and fishing. The steep access to the beach means that heavy equipment, including picnic tables, should not be carried down.

Wildlife and walks
The undulating cliffs form a challenging section of the Dorset Coast Path. To the east lies Lulworth Cove and the Isle of Purbeck, to the west White Nothe headland. The reward for tackling this stretch of Heritage Coast is a fine view across Weymouth Bay and down to the glorious beaches below. The chalk habitat creates picturesque downland with its accompanying flora and fauna.

Track record

West	✓	✓	✓	✓	✓	✓	✓	✓
East						✓	✓	✓

57

STUDLAND
Dorset
OS Ref: SZ035835

Five kilometres of excellent sandy beach are backed by unspoilt dunes in this Area of Outstanding Natural Beauty. From the entrance to Poole Harbour, the beach sweeps south towards the chalk cliffs of Handfast Point. The beach can be divided into three areas – South Beach, Middle Beach and North or Knoll Beach. Visitors should note that the eastern end of the beach is used by naturists. Behind Knoll Beach a brackish lake and marsh area forms the Studland Heath National Nature Reserve. Dogs must be kept on a lead and byelaws require that dog faeces is removed by the owners. A leaflet about Studland and the surrounding area is available from the National Trust.

Water quality
No sewage is discharged in the vicinity of this beach.

At the south-western tip of Studland Bay off Handfast Point stand isolated stacks of chalk which were once connected to The Needles on the Isle of Wight.

Bathing safety
Safe off the main beach; strong currents at the entrance to Poole Harbour make the northern end unsafe. The beach is patrolled by National Trust wardens from Easter to September and voluntary lifeguards operate at weekends from May to August.

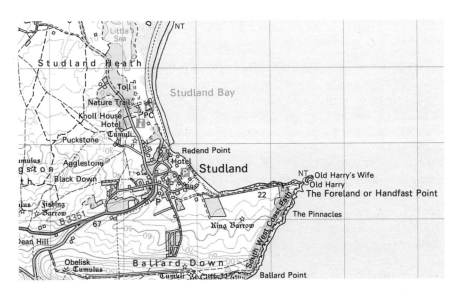

Litter
The beach is very clean due to the efforts of the National Trust.

Access
Each section of the beach is signposted from Studland village. It is a short walk from the car parks to the sands. There is a wheelchair ramp at Knoll Beach.

Parking
Four car parks provide parking for 3,500 cars.

Toilets
There are five blocks of toilets. Those at Middle and Knoll Beaches have facilities for disabled visitors, with facilities for nursing mothers at Knoll Beach.

Food
There are many cafés and kiosks.

Seaside activities
Swimming, windsurfing and sailing. Windsurf boards are available for hire.

Wildlife and walks
The Studland Heath National Nature Reserve behind the beach contains a brackish lagoon, Little Sea. The reserve cannot be reached from the beach but must be entered from the road which bounds its western edge. It is home to a wide variety of wildlife including the rare smooth snake and adders, and walkers are advised to wear stout shoes and to stay on the marked paths. The Dorset Coast Path starts and finishes at the entrance to Poole Harbour. It follows the bay south and on to The Foreland. From the path there are splendid views of the cliffs and the chalk pillars, Old Harry and Old Harry's Wife, which are isolated from the adjacent headland of Handfast Point by the ever eroding waves. The path continues south towards Ballard Point from where fine views can be had of Swanage Bay. Durlstone Head (SZ035773) is a well established Country Park with visitor facilities that make it very easy to view nesting seabirds.

Track record   ✓ ✗ ✓ ✓ ✓ ✓ ✓ ✓

SHELL BAY and POOLE SANDBANKS
Dorset
OS Ref: SZ038863, SZ048880

These two extremely popular and well managed beaches with consistently good or excellent water quality face each other across the entrance to Poole Harbour. From the end of the Sandbanks spit, a fringe of soft golden sand stretches over five kilometres north-east to merge with the beaches of Bournemouth. To the south-west, the cliffs give way to the low-lying Sandbanks Peninsula where the beach is edged by dunes and overlooked by holiday development and the Sandbanks Pavilion and recreation area. Less than 500 metres of water separates the spit from South Haven Point, and a car and passenger ferry connects the two, giving access to the beautiful Shell Bay, renowned for its warm shallow water.

Water quality

Shell Bay
Poole Sandbanks

Bathing safety

Poole Sandbanks: bathing is safe, except at the extreme western end of the beach near the harbour entrance. Warning signs indicate where not to swim.

Shell Bay: The beach is patrolled by lifeguards from May to September and first aid is available daily.

Litter
The beaches are cleaned daily. Dogs are banned from May to September.

Access
Poole Sandbanks: there is easy access along the length of the beach; paths lead down the cliffs to the promenade.
Shell Bay: by ferry or from nearby car park.

Parking
Numerous car parking opportunities.

Toilets
Toilets including facilities for disabled visitors along the beach; a mother-and-baby room is available at Sandbanks.

Food
Cafés and kiosks close to the beach.

Seaside activities
Swimming, windsurfing, sailing and fishing; windsurf boards and boats for hire. Poole Harbour has several windsurfing and sailing schools. There is also a putting green, crazy golf and a variety of children's amusements.

Wet weather alternatives
Tower Park leisure complex incorporating Splashdown, Ice-Trax, Mega-Bowl, multi-screen cinema; four sports centres, Dolphin swimming pool, aquarium complex,

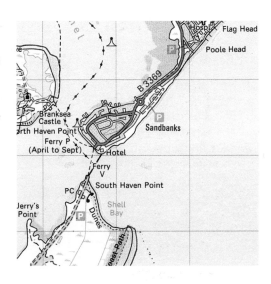

Royal National Lifeboat Museum, Waterfront and Scaplen's Court Museum, Arts Centre, Poole Pottery and Poole Park. Excellent shopping in the Dolphin Shopping Centre.

Wildlife and walks
The extensive Studland Heath National Nature Reserve backs Shell Bay. There is also a pedestrian ferry to Brownsea Island where tern colonies and lagoons can be seen. 80 hectares of this 202-hectare National Trust-owned island is a nature reserve run by the Dorset Trust for Nature Conservation. Many different types of habitat are found on the island including heathland, woodland, freshwater lakes, saltmarsh and the seashore. There is a nature trail and guided walks are available during the summer. Further information is available from the National Trust shop on the island's landing quay.

Track record
Shell Bay

					✓	✓	✓

Poole Sandbanks

✓	✓	✓	✓	✓	✓	✓	✓

Poole's pedestrian promenade is set against a dramatic steep pine- and shrub-covered backdrop making this a delightful setting for a stroll at any time of the year.

DURLEY CHINE, BOURNEMOUTH
Dorset
OS Ref: SZ078903

This sandy beach with sandstone cliffs either side of the wooded chine is easily reached down a zigzag path and steps after a 15-minute walk from the town centre. All the facilities for the day are found on the beach, including beach huts which can be hired daily or weekly. Dogs are banned between May and September.

A long promenade backs the sandy beach at Durley Chine.

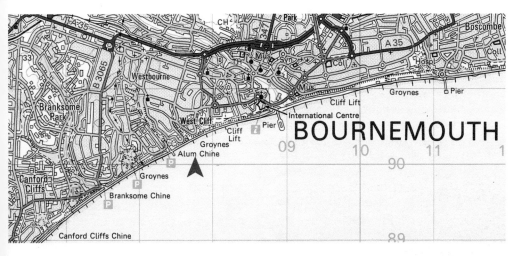

Water quality

No sewage is discharged in the vicinity of this beach.

Bathing safety

There is a buoyed area for swimmers and voluntary lifeguards operate in the summer.

Litter

The beach is cleaned twice daily by hand and by machine in the summer.

Access

From the A338 westbound, the first left at the end of the dual carriageway is signposted for Durley Chine.

Parking

Roadside parking in lower Durley Chine and along the overcliff drive.

Public transport

The yellow buses (numbers 17/18, and 12 in the season) stop at the top of Durley Chine. The nearest rail station is Bournemouth Central.

Toilets

Toilets are available including facilities for disabled visitors and a mother-and-baby room at nearby West Beach.

Food

A kiosk serves hot and cold snacks and Durley Inn has a bar and hot and cold meals.

Seaside activities

Swimming and boating.

Wet weather alternatives

Many facilities in the town centre one kilometre away.

Wildlife and walks

On either side of Durley Chine are wooded areas and the cliff top is open and grassed. Short walks can be taken in the immediate area: detailed leaflets on routes, flora and fauna are available at the Visitor Information Bureau. There are ten kilometres of promenade going west to near Sandbanks and east to Southbourne.

Track record □□□□□□ ✓✓

FISHERMAN'S WALK (SOUTHBOURNE), BOURNEMOUTH
Dorset
OS Ref: SZ128913

This sandy beach backed by low sandstone cliffs has good facilities including showers and changing rooms. Essentially a quiet beach, it is an excellent spot for body-boarding in the sea or for scenic cliff-top walks. Dogs are banned between May and September.

Water quality
No sewage is discharged in the vicinity of this beach.

Toilets
There are toilets including facilities for disabled visitors.

Bathing safety
Safe; the beach is patrolled by voluntary and Council lifeguards.

Food
A kiosk serves hot and cold snacks.

Litter
Cleaned by hand and machine twice daily during the summer.

Seaside activities
Swimming.

Access
From the A338 east on to Castle Lane East, the A3060. Follow signs for Southbourne Beaches.

Wet weather alternatives
The town centre attractions are within easy reach.

Parking
There is roadside parking on the overcliff road.

Wildlife and walks
Undercliff and overcliff walks can be taken using zigzag paths, and walkers can meander in and out of Shelley Park, Woodland Walk and Fisherman's Walk. Three kilometres walk east along the undercliff is Hengistbury Head.

Public transport
Yellow buses run landward to the end of Fisherman's Walk.

Track record □□□□□□✔✔

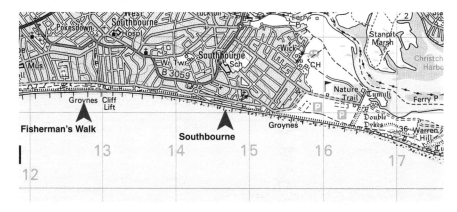

SOUTHBOURNE, BOURNEMOUTH
Dorset
OS Ref: SZ147911

A sandy beach backed along its length by steeply sloping shrub-covered cliffs, Southbourne is close to the holiday centre of Bournemouth.

Water quality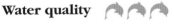

 Bathing safety
Generally safe bathing.

 Access
Southbourne is easily reached by car and public transport.

 Parking
There is plenty of parking.

 Toilets
There are extensive toilet facilities along the promenade.

 Food
Numerous facilities along the promenade into Bournemouth.

Seaside activities
 Swimming, surfing, windsurfing, sailing and fishing.

Track record ☐☐☐☐ ✓✓✓✓
Not EU designated.

Southbourne offers clean beaches, safe swimming and all the attractions of a major seaside resort.

HENGISTBURY HEAD, EAST BOURNEMOUTH
Dorset
OS Ref: SZ170906

The one-and-a-half-kilometre-long Hengistbury headland separates Poole Bay and Christchurch Bay and encloses Christchurch Harbour on its landward side. Most of the headland remains undeveloped and has been designated a Site of Special Scientific Interest because of the wide variety of plant and animal life it supports. There are two distinct beach areas: Hengistbury Head itself is a south-facing pebble beach below imposing sandstone cliffs. This three-kilometre stretch of beach is undeveloped, in sharp contrast to the sand spit stretching north from the headland to the entrance of Christchurch Harbour where a string of beach huts face the groyne-ribbed sands. A ferry from Mudeford crosses the harbour entrance to drop passengers at the northern end of the beach where there is a quay and short promenade.

Water quality

Bathing safety
On the seaward-facing side of the headland bathing is safe except near the entrance to the harbour. Lifeguard cover from Southbourne.

Litter
Occasionally affected by marine litter from nearby boats.

Access
From the A338, follow the A3060 sign for Tuckton Bridge.

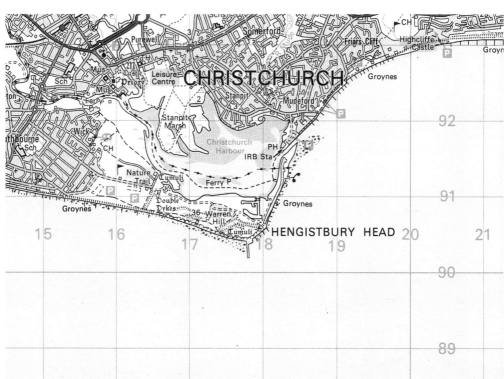

The south-facing pebble beach at Hengistbury is completely undeveloped – a picture of unspoilt beauty.

Parking
There are 500 spaces at Hengistbury Head and 360 at Mudeford Quay.

Public transport
By yellow bus number 12 in summer and 22 all year. There are pathways at the end of the Southbourne promenade from the grassed areas to the beach.

Toilets
Several blocks on the main beach including facilities for disabled visitors.

Food
From a beach café.

Seaside activities
Swimming and windsurfing; there is a windsurfing school nearby. Barbecue facility available, pitch-and-putt and crazy golf.

Wildlife and walks
Hengistbury Head is of considerable archaeological interest with evidence of Iron Age and Roman settlement. There are information signs to interpret the history and wildlife of the area, and nature trail. An excellent viewpoint at OS Ref: SZ178904 gives splendid views.

Track record ✓✓✓✓✓✓✓✓

RATING	NAME	TRACK RECORD	SEWAGE OUTLET	REMARKS
	AVON			
–	**Clevedon** Bay	✗✗✗✗✓✗✗☐		Rocks and mud.
⌢⌢	Swimming pool - EU ST398712	☐☐☐☐☐✗✗✓		Rocks and mud.
	Weston-super-Mare		Screened and disinfection, 75,000, remote from main beach. Improvements planned for 2000.	Main beaches cleaned regularly.
f	Uphill Slipway - EU ST312588	☐☐☐☐☐✓✓✗✗		Sandy.
f	Sanatorium ST314600	☐☐☐☐☐✗✓✗✗		Sandy.
⌢	Main Beach - EU ST316607	☐☐☐☐☐✗✗✗✓		Sandy with rocky coves at north end. Beach cleaned regularly.
f	Grand Pier ST317615	☐☐☐☐☐✗✗✗✗		Sandy.
f	Marine Lake	☐☐☐☐☐✓✓✓✗		Sandy. Rocks at north end.
⌢	Kewstoke Sand Bay (near Weston) - EU ST330635	✓✗✓✓✓✓✓✗✓		Sandy. Beach affected by sewage-related debris.
	SOMERSET			
f	**Berrow** North - EU ST293545	☐☐☐☐☐✓✓✓✗		Sandy.
–	South ST290535	✓✓✗✓✓✓✓✗☐		Sandy. Sewage-related debris sometimes a problem.
⌢	**Brean** - EU ST296585	✓✓✓✓✓✓✓✓✓		Sandy.
f	**Burnham-on-Sea** Yacht Club ST301480	☐☐☐☐☐✗✗✓✗		Sandy.
⌢⌢	Jetty - EU ST302488	☐☐☐☐☐✗✓✓	Screened primary/ chemical, 36,000, HWM.	Sandy. Beach cleaned regularly. Bathing mostly dangerous.
–	**East Quantoxhead**		Macerated, 800, LWM.	Rocks and sand.
–	**Doniford**	☐☐☐☐☐✗✗☐	Fine screened, 5,000, 100 above LWM.	Sand and mud.
–	**Watchet**	☐☐☐☐☐✗✓☐	Raw, 4,500, 100 above LWM.	Sand and mud.
⌢⌢	**Blue Anchor** - EU ST023435	✓✗✓✓✓✗✓✓✓	Raw, 4,500, 100 above LWM. Improvements planned.	Sand and shingle.
⌢⌢	**Dunster** North West - EU SS997455	☐☐☐☐☐✓✓✓✓		Sand and shingle.
–	South East	✗✗✗✗✓✓✓☐		Sand and shingle.
	Minehead		Screened and disinfection, 35,000, LSO, remote from the beaches.	Sandy.
⌢⌢	Terminus - EU SS973465	☐☐☐☐☐✓✓✓✓		Sandy.

RATING	NAME	TRACK RECORD	SEWAGE OUTLET	REMARKS
–	The Strand SS978463	✓✓✓		Sandy.
⌒⌒⌒⌒	**Porlock Bay** Porlock Weir - EU SS864479	✓✗✓✓✓✓✓✓	3, all raw, 850, 1,200 and 450, all at LWM.	Pebbles. Not featured due to adjacent sewage outfalls.
	DEVON (NORTH)			
f	**Lynmouth** - EU SS725497	✗✗✓✗✗✗✓✗✗	Raw, 4,300, 110 below LWM. Improvements planned for 1997.	Pebbles.
f	**Combe Martin** - EU SS577473	✗✗✗✗✓✗✗✓✗	Raw, 3,600, 65 below LWM. Improvements planned for 1997.	Pebbles and sand.
f	**Ilfracombe** Hele Beach - EU SS535479	✗✗✓✗		Shingle.
⌒	Capstone Beach - EU SS518479	✗✗✓✓✓✓✗✗✓	Improvements planned for 1996.	Shingle.
⌒	Tunnels - EU SS514478	✓✓✓✓	2, both raw, 22,000 and 744, 235 below and 30 below LWM. Improvements planned for 1996.	Sandy.
–	Rockham Bay			Rocky.
⌒⌒	Barricane Bay	✓		Sandy, surrounded by rocks.
⌒⌒⌒⌒	**Woolacombe Village beach** - EU SS456437	✓✓✓✓✓✓✓✓	Secondary, 13,200, 100 below LWM.	Sandy backed by dunes. Not featured due to dangerous bathing conditions at low tide.
⌒⌒⌒⌒	**Putsborough Beach** - EU SS447408	✓✓		Shingle. Not featured due to insufficient information.
⌒⌒	**Croyde Bay** - EU SS434393	✓✓✓✓✓✓✓✓	Screened, 6,400, below LWM. Improvements planned for 2000.	Sandy, bounded by rocks at either end. Strong undertow at all times.
⌒⌒	**Saunton Sands** - EU SS445376	✓✓✓✓✓✓✓✓		Sandy.
f	**Instow** - EU SS471304	✗✗✗✓✗✗✗✗✗	Screened, 8,500, LWM. Improvements planned.	Polluted by Rivers Taw and Torridge.
⌒⌒	**Westward Ho!** - EU SS432294	✓✓✓✓✓✓✓✓	Screened, 4,600, 10 below LWM.	Sand and pebbles.
–	**Clovelly**		Raw, 1,300, at LWM.	Sand at low tide only.
⌒⌒⌒⌒	**Shipload Bay** SS2428	✓✓ ✓		Sand and shingle. Bathers beware of currents. Not featured because of difficult access.
⌒⌒⌒⌒	**Hartland Quay** - EU SS2428	✓✗✓✓✓✓✓✓		Rocks, boulders and stunning rock formations. Not featured because unsuitable for bathing.
⌒⌒⌒⌒	**Welcombe Mouth**	✓		Pebbles and rocks; some sand at low tide. Not featured because area is environmentally sensitive.
	CORNWALL			

RATING	NAME	TRACK RECORD	SEWAGE OUTLET	REMARKS
	CORNWALL			
⌒	**Bude Crooklets** - EU SS203072	✗✗✗✓✓✗✓✓✓		Sandy.
⌒⌒⌒	**Bude Summerleaze** - EU SS204066	☐☐☐☐☐✗✓✗✓	Primary, 12,700, LSO. .	See Bude Sandy Mouth. (page 16)
⌒	**Widemouth Bay** - EU SS198024	✓✓✓✓✓✓✓✓✓		Sandy, backed by low cliffs and grassy fields.
–	**Crackington Haven** SX142969	☐☐☐☐☐✓✗✗☐		Sandy.
–	**Boscastle**		Raw, 1,300, at LWM remote from harbour.	
–	**Tintagel**		Raw, 1,500, at LWM.	Shingle.
–	**Trebarwith Strand** SX048863	☐☐☐☐☐✓✓✗		Sand and rocks. Swimming can be dangerous.
–	**Port Isaac**		Secondary, 1,800, LWM..	Fishing port.
⌒⌒	**Polzeath** - EU SW936792	✓✓✓✓✓✓✓✓✓	Screened and septic tank, 1,700, at LWM. Improvements planned.	Sandy. Beach cleaned all year round. Bathing can be dangerous at low water.
–	**Padstow** SW919764		Screened, 3,800. Improvements planned.	Small harbour. No swimming.
⌒⌒	**Trevone Bay** - EU SW892761	✗✗✗✓✓✗✓✗✓	Raw, 1,000, at LWM. Improvements planned.	Sandy. Bathing can be dangerous.
⌒⌒⌒	**Mother Ivey's Bay** - EU SW863760	✓✓✓✓✓✓✓✓		Sandy. Bathing generally safe but dangerous rip currents. Not featured due to insufficient information.
⌒⌒	**Mawgan Porth** - EU SW848674	✗✗✓✗✗✗✓✗✓		Sandy. Surfing dangerous at low tide.
	Bedruthan Steps			Sand and rocks. Bathing dangerous.
⌒	**Watergate Bay** - EU SW841649	✓✓✓✓✓✗✓✓✓		Sandy.
–	**Porth Beach** SW829627	☐☐☐☐☐✗✓✓		Sandy.
⌒	**Newquay Bay** Towan Beach - EU SW810620	✓✓✓✓✓✓✓✓✓	Screened, 50,000, 75 below LWM. Improvements planned.	Sandy.
⌒⌒⌒	Fistral Beach - EU SW796623	✓✓✓✓✓✓✓✓		Sandy. Strong currents when rough. Not featured due to insufficient information.
⌒⌒	**Crantock** - EU SW784608	✓✓✓✓✓✓✓✓		Sandy. Swimming dangerous at low water and near estuary.
⌒⌒	**Holywell Bay** - EU SW765595	☐☐☐☐☐✓✓✓✓		Sandy. Surfing dangerous at high tide due to steep shelf.
⌒⌒⌒	**Perranporth** Penhale sands - EU SW762570	☐☐☐☐☐✓✓✓✓		Sandy. Not featured due to insufficient information.
⌒⌒	Village End Beach - EU SW757548	☐☐☐☐☐✗✓✓✓	Macerated, 12,000, at LWM. Improvements planned for end 1995.	Sandy. Bathing dangerous at low tide.
f	**Trevaunance Cove** - EU SW723517	✗✗✓✓✓✗✗✗✗	Screened, 4,000, at LWM. Improvements planned for 1996.	Sandy and pebbly at high tide.

RATING	NAME	TRACK RECORD	SEWAGE OUTLET	REMARKS
⌒⌒⌒	**Porthtowan Sandy** - EU SW691481	✓✓✓✓✓✓✓✓		Pebbly beach. Surfing dangerous at low water. Not featured because of reported sewage-related debris.
⌒⌒⌒	**Portreath** - EU SW653455	✓✓✓✓✓✓✓✓	Screened, 26,300, at LWM east of village. Improvements planned for 2000.	Sandy. Swimming dangerous near pier. Not featured because of insufficient information.
–	**Deadman's Cove** (Cambourne)		Raw, 19,500, at LWM. Improvements planned.	Sand and rocks.
⌒	**The Towans** - Godrevy - EU SW581417	✓✓✓✓✓✓✓✓		Sandy. Swimming dangerous at low water.
⌒	**Carbis Bay** Port Kidney Sands - EU SW540385	☐☐☐☐☐✗✓✓✓		Sandy.
⌒⌒	Station Beach - EU SW528389	☐☐☐☐☐✓✓✓✓		Sandy and sheltered.
f	**St Ives** Porthminster - EU SW522402	✓✓✓✗✓✓✓✓✗		Sandy. Sheltered. Well managed beach.
f	Porthgwidden - EU SW522411	✗✓✗✗✗✗✓✗✗		Sandy beach.
⌒	Porthmeor - EU SW5141	✓✓✓✓✓✓✓✓✓	Screened, 50.	Sandy. Bathing is dangerous on ebb tide.
–	**St Just Priest's Cove** SW772604			Shingle.
–	**Porthgwarra**			Sandy at low tide.
⌒⌒⌒	**Porthcurno** - EU SW387223	☐✓✓✓✓✓✓✓✓	Macerated, 200, at LWM.	Sandy. Not featured due to insufficient information.
–	**Lamorna Cove**		Tidal tank, at LWM.	Sand and rocks.
–	**Mousehole** SW470263		Raw, 2,000, at LWM. Improvements planned for 1995.	Fishing port.
f	**Marazion and Mounts Bay** Wherrytown - EU SW467294	☐☐☐☐☐✗✗✗✗		Pebbles.
f	Heliport - EU SW485311	☐☐☐☐☐✗✓✗✗		Fine shingle and coarse sand.
f	**Penzance** - EU SW475298	✗✗✗✗✗✗✗✗✗		Shingle and coarse sand.
⌒⌒	**Little Hogus** - EU SW513310		12, raw, 37,585, 11 at LWM, 1 at 50 below LWM. Improvements planned for 1995.	Sand and shingle.
⌒⌒⌒	**Perran Sands** - EU SW539293	✓✓✓✓✓✗✓✓✓	Raw, 1,000, at LWM.	Sandy. Not featured due to adjacent sewage outfall.
f	**Porthleven West** - EU SW632253	✗✗✗✓✗✗✓✗✗	Raw, 3,500, 50 below LWM. Improvements planned for 1995.	Flint and pebbles. Bathing dangerous.
⌒⌒	**Poldhu Cove** - EU SW665198	☐✓✓✓✓✓✓✓		Sandy. Bathing dangerous at low tide.
⌒⌒	**Polurrian Cove** - EU SW668187	✓✓✓✓✓✓✓✓	Macerated, 1,600, LWM.	Sandy.
–	**Kynance Cove**			Sandy.

RATING	NAME	TRACK RECORD	SEWAGE OUTLET	REMARKS
–	**Polpeor** SW7012			Rock and shingle cove.
–	**Lizard Church Cove** SW661705	✓✓✓✓✓✓✓✓✓	Raw, 1,600, 500 below LWM.	Rocky fishing cove.
f	**Coverack** - EU SW783186	✓✓✓✓✓✓✓✓✗	Primary, 800, 100 below LWM.	Sand and shingle.
∩∩∩∩	**Porthoustock** - EU SW807217	✓✓✓✓✓✓✓✓		Shingle with sand at low tide. Not featured due to insufficient information.
f	**Porthallow** - EU SW797233	✗✗✗✗✓✗✓✗✗	Various private outflows to stream, raw/septic tanks, 100. Improvements planned.	Grey stones.
∩	**Maen Porth** - EU SW790296	✓✗✓✓✓✓✓✗✓		Sand and shingle.
	Falmouth			
∩∩∩∩	Swanpool Beach - EU SW790233	✓✗✓✓✓✗✗✓	2, macerated, 36,500, at LWM and 50 below LWM. Improvements planned.	Sand and shingle. Not featured due to insufficient information.
∩∩∩∩	Gyllyngvase - EU SW809316	✓✗✓✓✓✓✓✓		Sandy. Not featured due to insufficient information.
–	Feock Loe Beach SW826320	✓✓✓		Sand and shingle.
–	**St Anthony's Head**			Fine shingle at low tide.
–	**Towan Beach**		Screened, LSO.	Sand and rock.
f	**Portscatho**		2, raw, 1,988 and 52, both at LWM.	Sand and rock.
∩∩∩∩	**Porthcurnick Beach**			Sand, some rocks. Not featured due to insufficient information.
∩	**Pendower Beach** - EU SW898381	✓✓✓		Sand and rock.
	Carne Beach (Pendower) SW905383	✓✓✓		Rocky.
f	**Portloe** SW938394		2, macerated, 200, at LWM.	Sand and rock. Fishing village.
f	**Portholland Beach**			Shingle, sand at low tide.
∩∩	**Porthluney Cove** - EU SW973413	✓✓✓		Sandy.
∩∩∩∩	**Hemmick Beach**			Small, sandy bay. Not featured due to insufficient information.
∩∩	**Little Perhaver** - EU SX013417	✓✓✓	2, secondary, 2,600, at LWM south of village.	Sandy.
∩∩	**Portmellon** - EU SX016439	✓✓✓✓✓✓✓✓✓		Sand and shingle.
f	**Mevagissey** SX016439	✗✗	Raw, 3,000, at LWM east of harbour. Improvements planned.	Fishing harbour. No beach.
∩	**Polstreath** - EU SX017454	✓✓✓✓✓✓✓✓✓		
∩∩	**Pentewan** - EU SX018467	✗✗✗✗✓✓✓✓		Sandy.
∩∩∩∩	**Porthpean** - EU SX032507	✓✓✓✓✓✓✓✓		Small sandy bay. Not featured due to insufficient information.

RATING	NAME	TRACK RECORD	SEWAGE OUTLET	REMARKS
⌒⌒⌒⌒	**Charlestown** - EU SX042516	□□□□□ ✓✓✓		Sandy. Not featured due to insufficient information.
⌒⌒⌒⌒	**Duporth** - EU			Sandy. Not featured due to insufficient information.
⌒⌒⌒⌒	**Crinnis Beach (Par)** Golf links - EU SX063522	✓✓✓✓✓✓✓✓		Sandy. Not featured due to insufficient information.
⌒⌒⌒⌒	Leisure Centre - EU SX056521	□□□□□ ✓✓✓		Sandy. Well managed beach. Swimming dangerous near stream. Not featured due to insufficient information.
⌒⌒	Par Sands - EU SX083533	✗✓✓✓✓✗✓✓	Secondary, 21,000, LSO.	Sandy.
⌒⌒⌒⌒	**Polkerris** - EU SX092521	✓✗✓✓✓✓✓✓	Screened, 60, 5 below LWM. Improvements planned.	Sandy. Not featured due to insufficient information.
⌒⌒	**Polridmouth Beach**			Sandy beach with shelter from south-westerly winds.
⌒	**Fowey** Readymoney Cove - EU SX118511	✗✗✓✓✓✗✓✗✓	40, raw, 2,500, generally at LWM. Improvements planned for 1995.	Sandy.
⌒	**Lantic Bay**			Sand and shingle. Strong undertow.
–	**Lansallos Bay**			Sandy.
f	**Polperro** SX210509	□□□□□□ ✗✗	Macerated, 3,500, LWM.	Pebbles.
⌒	**East Looe** - EU SX257532	✓✓✓✗✓✓✓✗✓		Sandy. Beach cleaned regularly.
⌒	**Millendreath** - EU SX268541	□✓✓✗✓✓✓✓		Sandy. Beach cleaned daily in the season.
⌒⌒⌒⌒	**Seaton Beach** - EU SX268541	✗✗✗✓✓✓✗✓✓	Raw, 1,300, at LWM. Improvements planned for 1996.	Grey sand and pebbles. Not featured due to insufficient information.
⌒⌒⌒⌒	**Downderry** - EU SX314538	□✗✓✓✓✓✓✓	Raw, 1,000, below LWM east of beach. Improvements planned for 1996.	Sandy. Beach cleaned regularly. Not featured due to adjacent sewage outfall.
⌒⌒	**Portwrinkle, Freathy** (Whitsand Bay) - EU SX359538	□✗✓✓✓✓✓✓	Macerated, 800, LWM. Improvements planned for mid 1995.	Sandy backed by cliffs. Bathing is unsafe.
–	**Cawsand Bay**		3, raw, 260, LWM. Improvements planned.	Pebbles and rocks.
–	**Kingsands Bay**		2, raw, 440, 5 and 12 below LWM. Improvements planned.	Sand and shingle.
	DEVON (South)			
f	**Plymouth Hoe** East and West - EU SX478537	✗✗✗✓✗✗✗✗✗	Many, primary and raw, 100,000, from LWM to 50 below LWM. Improvements planned for 1995.	Shingle. Shingle.
⌒⌒⌒⌒	**Bovisand Bay** - EU SX493505	✓✓✓✓✓✓✓✗✓		Sand and rocks. Not featured due to reported sewage-related debris.

73

RATING	NAME	TRACK RECORD	SEWAGE OUTLET	REMARKS
⌒⌒	**Wembury** - EU SX516485	✓✗✓✓✓✓✗✓	Secondary, 4,400, 100 below LWM. Discharge point remote from beach.	Silvery sand and rocks.
f	**Mothecombe** - EU SX610473	✓✓✓✓✓✓✓✗		Sandy. Bathing safe only on incoming tide.
⌒⌒	**Bigbury-on-Sea, South** - EU SX651441	✓✓✓✓✓✓✓	Secondary, 1,260, 50 below LWM.	Sandy. Swimming dangerous near river mouth.
⌒⌒⌒⌒	**Bantham** - EU	✓✓✓✓✓✓✓✓		Sand and mud. Not featured because bathing dangerous.
⌒	**Hope Cove** - EU SX675397	✓✓✓✓✓✓✓✓		Sandy.
⌒⌒	**Soar Mill Cove**	✓✓		Stream-crossed sands, rockpools and cliffs.
⌒⌒	**Salcombe North Sands** - EU SX731382	✗✓✓✗✓✗✓✓	4, secondary, 3,400, at LWM and 50 below.	Sandy.
⌒⌒	**Salcombe South Sands** - EU SX720850	✗✓✗✓✓✓✗✓	Secondary, 70, 7 below LWM.	Sandy.
⌒⌒⌒⌒	**Hallsands**			Shingle. Not featured due to insufficient information.
⌒⌒⌒	**Beesands**			Shingle, steeply shelving. Not featured due to insufficient information.
⌒⌒⌒⌒	**Torcross** - EU SX823419	✓✓✓✓	Raw, 300, at LWM south of village.	Fishing port. See Slapton Sands.
–	**Leonard's Cove**		2, raw, 1,000 and 1,000, both at LWM at Stoke Fleming.	Shingle.
⌒	**Dartmouth Castle & Sugary Cove** - EU SX886502	✓✓✓✓✓✓✓✓	5, macerated, 11,900, at LWM to 50 below. Improvements planned.	Shingle.
⌒	**St Mary's Bay** - EU SX932551	✓✓✓✓✓✓✓✓	Macerated, 90,000, 220 below LWM off Sharkham Point. Improvements planned for 2000.	Sand and pebbles.
⌒	**Churston Cove** SX919569	✓✓		Shingle.
f	**Broadsands Beach** - EU SX897574	✓✓✓✓✓✓✓✗		Muddy sand and pebbles.
⌒	**Goodrington Sands** - EU SX893594	✓✗✓✓✓✓✓✓	Stormwater only.	Sand and pebbles.
f	**Paignton** Paignton Sands - EU SX894606	✓✓✗✓✓✓✓✗	Stormwater only.	Red sands.
f	Preston Sands - EU SX896617	✓✓✓✓✓✗	Stormwater only.	Red sands.
⌒⌒⌒	**Hollicombe** - EU 8988621	✓✓✓✓✓✓✓✓		Not featured due to insufficient information.
⌒	**Torre Abbey Sands** - EU SX909635	✓✓✓✓✓✗✓✓		Sandy.
⌒⌒⌒⌒	**Beacon Cove** - EU SX919630			Shingle. Not featured due to insufficient information.
⌒⌒	**Meadfoot Beach** - EU SX930630			Sandy at low tide.

RATING	NAME	TRACK RECORD	SEWAGE OUTLET	REMARKS
🐦🐦	**Anstey's Cove/ Redgate Beach -** EU SX930648	✓✓✓✓✓✓✓✓✓	Screened, 100,000, 50 below LWM. Improvements planned.	Sand and shingle.
🐦	**Babbacombe -** EU SX930654	✓✓✓✓✓✓✓✓✓		Shingle.
🐦🐦	**Shaldon -** EU SX935723	✗✗✗✓✓✗✓✓✓	Secondary, 50,000, LSO.	Sandy.
🐦	**Teignmouth -** EU SX943728	✓✗✓✓✓✓✓✓✓		Sandy.
f	**Holcombe -** EU SX956746	✗✓✓✓✗		Rocky.
🐦	**Dawlish** Town - EU SX965768	✓✓✓✓✓✓✗✓✓		
🐦	Coryton Cove - EU SX961760	✓✓✓	Raw, 12,000, 100 below LWM. Improvements planned.	Red sand and shingle.
🐦🐦🐦🐦	Dawlish Warren - EU SX983787	✓✓✓✓✓✓✓✓✓		Sand and dunes. Bathing dangerous near River Exe. Not featured due to adjacent sewage outfall.
🐦	**Exmouth -** EU SY983787	✗✓✓✓✓✓✓✗✓	Primary, 42,700, 170 below. Improvements planned for mid 1995.	Sandy, sheltered from all but easterly winds. Strong tides.
🐦	**Sandy Bay -** EU	✓✓✓✓✓✓✓✗✓		Sandy. This area will benefit from the Exmouth scheme.
f	**Budleigh Salterton -** EU SY069819	✓✗✓✓✓✓✓✗✗		Pebbles. This area will benefit from the Exmouth scheme.
🐦	**Ladram Bay -** EU SY119895	✓✓✓✓✓✓✓✓		Pebbles.
f	**Sidmouth -** EU SY127872	✓✓✓✓✗	Macerated/screened, 14,000, 400 below LWM. Improvements planned.	Pebbles with sand.
🐦	Jacob's Ladder - EU SY119869	✓✓✓✓✓✓✓✓✗		
–	**Branscombe** SY2188			Pebbles.
f	**Beer -** EU SY231891	✓✓✓✓✓✓✓✓✗	Raw, 2,000, at LWM 1 km south of the town.	Pebbles.
🐦🐦	**Seaton -** EU SY245898	✓✗✓✓✓✓✓✓✓	Secondary, 11,000. Discharged into estuary.	Pebbles. Steep beach.
	DORSET			
	Lyme Regis Monmouth Beach SY337915	✗✗✗✗✗✗ ✗✗		Pebbles, shelves slightly.
–	Church Beach SY343921	✗✗✗		Sandy.
🐦🐦	Cobb/Town Beach - EU SY339918	✓✗✗✗	Secondary/disinfection, 6,000, 400 below LWM. Improvements planned for 1995.	Sandy shallow bay.
🐦	**Charmouth West -** EU SY636930	✗✓✓✓✓✓✓✓✓		Sand and pebbles with slight shelving.
🐦🐦	**Charmouth East** SY367929	✗✓✗✓	Screened, 8,000, LSO.	Sand and pebbles, slight shelving.

RATING	NAME	TRACK RECORD	SEWAGE OUTLET	REMARKS
ᐱ	**Seatown** - EU SY446910	✓✓✓✓✓✓✓✓		Pebble beach with steep shelving.
ᐱᐱ	**Eypemouth** - EU SY446910	✗✓✓✓✓✓✓✓		Pebble beach with a rocky margin.
ᐱᐱᐱᐱ	**Burton Bradstock** SY490887	□□□□□✓✓✓		Steeply shelving shingle. Not featured due to insufficient information.
ᐱᐱᐱᐱ	**Chesil Cove** SY682735	□□□□✓✓✓✓	Screened, 86,000, LSO. Improvements planned.	Pebbles. Not featured because unsuitable for bathing
ᐱᐱᐱᐱ	**Church Ope Cove** - EU SY697710	✓✓✓✓✓✓✓✓		Shingle, pebbles, boulders. Not featured because unsuitable for bathing.
ᐱᐱ	**Portland Harbour** Sandsfoot - EU SY673772	✓✓✓✓✓✓✗✗✓		Sandy.
ᐱᐱ	Castle Cove - EU SY676775	□□□□□✓✓✓		Sandy.
ᐱ	**Weymouth South** SY682789	□□□□□✓✓✓		Sandy.
ᐱᐱᐱᐱ	**Lodmoor West** SY687806	□□□□□✓✓✓		Shingle and pebble. Not featured due to insufficient information.
ᐱᐱᐱᐱ	**Lodmoor** - EU SY688807	□□□□□✓✓✓		Shingle and pebble. Not featured due to insufficient information.
ᐱᐱ	**Bowleaze** - EU SY704818	✓✓✓✓✓✓✓✓		Fine shingle and pebble.
ᐱᐱ	**Ringstead Bay** - EU SY751813	✓✓✓✓✓✓✓✗✓		Shingle and pebble.
ᐱ	**Lulworth Cove** - EU SY824799	✓✓✓✓✓✓✓✓	Raw, 2,000, below LWM outside Cove. Improvements planned.	Shingle.
–	**Worbarrow Bay**			Sometimes badly littered.
f	**Kimmeridge Bay** - EU	✓✓✓✓✓✓✗✗		Rocky. Cliffs are unstable.
f	**Swanage** South	□□□□□✓✓✗✗		Sandy.
ᐱᐱ	Central - EU SZ032791	✓✓✓✓✓✓✗✓		Sandy.
f	North SZ031797	□□□□□✓✓✗✗	Macerated, 12,000, 100 below LWM.	Sandy.
ᐱᐱ	**Poole** Rockley Sands - EU SY972908	✗✓✓✓✓✓✓✓		Sandy.
ᐱᐱ	Lake - EU SY983904	✓✓✓✓✓✓✓✓		
ᐱᐱᐱ	Harbour - EU SZ049885	✓✓✓✗✓✓✓✓		See other Poole beaches in featured section.
ᐱ	Branksome Chine SZ066897	□□□□□✓✓✓		Sand and shingle. Muddy at low tide.
ᐱᐱᐱᐱ	**Bournemouth** Alum Chine SZ076903	□□□□□✓✓✓		See other Bournemouth beaches in featured section.
f	Bournemouth Pier - EU SZ088906	✓✓✓✓✓✓✓✗	Stormwater only.	Sandy.
ᐱᐱ	Boscombe Pier - EU SZ112911	□□□□□✓✓✗✓		Sandy.

RATING	NAME	TRACK RECORD	SEWAGE OUTLET	REMARKS
⌒⌒	**Christchurch** Mudeford Sandbank - EU SZ183912	✓✓✓✓✓✓✓✓		Sandy. Beach cleaned regularly.
f	Mudeford Quay	⬜⬜⬜⬜⬜✓✗✗✗		Sand and shingle.
⌒	Avon Beach - EU SZ183912	✓✗✗✓✓✓✓✓		Sand and shingle. Beach cleaned regularly.
⌒⌒	Friars Cliff - EU SZ192252	⬜⬜⬜⬜⬜✓✓✓		Sandy. Beach cleaned regularly.
⌒⌒	**Highcliffe Castle** - EU SZ200929	⬜⬜⬜⬜⬜✓✓✓		Sandy.
⌒⌒	**Highcliffe** SZ216931	✓✓✓✓✓✓✓✓		Shingle and mud.
	ISLE OF WIGHT			
⌒⌒⌒	**Totland** - EU SZ322871	✗✓✓✓✓✓✓✓	1, 2,000, 300 below LWM, Improvements planned.	Shingle. Not featured due to insufficient information.
⌒	**Colwell Bay** - EU SZ328879	✗✓✗✓✓✓✓✓		Shingle.
−	**Yarmouth**		Stormwater only.	Shingle beach.
−	**Norton** SZ347898	⬜⬜⬜⬜⬜✓✓✓	Macerated, 15,000, 230 below LWM.	Sandy.
⌒⌒	**Gurnard Bay** - EU SZ477959	✗✗✗✓✗✗✗✓✓	Macerated, 5,800, 400 below LWM.	Shingle.
⌒⌒	**Cowes** West - EU SZ488967	✗✗✗✗✗✗✗✓✓	Screened, 15,000, LSO.	
⌒	East SZ506964	⬜⬜⬜⬜⬜✓✓✓		Sailing centre.
f	**Ryde** West SZ588930	✗✗✗✗✓✗✗✓✗		Sandy.
⌒	East - EU SZ601927	⬜⬜⬜⬜⬜✓✓✓	Macerated, 21,000, LSO.	Sandy.
−	Seaview			Sandy and rocks.
⌒⌒	**Bembridge** - EU SZ657881	✗✗✗✗✓✗✓✓✓	Macerated/tidal tank, 7,000, LSO. Improvements planned.	Sailing centre.
⌒	**Whitecliff Bay** - EU SZ641862	✓✓✗✗✓✓✓✓		Sandy.
f	**Sandown Yaverland** SZ610849	⬜⬜⬜⬜✓✓✓✗	Primary, 50,000, 250 below LWM.	Sandy.
⌒	**Sandown Esplanade** - EU SZ601842	✓✓✓✓✓✓✓✓		Sandy.
f	**Shanklin** (Welcome Beach) SZ589827	✓✗✓✓✓✓✓✗✗		
⌒	**Shanklin** - EU SZ585811	⬜⬜⬜⬜⬜✓✓✓		Sandy.
f	**Ventnor** - EU SZ562773	✗✗✗✗✓✗✗✗✗	Macerated, 5,300, LWM. Improvements planned.	Sandy.
⌒⌒	**Compton Bay** SZ3841	✓✓✓✓✓✓✓✓		Shingle beach. Beach cleaned regularly.
⌒	**St Helens** - EU SZ637892	✓✗✗✗✓✓✗✓✓	Raw, 1,500. Improvements planned.	Sandy.
⌒⌒⌒	**Seagrove Bay** - EU SZ632912	✓✓✗✗✗✗✗✗✓		Not featured due to insufficient information.

Hayling Island is representative of the south coast's best beaches.

South-East England

THE SOUTH-EAST COAST OF ENGLAND IS RICH IN CONTRASTS: THE AREA BETWEEN BARTON-ON-SEA IN HAMPSHIRE AND HEACHAM IN NORFOLK ENCOMPASSES SOME OF THE MOST VARIED AND BEAUTIFUL COASTAL SCENERY IN THE COUNTRY, RANGING FROM LONG SHINGLE BANKS TO SAND DUNES AND SALT MARSHES.

•

Low clay cliffs predominate in Suffolk, while creeks and mud flats are found on the Essex coast and the Thames Estuary. Where the chalk hills of the North Downs reach the coast they form the formidable white cliffs of Dover, one of the most potent of national symbols and an impressive setting for many busy holiday resorts. Then there is Lowestoft Ness in Norfolk, the most easterly point of Britain, continually being eroded by the North Sea. Much of the Norfolk coast is designated an Area of Outstanding Natural Beauty and is managed to promote sustainable tourism.

The Solent is busy with boating traffic and the naval base of Portsmouth is a storehouse of British maritime history, home to famous ships such as the *Mary Rose*, HMS *Warrior* and HMS *Victory*. There are other ports of a very different nature – the ferry terminals of Felixstowe, Dover and Folkestone provide a gateway to Europe, while the Thames Estuary reminds us of our rich maritime past and is the site of popular boating areas such as the Medway, the Blackwater Estuary and the Swale.

These are some of the most heavily developed and densely populated coastal stretches, and not without severe problems. Heavy shipping traffic in the Channel means that marine litter and oil are constantly being washed up on to the beaches. International legislation is in place to prevent such pollution, but the signs are that it is being widely ignored. Extensive stretches of the coastline suffer from pollution by sewage, although action is being taken at many sites in the south. One source of this pollution, the dumping of sewage sludge off the Thames Estuary, must end by 1998, but other discharges, domestic, nuclear and industrial, are still a cause for concern. The disturbance around Shakespeare Cliff from the construction of the Channel Tunnel will have a severe long-term effect on marine and coastal life. On a coastline under such pressure from diverse human activities including tourism, industry and residential development, efforts are needed to bring about an improvement in the coastal environment, and to ensure that those areas which have survived unspoilt are allowed to remain so.

STOKES BAY, GOSPORT
Hampshire
OS Ref: SZ595985

The arc of Stokes Bay, with its almost manicured shingle, curves from Browndown Point south to Fort Gilkicker, a fortification built in 1860 to protect the western approaches to Portsmouth docks. The narrow band of shingle, which shelves quite steeply to some sand at low tide, widens landward towards the south-east of the bay; the longshore drift currents continually move it in this direction and this has led to the build-up of a wide area of flat shingle stretching towards Fort Gilkicker. The beach, overlooking Ryde on the Isle of Wight, has a wide-open feel about it. The promenade is level with the shingle and is backed by flat, grassed recreational areas bordered by the trees and shrubs of the adjacent park and school. Dogs are banned from certain areas of the beach.

Water quality

One outfall serving 200,000 people discharges secondary treated sewage one kilometre below LWM from Peel Common, to the north of Lee-on-the-Solent.

Bathing safety

Safe bathing, with swimming and windsurfing restricted to signposted areas of the beach. There is an inshore rescue boat station at southern end of the bay.

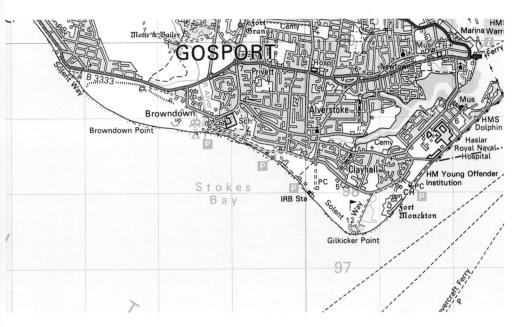

Litter

The beach is cleaned regularly by the local authority. Heavy use of the Solent by shipping leads to some littering problems on the beaches.

Access

Stokes Bay is signposted from the B3333 between Lee-on-the-Solent and Gosport. There is easy parking off the road behind the beach and level access on to the shingle.

Parking

Car parks are signposted at each end of the beach and at its centre, with over 300 spaces. There is also some parking adjacent to the promenade towards the western end.

Popular for watersports, Stokes Bay attracts dinghy sailors throughout the year.

Toilets

At the car park adjacent to the No 2 Battery Fort at Browndown, on the promenade near the sailing club and at Gilkicker.

Food

A café on the promenade.

Seaside activities

Swimming, windsurfing, sailing, canoeing and diving. Two public slipways. Children's paddling pool, miniature golf and tennis courts behind the beach.

Wet weather alternatives

In Gosport there is a local museum, the submarine museum and Fort Brockhurst.

Wildlife and walks

The Solent Way footpath can be followed south-east past Fort Gilkicker towards Portsmouth Harbour or north-west to Lee-on-the-Solent and beyond.

Track record ✓ ✗ ✓ ✓ ✓ ✓ ✓ ✓

HAYLING ISLAND, WEST BEACH
Hampshire
OS Ref: SZ710987

Eight kilometres of pebble beach with sand at low tide stretch along Hayling from Eastoke Point at the entrance of Chichester Harbour to Sinah Common at the entrance of Langstone Harbour. The western end of the beach is undeveloped, backed by dunes and a golf course.

Water quality

Bathing safety
Unsafe at either end of the beach due to the harbour currents. Coastguard is on the foreshore.

Litter
Litter is hand-picked twice daily during the season. There is a dog ban from May to September and poop scoop byelaws along the foreshore.

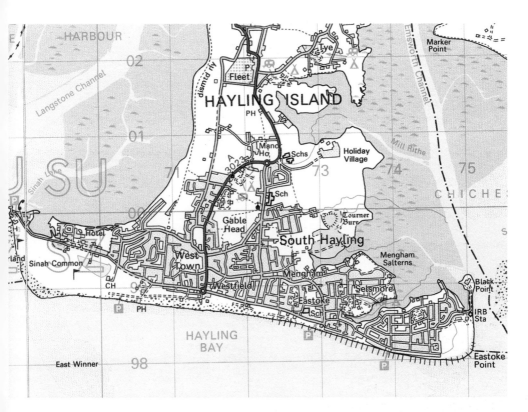

Access
From the A27; the beach is a short walk from the foreshore car park.

Parking
There is plenty of parking on the foreshore.

Public transport
A number of buses run from Havant which is also the nearest rail station.

Toilets
There are public toilets including facilities for disabled visitors.

Food
There are several kiosks and cafés.

Seaside activities
Swimming, windsurfing, sailing and water-skiing. Golf course.

Wet weather alternatives
Amusement arcades.

Wildlife and walks
In spite of its popularity with visitors, many areas of the island are still unspoilt. The walk along the old railway line to the north of the town takes you along the east shore of Langstone Harbour and leads to a nature reserve covering an area of marshland with a variety of plant and animal life.

Windsurfers and bathers share the west beach at Hayling Island.

Track record ✓✓✓✓✓✓✓✓

SELSEY BILL
Sussex
OS Ref: SZ860925

From the low headland of Selsey Bill with its excellent views of the Isle of Wight, the beach extends in both directions. The groyne-ribbed east beach is the most popular, backed by the sea wall, with shingle and sand stretching to Pagham Harbour. The lifeboat station and the fisherman's compound add to the interest. The west beach is backed by private land and stretches away to East Wittering round Bracklesham Bay.

Water quality

Bathing safety
Bathing is safe one kilometre to either side of the headland, but fast currents around Selsey Bill make it unsafe to bathe there.

Access
There is direct access to the beach from the sea wall.

Parking
A car park at Selsey has around 500 places.

Toilets
There are toilets available at Selsey.

Food
Many kiosks can be found on or near the seafront.

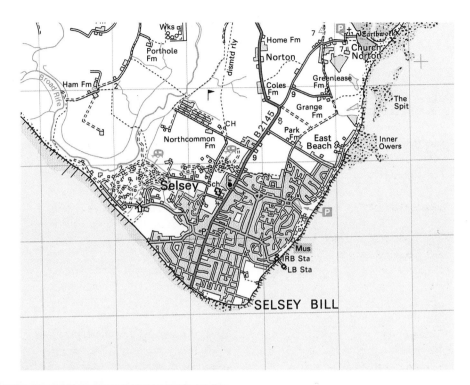

Seaside activities
Surfing, windsurfing and sailing.

Wildlife and walks
Pagham Harbour to the east is a nature reserve and a refuge for dozens of species of birds, butterflies and plants. The Sidlesham Ferry Nature Trail circles the western edge of the harbour and is well worth following to Pagham. The saltmarsh has a large number of visiting wildfowl in the winter.

Track record ✓✗✗✓✗✓✓✓

Miles of sand and shingle in every direction gives scope for superb walks.

85

JOSS BAY, BROADSTAIRS
Kent
OS Ref: TR399702

Asandy natural bay with low cliffs behind, this is a centre for canoeing and surfboarding, and there is good swimming too. Charles Dickens wrote his novel *David Copperfield* in this area, and the twisting narrow streets of Broadstairs are full of reminders: every year in June there is a week-long Dickens Festival. A variety of bays and beaches abound providing widely differing characteristics and opportunities for recreation.

Water quality

 Bathing safety
Swimming is safe, with lifeguards in the summer season.

 Litter
The beach is cleaned regularly by hand.

 Access
Via the M2 Thanet Way to Broadstairs, then follow road signposts.

 Parking
There is a large car park adjacent to the beach.

 Toilets
Toilets are available.

 Food
A café and kiosk serve hot and cold snacks.

 Seaside activities
Swimming, surf ski hire and volleyball.

 Wet weather alternatives
Local museums; theme park in Margate; day trips to Dunkirk in France via the Sally Line Ferries.

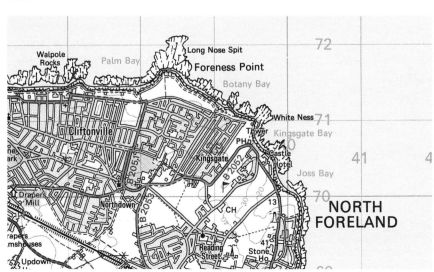 **Wildlife and walks**
The coastal nature path can be reached by following the signs from either end.

Track record ✗ ✗ ✓ ✓ ✓ ✓ ✓ ✓

BOTANY BAY, CLIFTONVILLE
Kent
OS Ref: TR391712

The Isle of Thanet was a real island in Roman times, separated from the mainland by one and a half kilometres of the Wantsum Channel. Over the centuries this channel silted up and today Thanet is an island in name only. Botany Bay is a sandy natural cove, with steps leading down to the beach from Kingsgate Avenue.

Water quality
No sewage is discharged in the vicinity of this beach.

 Bathing safety
There is lifeguard cover between the third Saturday of June and the first week in September.

Litter
The beach is cleaned regularly by hand and dog bins are provided which are emptied daily.

Access
Via the M2 Thanet Way to Margate then follow signposts to Northdown Park/Botany Bay.

P Parking
On-street parking.

Public transport
The nearest rail and coach station is at Victoria, Margate. Local buses to Kingsgate stop at Botany Bay.

 Toilets
By the steps to the beach.

 Food
There is a pub nearby.

 Seaside activities
Swimming.

 Wet weather alternatives
As Joss Bay opposite.

 Wildlife and walks
As Joss Bay opposite.

Track record ✔✔✔✔
Not EU designated.

The bays and beaches around the Kent coast form a continuous holiday playground.

MINNIS BAY
Kent
OS Ref: TR286697

Minnis Bay is a popular family beach, sandy with some rocks and a grassy area where beached dinghies are parked. It has a small slipway which can be used for two and a half hours either side of high water.

Water quality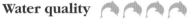

Bathing safety
Safe, with lifeguard cover from the third Saturday in June to the first weekend in September.

Litter
The beach is cleaned regularly by hand. Dogs are banned from May until September and dog-dirt bins are provided. These are emptied daily.

The wide sands of Minnis Bay are equally beautiful in the winter months.

Access
Via the M2 Thanet Way to Birchington and follow the signs for the bay.

Parking
Parking is adjacent to the beach.

Public transport
The nearest rail and coach station is at Birchington, Victoria. A promenade and stairway lead to the beach.

Toilets
These are adjacent to the beach and include facilities for disabled visitors.

Food
There is a beach café, a pub and a kiosk.

Seaside activities
Swimming, windsurfing and putting. Beach chalets are available for hire.

Wet weather alternatives
Powell Cotton Natural Life Museum, Margate Museum and Amusement Park. Day trips from Ramsgate to Dunkirk via Sally Line Ferries.

Wildlife and walks
Access to the Coastal Nature Path is signposted from the car park.

Track record ✓✓✓✓✓✓✓✓

SHEERNESS (BEACH STREET)
Kent
OS Ref: TR925750

A substantial sea defence wall which forms the promenade is a distinctive characteristic of this gently sloping sand and shingle beach at the mouth of the busy Thames and Medway Estuaries. The beach is separated from the town centre by gardens, a leisure complex, swimming pool and a large sand pit play area. The beach is a bathing-only zone, 600 metres in length and dogs are banned between May and September.

Water quality
No sewage is discharged in the vicinity of this beach.

Bathing safety
There is a lifeguard patrol between May and September, 9.00am to 5.00pm seven days a week and first aid is available in the leisure complex and swimming pool. A flag system operates to warn of dangerous conditions and swimmers should keep away from the groynes.

Litter
The beach is cleaned daily during the summer season.

Access
From the M20, follow the signs for the A249 into the centre of Sheerness; the beach is signposted. Steps lead down to the beach and lifeguards will assist disabled visitors.

Parking
There are 236 spaces in three car parks adjacent to the beach.

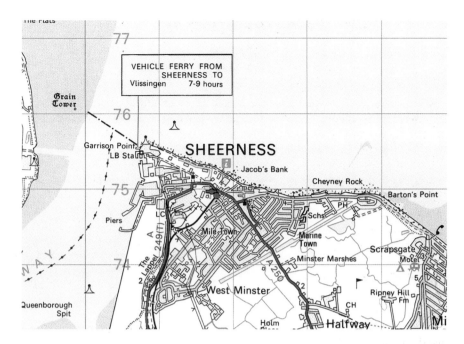

Public transport

Sheerness rail station is 150 metres from the beach. Buses arrive six times a day to the Tesco site 150 metres from the beach.

Toilets

There are toilets in the leisure complex, at the swimming pool and on the street, with facilities for disabled visitors.

Food

There is a wide variety of cafés and restaurants in the High Street, and a beach kiosk serves snacks.

Seaside activities

Bathing, paddling, sandpit, climbing frame, windsurfing and sailing.

The massive sea wall above Sheerness Beach is a superb vantage point for views across the Thames Estuary.

Wet weather alternatives

The leisure complex and indoor heated pool, Minster Abbey Gatehouse, crazy golf, tennis and children's playground.

Wildlife and walks

From Sheerness it is possible to walk right around the Isle of Sheppey, or walk one of the two coast trails. The nearby Minster Cliffs are an outstanding site for a relaxing picnic. The Medway Estuary and Swale marshes are rich in wildlife and naturalists should visit the Swale National Nature Reserve at the eastern tip of Sheppey or the RSPB's Elmley Reserve. Turn right one kilometre from Kingsferry Bridge on to the A249. Once visitors are off the road they will by surprised by the wilderness of Southern Sheppey. The area is internationally important for wading bird populations.

Track record ☐☐☐☐☐ ✓✓✓

BRIGHTLINGSEA
Essex
OS Ref: TM076161

This small semi-rural beach close to the centre of Brightlingsea has a tidal-washed paddling pool which is very popular with children. Brightlingsea stands on an island, surrounded on three sides by water and can only be reached by a single road. Dogs are banned from May to September.

Water quality
One sewage outfall serving 9,000 people discharges secondary treated sewage to the Colne.

Bathing safety
Strong currents can make bathing dangerous; there is no lifeguard cover.

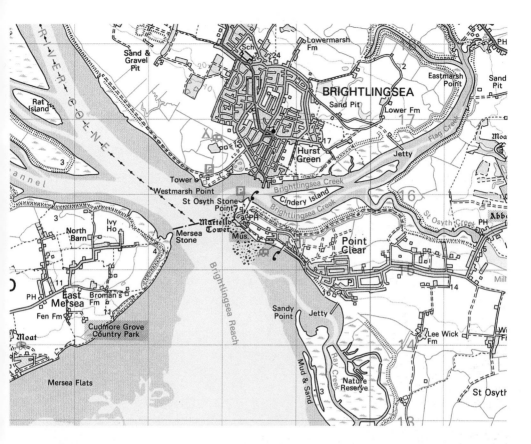

Litter

The beach is cleaned regularly.

Access

 Brightlingsea is between Colchester and Clacton off the B1029.

Parking

 There is free parking nearby.

Public transport

 Buses run from Clacton and Colchester.

Fishing and boat-building have been major local industries in Brightlingsea for many years, and there are facilities for launching craft of all descriptions.

Toilets

Toilets are available including facilities for disabled visitors.

Food

There are two small kiosks a short distance from the beach.

Seaside activities

Swimming.

Wet weather alternatives

There is a sports centre locally and a museum.

Wildlife and walks

There is a walk along the sea wall towards Wivenhoe and a nature trail along an old disused railway line.

Track record

FELIXSTOWE (SOUTH AND NORTH)
Suffolk
OS Ref: TM300341

The seaside resort is strung out around a gently curving bay, shingle and sand beach with groynes. This is a sheltered spot ideal and safe for bathing, the promenade is nearly five kilometres long and backed by beautiful gardens which are the pride of the town.

Water quality
Two sewage outlets serving 8,400 and 27,000 people discharge macerated sewage 630 metres below LWM. Improvements are planned for 1997.

Bathing safety
Generally safe along most of the beach, except at Landguard Point where there are strong currents. Lifeguards operate from May to September.

FELIXSTOWE

VEHICLE FERRY
FROM FELIXSTOWE TO
Zeebrugge 5 to 8 hours

Litter
Dogs are banned from certain zones of the beach, which is cleaned daily during the summer.

Access
Via the A45. There is easy access from the promenade.

Parking
Several seafront car parks.

Toilets
Toilets, including facilities for disabled visitors and mother-and-baby rooms, in the leisure centre.

Felixstowe combines the elegance of a Victorian bathing resort with the industry of a European container port.

Food
There are a variety of cafés, restaurants and kiosks along the seafront.

Seaside activities
Swimming and windsurfing.

Wet weather alternatives
Museum, indoor leisure centre, theatre with children's shows, cinema.

Wildlife and walks
There are seven walks around Felixstowe including circular walks. The Suffolk Heritage Coast Path starts from here.

Track record ✗ ✓ ✓ ✓ ✓ ✓ ✓ ✓

SOUTHWOLD (THE DENES)
Suffolk
OS Ref: TM508754

All that remains of Southwold's pier is a short skeleton and the buildings on the promenade, but it is still the focal point for this five-kilometre-long beach of sand and shingle. To the north, rainbow-coloured beach huts line the sea wall which edges the groyne-ribbed beach of soft sand. As the beach curves northwards, sand cliffs rise to replace the sea wall. South of the pier the sand and shingle stretch to the harbour at the mouth of the River Blyth. Wheeled changing-huts line the promenade below scrub-covered slopes. The attractive town of Southwold sits aloft, built around seven greens and shadowed by its lighthouse.

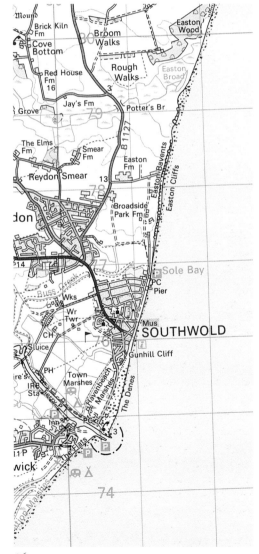

Water quality
One outfall discharges secondary treated sewage.

Bathing safety
Safe bathing except near the groynes and at the river mouth. The District Council provides a Lifeguard Service for this beach during the bathing season.

Access
The seafront is signposted from the town; there are steps and a steep ramp on to the beach.

Parking
Three car parks have a total of 300 spaces adjacent to the pier and harbour.

Public transport
The nearest rail station is at Halesworth.

Toilets
On the promenade, including facilities for disabled visitors.

Food
Café, bar, shop and take-away at the pier.

Colourful beach huts form the backdrop to the sand and shingle beach.

 Seaside activities
Swimming, surfing, windsurfing, sailing and fishing. Amusement arcade. Boating lake.

 Wet weather alternatives
St Edmund's Hall and museum contain relics connected with local history.

Wildlife and walks
There are walks along the river and across the meadows. The climb to the summit of Gun Hill is well worth the effort for the reward of some good views. The Suffolk Coastal Path runs north towards Lowestoft and south to Dunwich Forest and Minsmere, approximately five kilometres from Southwold.

Track record ☐☐☐☐ ✓✓✓✓

97

LOWESTOFT, SOUTH BEACH
Suffolk
OS Ref: TM545917

Fine pale sand interspersed with traditional wooden groynes characterise this beach, located between the South Pier and the Claremont Pier and including an especially safe children's corner with beach activities and Punch and Judy. Adjacent to the beach is the recently refurbished Royal Green, an events arena with a wide programme for visitors and residents. The newly opened Fast Point Pavilion offers indoor facilities and entertainment; the South Pier is also open to the public.

Water quality
No sewage is discharged in the vicinity of this beach.

Bathing safety
Safe, with lifeguard cover between May and September from 10.00am to 6.00pm.

Litter
The beach is cleaned daily by hand. Dogs are banned between May and September.

A safe bathing area for children means parents can relax at Lowestoft.

98

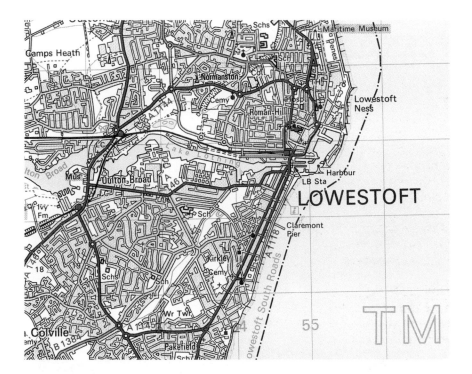

Access
Three ramps and two sets of steps lead to the beach.

Parking
Esplanade parking very close to the beach.

Public transport
Lowestoft Central is the nearest rail station, National Express coaches and local buses (numbers L13, L23, L18 and L19) stop here.

Toilets
There are mother-and-baby rooms at the East Pavilion, facilities for disabled visitors at Waterloo Road and other toilets close to the South Pier.

Food
A variety of cafés and restaurants are nearby.

Seaside activities
Swimming, surfing, windsurfing (zoned areas). Punch and Judy and children's activities on the beach. Beach chalets can be hired.

Wet weather alternatives
The East Point Pavilion houses a children's indoor play and Heritage attraction. Nearby are the Pleasurewood Hills Family Theme Park, Suffolk Wildlife Park and many local museums.

Wildlife and walks
The Suffolk Heritage Coast Footpath to the south of Lowestoft traverses superb coastline and heathland in an Area of Outstanding Natural Beauty. Lowestoft links into the southern end of the Norfolk and Suffolk Broads.

Track record ✓✓✓✓✓✓✓✓

RATING	NAME	TRACK RECORD	SEWAGE OUTLET	REMARKS
	HAMPSHIRE			
–	**Barton-on-Sea** SZ239928	☐☐✓✓✓✓✓	Primary and disinfection, at LWM. Improvements planned.	Pebbles and shingle.
⌒⌒⌒⌒	**Milford-on-Sea** - EU SZ283915	✗✗✗✗✓✗✗✓✓	Improvements planned.	Not featured due to insufficient information.
⌒⌒	**Lepe** - EU SZ456985	✓✓✓✓✓✓✓✓✓		Sand and shingle.
⌒⌒	**Calshot** - EU SU481012	✓✗✗✓✓✓✓✓✓		Mud.
–	**Solent Breezes** SU505038	☐☐☐☐☐✓✓✓		
⌒⌒	**Hill Head** - EU SU548180	☐☐☐☐☐✓✓✓		
⌒⌒	**Lee-on-the-Solent** - EU SU5700			Groyne-ribbed shingle with sand at low tide.
f	**Southsea** (South Parade Pier) - EU SZ653982	✓✗✗✓✓✓✓✓✗✗	Improvements planned.	Shingle.
⌒⌒⌒	**Eastney** - EU SZ675988	✓✓✗✓✓✓✓✓✓	Screened, 200,000, LSO.	Not featured due to insufficient information.
–	**Hayling Island** East SZ729984	✓✓✓✓✓✓✓✓✓		Shingle, sand at low tide.
	WEST SUSSEX			
⌒⌒⌒	**West Wittering** - EU SZ768980	✓✓✓✓✓✓✓✓✓		Sandy. Not featured due to insufficient information.
⌒⌒⌒⌒	**East Wittering** - EU SZ805963	☐☐☐☐☐✓✓✓		Sandy with shingle bank. Not featured due to insufficient information.
⌒⌒	**Bracklesham Bay** - EU			Sandy.
⌒	**Pagham** - EU SZ892972	✓✓✗✗✓✓✓✓✓		Shingle.
⌒⌒	**Bognor Regis** - EU SZ923985	✓✓✓✓✓✗✓✓✓	Primary, 71,500, LSO.	Sandy. Beach cleaned regularly.
–	**Felpham** (Yacht Club) SZ985993	☐☐☐☐✗✓✓✓	Stormwater only. Improvements planned for 1995.	
⌒⌒	**Middleton-on-Sea** - EU SZ985999	✗✗✗✓✓✓✗✓✓		Sand and shingle.
⌒	**Littlehampton** - EU TQ040013	☐✗✗✗✓✓✓✓✓	Macerated/screened, 53,000, LSO.	Sand and shingle. Beach cleaned regularly.
–	**Goring-by-Sea**		Primary, 45,000, LSO. Improvements planned.	Sand and shingle.
f	**Worthing** West - EU TQ139021	✗✗✗✓✓✓✗✗✗	Primary, 45,000, LWM. Improvements planned.	Shingle and sand. Beach cleaned regularly.
–	East TQ168029	☐☐☐☐☐✓✗✗✗	2, screened and stormwater, 80,000, LSO. Improvements planned.	Sand and shingle. Beach cleaned regularly.
f	**Lancing** (South) - EU TQ183036	✗✗✗✗✗✗✗✗✗	Improvements planned for mid 1995.	Shingle and sand.
–	**Shoreham** (Kingston Beach) TQ235046	☐☐☐☐☐✗✗✓		Shingle and sand.

RATING	NAME	TRACK RECORD	SEWAGE OUTLET	REMARKS
−	**Shoreham-By-Sea Beach** TQ214047	✗ ✓✓✓✗✓	Improvements planned for mid 1995.	Commercial port.
	EAST SUSSEX			
f	**Southwick** - EU TQ214044	✗✗✗✓✗✗✓✓✗	Screened, 54,000, 50 below LWM. Improvements planned for mid 1995.	Shingle.
f	**Hove** - EU TQ288043	✗✗✗✗✗✗✗✓✗	2, stormwater only.	Shingle. Beach cleaned regularly.
f	**Brighton** Kemp Town - EU TQ323035	✓✗✗		
−	Palace Pier TQ314038	✓✗✗✓✗✗✓✗	3, stormwater only. Improvements for 1995.	
⌒	**Saltdean** - EU TQ381018	✓✓✓✓✓✓✓✓	Screened. Improvements for 2000.	Rocky with some sand. Beach cleaned regularly.
−	**Portobello**		Screened, 300,000, LSO.	
⌒	**Newhaven West Key** - EU TV449998	✓✗✗✗✗✗✓✓✓	Primary, 7,500, LSO.	Sandy beach within breakwater. Beach cleaned regularly.
f	**Seaford** (Dane road) - EU TV488982	✓✓✓✗	Screened, 21,500, LSO.	Shingle beach is steep. Beach cleaned regularly.
⌒⌒	**Cuckmere Haven** TV520975			Pebbles. Bathing not safe at the mouth of the river.
⌒⌒⌒	**Birling Gap**	✓✓✓		Not featured because severely affected by marine litter.
−	**Eastbourne** East of Pier TV625998	✓✗✓	Macerated/screened, 90,000, 640 below LWM. Improvements under construction.	Shingle and sand.
⌒	Wish Tower - EU TV614982	✓✓✓✓✓✓✓✓		Shingle with sand below the tide. Beach cleaned regularly.
⌒⌒	**Pevensey Bay** - EU TQ657037	✓✗✓✓✗✓✓✓	Macerated/tidal tank, 9,590, 360 below LWM. Improvements planned for mid 1995.	Shingle with sand. Beach cleaned regularly.
⌒⌒	**Normans Bay** - EU TQ682053	✓✓✓✓✗✓✓✓		Shingle with sand at low water. Beach cleaned regularly.
−	**Cooden Beach**		Improvements planned for 1998.	Shingle with sand at low tide.
⌒	**Bexhill** (Egerton Park) - EU TQ737068	✓✓✓✓✓✓✓✓	Improvements planned for 1998.	Sand and shingle. Beach cleaned regularly.
−	**Hastings** Bulverhythe TQ784086	✓✗✓	LSO.	Shingle.
−	St Leonards Beach TQ797087	✓✓✓✓	Improvements planned for 1998.	Shingle, sand and rocks.
f	Queens Hotel - EU TQ819092	✓✓✗✗✗✗	2, 40,000, 50 above and 140 below LWM. Improvements planned.	Sand and shingle.

RATING	NAME	TRACK RECORD	SEWAGE OUTLET	REMARKS
–	**Hastings** Fairlight Glen TQ862108	✗✓✓		Shingle and sand with rockpools at low tide.
⌒⌒	**Winchelsea** - EU TQ912154	✓✓✓✓✓✓✓✓		Pebble and shingle with rockpools at low tide. Unsafe in rough weather.
⌒⌒	**Camber Sands** - EU TQ973184	✓✗✓✓✓✗✓✓✓		Sand dunes. Beach cleaned regularly.
–	**Broomhill Sands**		Secondary, 9,500, 300 above LWM.	Sandy and coarse shingle.
–	KENT **Greatstone Beach** TR082229	✓✗✓		Silty sand.
⌒⌒	**Littlestone-on-Sea** - EU TR084239	✗✗✗✗✓✗✓✓✓	Secondary and UV disinfection, 5,170, LWM.	Sandy.
⌒⌒	**St Mary's Bay** - EU TR093277	✗✗✗✓✓✗✗✓✓		Sand and shingle.
	Dymchurch Dymchurch Hythe Road TR128319	✓✓✓		
⌒⌒	Dymchurch Beach - EU TR113304	✗✗✗✗✓✗✓✓✓	Secondary and UV disinfection, 6,900, between HWM & LWM.	Shingle and sand.
–	Dymchurch Redoubt TR101290	✓		Pebbles and sand.
⌒⌒⌒⌒	**Hythe** - EU TR160340	✗✗✗✓✗✓✓✓	Screened, LSO.	Shingle and sand. Not featured due to insufficient information.
⌒	**Sandgate** Sandgate Beach - EU TR188348	✗✗✗✓✓✓✓✗✓✓		Shingle.
–	Sandgate Town Centre TR203351	✓✗✗	Improvements planned for mid 1997.	Shingle.
f	**Folkestone** - EU TR237363	✗✗✗✗✗✗✗✓✗	Screened, at HWM. Improvements planned.	Sandy.
⌒	**The Warren** TR248376	✓✓	Improvements planned for mid 1997.	Danger from falling rocks.
–	**Shakespeare Cliff**		Macerated, 30,000, 635 below LWM.	Sand and shingle.
⌒⌒	**Dover Harbour** TR321412	✓✓✓✓		
⌒⌒	**St Margaret's Bay** - EU TR368444	✗✓✓✓✓✓✓✓✓		Shingle cove.
f	**Deal Castle** - EU TR378527	✗✗✗✗✗✗✓✗✗	3, screened/macerated, 34,480, LSO. Improvements planned for late 1995.	Steep shingle.
f	**Sandwich Bay** - EU TR358540	✗✗✗✗✗✗✗✗✗	Improvements planned for late 1995.	Sandy.
⌒⌒	**Ramsgate** Ramsgate Sands TR387649	✓✓✓		Sandy.
f	Ramsgate Beach - EU TR372640	✓✗✗✗✗✗✗✗✗	3, screened/macerated, 20,000, 150 below LWM. Improvements planned for mid 1995.	Sandy.

RATING	NAME	TRACK RECORD	SEWAGE OUTLET	REMARKS
⌒⌒	**Broadstairs East Cliff.** TR401688	☐☐☐☐☐✓✓✓✓		
⌒	**Broadstairs Beach** - EU TR372640	✗✗✗✓✗✗✓✗✓	Screened, 24,160, LSO.	Sandy.
⌒⌒	**Palm Bay** TR373714	☐☐☐☐☐✓✓✓✓	Screened, 56,700, LSO.	Sandy. Not featured due to insufficient information.
⌒	**Walpole Bay** TR365715	☐☐☐☐☐☐✗✓✓		Sand, rocks.
⌒⌒	**Margate** The Bay - EU TR347708	✓✓✓✓✓✗✓✓✓		Sandy.
⌒⌒	Fulsam Rock - EU TR356715	☐☐☐☐☐☐☐✓✓		Sandy.
⌒	**Westbrook Bay** TR320705	☐☐☐☐☐✓✓✓✓		Sandy.
⌒⌒	**St Mildred's Bay** - EU TR328705	✓✗✓✓✓✓✓✓✓		Sandy.
⌒⌒	**Westgate Bay** TR320702	☐☐☐☐☐✓✓✓✓		Sandy.
f	**Herne Bay** - EU TR186686	✓✗✗✗✗✗✗✓✗	Screened, 10,000, 460 below LWM. Improvements planned for mid 1995.	Pebbles and sand.
–	**Whitstable** TR1166		Screened, LSO.	Shingle. Unpredictable currents can make bathing dangerous.
⌒⌒	**Leysdown-on-Sea** - EU TR025717	✗✗✓✗✓✓✓✓		Sand, shingle and mud. Beach cleaned regularly.
–	**Minster Leas** TQ953739			Beach cleaned regularly.
	ESSEX			
⌒	**Canvey Island** TQ805824	☐☐☐☐☐✓✓✓✓	Secondary, 44,500, at LWM.	Muddy sand.
f	**Leigh-on-Sea** TQ841856	☐☐☐☐☐✓✓✓✗		Sandy. Beach cleaned regularly.
⌒	**Westcliff-on-Sea** - EU TQ864853	✗✗✗✓✓✗✓✓✓	Improvements under construction.	Sand and shingle. Beach cleaned regularly.
⌒	**Southend-on-Sea** TQ887850	☐☐☐✓✓✓✓✓✓	Primary, 198,000, 500 below LWM. Improvements planned.	Sand, shingle and mud. Beach cleaned regularly.
f	**Thorpe Bay** - EU TQ911847	✗✗✗✓✓✓✓✓✗	Primary, 550 below LWM. Improvements planned for 1998.	Sand and shingle. Beach cleaned regularly.
⌒⌒	**Shoeburyness East** - EU TQ945852	☐☐☐☐☐✓✓✓✓		Beach cleaned regularly.
⌒⌒	**Shoeburyness** TQ925841	☐☐☐☐☐✓✓✓✓	Improvements planned for 1998.	Sand and shingle. Beach cleaned regularly.
f	**West Mersea** - EU TM022120	☐☐☐☐☐☐✗✓✗✗	Primary, 12,000, at LWM. Improvements planned for 1995.	Sand and shingle.
⌒⌒	**Jaywick** - EU TM148128	✓✓✓✓✓✓✓✓	Macerated, 24,000, 650 below LWM. Improvements planned.	Sandy.

RATING	NAME	TRACK RECORD	SEWAGE OUTLET	REMARKS
–	**Clacton** Off Coastguard Station TM173142	☐☐☐☐☐✓✓✓	Improvements planned for 2000.	Sandy.
–	Groyne 41 TM175144	☐☐☐☐☐✗✓✓	Improvements planned for 2000.	Sandy.
⌒⌒	Connaught Gardens - EU TM187152	✓✗✓✓✓✓✓✓	2, 300 and 50 below LWM, stormwater only. Improvements planned for 1997.	Sandy.
⌒⌒	**Holland-on-Sea** - EU TM224176	✓✗✓✓✓✓✓✓	Macerated, 50,000, LSO.	Sandy.
⌒⌒	**Frinton-on-Sea** - EU TM237194	✓✓✓✓✓✓✓✓	2, 50 below LWM, stormwater only. Improvements planned.	Sandy.
⌒	**Walton-on-the-Naze** - EU TM255215	✓✗✓✓✓✓✓✓	Secondary, 25,000, 50 below LWM. Improvements planned.	Sandy.
⌒⌒	**Dovercourt** - EU TM251306	✓✗✗✓✓✓✓✓	Primary, 15,000, at LWM. Improvements planned.	Sandy.
–	**Harwich** (Sailing Club) TM263326	☐☐☐☐☐✓✓✓	Improvements planned.	
	SUFFOLK			
–	**Aldeburgh** TM4757		Macerated, 4,000, LSO.	Steep shingle ridges with some sand. Beach cleaned regularly.
–	**Dunwich** TM4770			Pebble.
–	**Southwold** The Flats		Secondary, 9,000.	Sand and shingle.
–	**Kessingland** TM536867	☐☐☐☐☐☐✓✓	Secondary, 5,000, LSO.	
⌒⌒	**Lowestoft** North beach - EU TM554947	✗✓✓✓✓✓✓✓	2, secondary, 140,000, LSO. Improvements planned for 1998.	
f	**Gorleston Beach** - EU TG532031	☐☐☐☐☐✗✓✗✗	Improvements planned.	
	NORFOLK			
–	**Great Yarmouth** Power station	☐☐☐☐☐✗✗✗		
f	South - EU TG533064		Improvements planned.	
f	Pier - EU TG533007		Improvements planned.	
⌒	North - EU TG535010	☐☐☐☐☐✓✓✓	Multiple, screened, 75,000, including discharge to river, LSO. Improvements planned.	Sandy.
⌒⌒	Caister Point - EU TG530120	☐☐☐☐☐✓✓✓	1, 97,000, LSO. Improvements planned.	
⌒	**Hemsby** - EU TG509174	☐☐☐☐☐✓✓✓		
–	**Sea Palling** TG249412			Sandy. Beach cleaned regularly.

RATING	NAME	TRACK RECORD	SEWAGE OUTLET	REMARKS
–	**Happisburgh**			Sandy.
⌢⌢	**Mundesley** - EU TG317366	✓✓✓✓✓✓✓✓	Secondary, 7,000, LSO. Improvements planned for 2000.	Sandy.
–	**Overstrand** TG249412	□□□□✓✓✗□		Sand and shingle.
f	**Cromer** - EU TG219042	✓✗✗✗✓✓✓✓✗	Preliminary, 9,000, 100 below LWM. Improvements under construction for 2000.	Sandy.
–	**East Runton**		Macerated, 5,500, at LWM. Improvements under construction.	Sandy.
–	**West Runton**		Macerated, 5,500, at LWM. Improvements under construction.	Sand and pebbles.
⌢⌢⌢⌢	**Sheringham** - EU TG162436	✗✗✗✗✓✓✓✓	Preliminary, 14,800, 260 below LWM. Improvements under construction.	Sand and shingle. Not featured due to sewage-related debris.
⌢	**Wells-next-the-Sea** - EU TF914456	✗✗✓✓✓✓✓✓	Secondary, 7,200, to inland drain. Improvements under construction.	Sandy.
–	**Hunstanton** North Beach Sailing Club TF672412	□□□□□✓✓✓□		
–	Boat Ramp TF667400	✓✓✗✓✓✓✓✓□		
–	South Beach Hunstanton Road TF660395	□□□□□✓✓✓□	Stormwater only.	Sand, stones and shingle.
⌢⌢	Hunstanton - EU TF6742	□□□□□✓✓✓✓		Sandy beach with its famous striped red and white cliffs. Beach cleaned regularly.
– ⌢	**Heacham** North Beach - EU TF663375	□□□□□✓✓✓✓		Shingle.
–	South Beach TF659362	□□□□□✓✓✓□		Shingle.
–	South Beach (near River) TF661368	□□□□□✗✓✓□	Secondary/tertiary, 32,000, to river. Improvements planned.	Gravel.
–	**Snettisham Beach** TF647335	□□□□□✓✓✓□	Near RSPB Reserve.	Shingle.

The area around Seahouses (p. 118) on the Northumbrian Coast is steeped in history.

THE EAST COAST

FROM THE VAST, OPEN SKIES AND WATERY MARSHLANDS OF THE WASH TO THE WILD AND REMOTE STRETCHES OF BEACH ALONG THE BORDERLANDS OF NORTHUMBRIA, THIS SECTION OF BRITAIN'S COASTLINE ENCOMPASSES THE SHARPEST OF CONTRASTS, EVOKING DESCRIPTIONS SUCH AS FABULOUS, SPECTACULAR, DRAMATIC AND MYSTERIOUS.

•

Sadly, much less complimentary terms have also been used in connection with this area – polluted, industrialised, spoilt and scarred are just some which come to mind. Here industry extends to the shore, bringing with it steel mills, power stations, oil and chemical works. The toxic chemicals they discharge pollute our seas and coasts and damage our wildlife.

There are, however, many beautiful beaches on the east coast with excellent water quality, particularly in Lincolnshire and Humberside, and visitors to these counties are rewarded by some of the most dramatic cliff walks in the country. To the north, the empty borderlands are characterised by rugged cliffs and offshore islands, for many years outposts for the early Christian faith. St Aidan, sent to Holy Island to convert the people of Northumbria, built a small church there, and over the years it developed into a Benedictine monastery, the remains of which can be seen today. Dozens of ruined castles attest to centuries of conflict between the Scots and the English: the most northerly English town, Berwick-upon-Tweed, changed its allegiance no less than 13 times over 300 years of struggle.

Further south, beyond the industrialisation of the Tyne Estuary, are limestone cliffs of great conservation value; strange rock formations give way to sweeping sandy beaches and the fishing villages of Robin Hood's Bay and Filey. The Humber Estuary has huge sweeps of salt-marshes, and at the margins of the Wash seals can be seen basking off Gibraltar Point. The Wash itself is one of the most important areas of mud-flats, sandbanks and salt-marsh in the United Kingdom, and of international significance as a wetland with a transient annual population of over 200,000 resident and migrating birds. In the past large areas of mudflats were lost to agriculture, but no further land reclamation has been carried out since the late seventies.

But the region is beset by many problems, not the least of which is the offshore dumping of millions of tonnes of dredged spoil, sewage sludge and fly ash each year (although on the positive side the dumping of fly ash and sewage sludge is due to end in 1998). Years of dumping coalmining waste has blackened the beaches of Durham and Cleveland; although the closure of mines along the east coast may lead to an improvement in the state of the beaches, it may, ironically, be to the detriment of groundwater which could become contaminated by leachates from the mines. Raw and partially treated sewage pollutes and contaminates many of the beaches and bathing waters: shellfish gathered from the Wash are legally required to be cleansed and steam-cooked before they can be sold. Few of the beaches in the region escape the problem of marine litter.

SKEGNESS
Lincolnshire
OS Ref: TF572634

Once a small fishing village, Skegness boomed when the Victorians discovered that sea air had a beneficial effect on the constitution. Ten kilometres of open sandy beach backed by dunes, safe bathing, boating lakes and landscaped seafront gardens stocked annually with locally prized flowers maintain the attraction today. Dogs are banned from the beach between May and September.

*Skegness was one of the first planned resorts in Britain,
the brainchild of the local squire, Lord Scarborough,
whose aim was to provide the burgeoning middle
classes with wholesome holidays by the sea.*

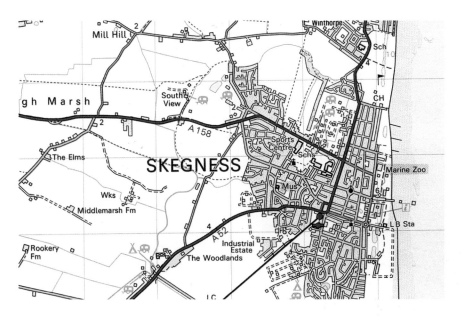

Water quality

No sewage is discharged in the vicinity of this beach.

Bathing safety
Generally safe. Lifeguards patrol regularly and are in contact with the coastguard and lifeboat.

Litter
The beach is cleaned daily.

Access
From the north and south, on the A52; from the west, on the A158. Ramps give disabled visitors easy access to the beach.

Parking
There are several attended car parks close by.

Public transport
The rail station is within walking distance, and local buses serve the beach.

Toilets
Several blocks, including disabled and baby facilities.

Food
There are many cafés and restaurants nearby.

Seaside activities
Donkey rides, beach ferry, boat hire, waterway trips, supervised beach games, model village, bowling greens, pitch and putt and crazy golf.

Wet weather alternatives
Beach chalets with facilities available for hire, Panda's Palace (children's indoor play area with a café), Natureland, Seal Sanctuary, cinema, theatres.

Wildlife and walks
Gibraltar Point Nature Reserve is five kilometres away. Local walks include one to Mablethorpe, much loved by Tennyson, and leaflets detailing these are available from the local Tourist Information Centre.

Track record ✓✓✓✓✓✓✓

SUTTON-ON-SEA
Lincolnshire
OS Ref: TF522821

An air of peace and unhurried gentility draws visitors back every year to the wide sandy beaches and attractive gardens of Sutton-on-Sea. Facilities in the gardens include bowls, crazy golf, putting and a popular paddling pool, while a gentle stroll through the quiet streets reveals shops selling locally made arts and crafts. There are also excellent launch facilities for both small boats and sailboards and safe bathing for young children and senior citizens.

Water quality
No sewage is discharged in the vicinity of this beach.

Bathing safety
Safe bathing with lifeguard patrol in the summer season.

Litter
The beach is cleaned daily; dogs are banned between May and September.

Access
On the A1111 from the A16. Steps and ramps lead to the beach.

Parking
Several car parks near the beach.

Public transport
Local and national buses stop here.

Toilets
Four sets of toilets including facilities for disabled visitors.

Food
Various cafés and restaurants nearby.

Seaside activities
Swimming, bowling, putting, 18-hole golf course, donkey rides, chalets for hire.

Wildlife and walks
There are many fine local walks, details of which may be had from the Tourist Information Centre.

Track record ✗ ✗ ✗ ✓ ✓ ✓ ✓ ✓

The ultra-flat coastline of England's eastern seaboard makes the skies seem vast and open: views from Sutton-on-Sea are panoramic in every direction.

DRURIDGE BAY
Northumberland
OS Ref: NZ279964

A ten-kilometre-long stretch of wide, sandy beach backed by extensive dune systems, Druridge Bay nestles between the fishing town of Amble and the village of Cresswell in rural Northumberland. The bay and its hinterland are renowned sites for birdwatching with many wetland areas attracting large numbers of waders and wildfowl, particularly during the winter months. Most of the duneland is owned or managed by the Local Authority, and conservation bodies are strongly represented locally, with five nature reserves and country parks in the area and another large one under construction on a former open-cast coalmining site.

Water quality
No sewage is discharged in the vicinity of this beach.

Bathing safety
Ice-cold water and unpredictable currents make bathing at Druridge Bay risky in all but the calmest of conditions. There are occasional patrols by the coastguard.

The Northumberland Wildlife Trust organises regular guided walks along the length of the beach, passing several of the nature reserves en route.

Litter

The beach is cleaned infrequently by hand.

Access

Off the A1068. The beach is easily reached on foot, but the soft sand may cause difficulties for wheelchair users.

Parking

Six nearby car parks are only ever full on the busiest and hottest of days.

Public transport

Widdrington rail station is a five-kilometre walk from the beach, which is not served by bus.

Toilets

Public toilets at Amble and Cresswell; Druridge Bay Country Park has facilities for disabled visitors.

Food

None in the immediate area of the beach but local villages have pubs and shops.

Seaside activities

Birdwatching, fishing, walking, boating, water-skiing and sailboarding at the country park.

Wet weather alternatives

Boat trips from Amble around Coquet Island RSPB National Nature Reserve. The country park has hides and a manned visitor centre. There is a mining museum at Woodhorn.

Wildlife and walks

Flocks of lapwings, and rarer migratory visitors, can regularly be seen on the sand flats of Druridge Bay. The wardens at Druridge Bay

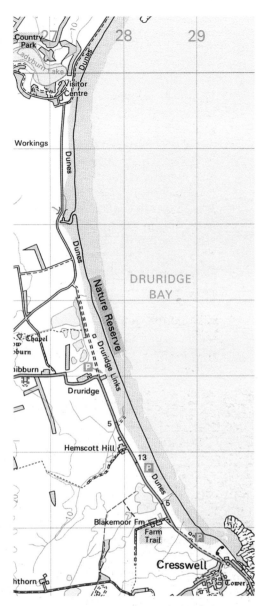

Country Park will advise on circular walks and birdwatching opportunities.

Track record ✓✓✓✓✓✓✓✓

LOW NEWTON (NEWTON HAVEN)
Northumberland
OS Ref: NU242245

This dune-fringed crescent of sand lies at the northern end of Embleton Bay, overlooked by the pretty village of Low Newton, a square of fishermen's cottages and pub now owned by the National Trust. Sheltered by a grassy headland to the north and an offshore reef, Low Newton's beach is favoured by watersports fanatics. Newton Pool, a freshwater lagoon behind the dunes, is an important nature reserve.

Water quality
No sewage is discharged in the vicinity of this beach.

Bathing safety
Safe on the incoming tide, but swimmers beware of undercurrents on the ebb tide.

Litter
Occasionally affected by oil drums and fishing debris, particularly in winter.

The curved sweep of Low Newton beach is overlooked by Dunstanburgh Castle, once home to John of Gaunt.

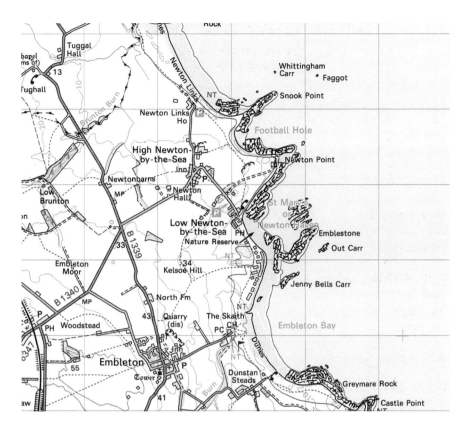

Access
From the car park on the approach road to Low Newton, signposted off the B1339 from High Newton. It is a short walk down to the village with direct access to the beach. A path leads along Low Newton beach to Embleton Bay.

Parking
One car park with 100 spaces between the village and the beach. Parking in the village is for residents and disabled badge holders only.

Public transport
Northumbria Buses run a service to Embleton from Alnwick.

Toilets
Adjacent to the beach.

Food
The village pub serves snacks; there is a tea room in High Newton ten minutes' walk away.

Seaside activities
Swimming, windsurfing, sailing, diving, canoeing and fishing.

Wildlife and walks
Bird hides at Newton Pool (one with access for disabled visitors) where a wide variety of species can be seen, particularly in winter. The Heritage Coast Path stretches south round Embleton Bay to Dunstanburgh Castle and north around Newton Point to the wide sweep of Newton Links and Beadnell Bay.

Track record ✓✓✓✓✓✓✓✓

115

BEADNELL BAY
Northumberland
OS Ref: NU233284

The golden sands of Beadnell Bay sweep south on a three-kilometre-long curve to the rocky outcrop of Snook Point, uninterrupted save for the stream that meanders across the beach. Beadnell village nestles at the north end of the bay; its tiny harbour has the distinction of being the only east coast harbour facing west. Eighteenth century lime kilns, restored by the National Trust, stand on the quayside.

Water quality
No sewage is discharged in the vicinity of this beach.

Litter
The beach is cleaned regularly.

Bathing safety
Swimming is safe. There are no lifeguards but lifebelts are positioned along the beach. Beach wardens supervise watersports and access to the water.

Access
Follow the B1340 Northumberland Coastal Route from the A1.

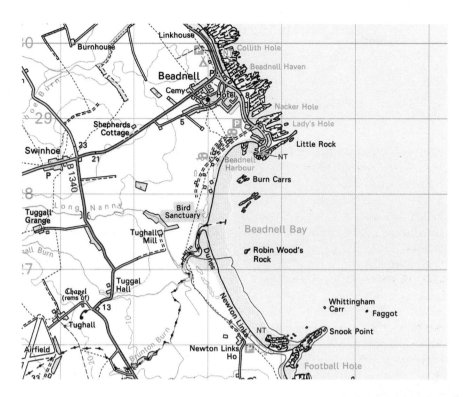

Parking
A large car park is located at the north end of the bay and a smaller one to the south at Newton Links.

Public transport
Nearest rail stations are Chathill, Alnmouth and Berwick. There are bus services to the bay.

Toilets
Beadnell car park has toilets including facilities for disabled visitors.

Food
An ice-cream van stops at the car park.

Seaside activities
Swimming, windsurfing, sailing, diving, water-skiing, canoeing and jet-skiing.

Wet weather alternatives
Preston Pele Tower near Chathill; the Marine Life Centre at Seahouses.

Wildlife and walks
The coastline presents many splendid walking opportunities: to the south, a path around the bay leads to Newton Haven, Embleton Bay and Dunstanburgh Castle. North, the rocky shore gives way to sand stretching to Seahouses, and beyond to Bamburgh Castle. The Farne Islands Nature Reserve lies offshore.

Brightly painted traditional east coast fishing cobles in the harbour at Beadnell.

Track record ✓✓✓✓✓✓✓✓

BAMBURGH AND SEAHOUSES
Northumberland
OS Ref: NU185353 and NU210330

A 45-metre rock outcrop towers above beautiful long sandy beaches and provides the magnificent setting for Bamburgh Castle. From the castle rock there are spectacular views of the sandy beaches stretching north to Holy Island and south to Seahouses. Seaward lies the panorama of the Farne Islands, their rocky cliffs falling steeply to the water below. Trips to the Islands can be made from the harbour at Seahouses. Between Bamburgh and Seahouses there are six and a half kilometres of superb beach with sand which squeaks when walked over. Backed by the St Aidan's and Shoreston Dunes, the sands give way to rocky shore at Seahouses.

Water quality
There is one outfall at Bamburgh serving approximately 1,000 people in the summer and 700 in winter, this discharges macerated sewage through a tidal tank at LWM.

Bathing safety
Bathing is safe only on the incoming tide due to undercurrents as the tide ebbs; beware of offshore winds. Lifebelts are available at Seahouses. There is an inshore rescue boat and lifeboat.

Litter
A little wood, plastic and fishing debris is sometimes washed on to the beach. Litter left by visitors is cleared by the National Trust and the beaches are cleaned daily in the summer by hand picking.

Access
There is access from both Bamburgh and Seahouses which lie on the B1340, with easy access to the beach across dunes.

P Parking
Bamburgh: Large car park with over 200 spaces. Three dune car parks with 25 spaces in each, plus space along the road above dunes.
Seahouses: Car park in village has 500 spaces. Space for 30 cars parking on verge of B1340 north of Seahouses.

Wildlife and walks
This fantastic section of coastline falls within the Northumberland Heritage Coast and is also designated as an Area of Outstanding Natural Beauty. Below the lofty position of Bamburgh Castle, a walk north along the shore leads to Budle Bay. The salt marsh, mud and sand flats are part of the Lindisfarne Nature Reserve which covers the whole of the Fenham Flats, Holy Island Sands and most of the island itself. The area provides feeding for thousands of waders and wildfowl. It is dangerous to cross the sands; access to the island is by the causeway which is covered for at least 11 hours each day. With its Castle and Priory, the island is steeped in history and its distinctive conical shape leaves a lasting impression on the memory. The beaches around the island are wide and sandy but unsafe for swimming because of strong currents. The

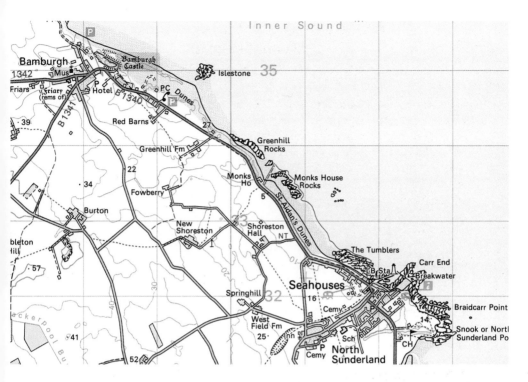

Farne Islands to the south of Holy Island are of international importance for their large colonies of seabirds and grey seals. The 30 islands that make up the Farnes are a National Trust Nature Reserve and landing is permitted on Inner Farne and Staple Island. Boats make the hour-long trip from the harbour at Seahouses in good weather. Further information about the service is available from the National Trust shop in Seahouses. Access is restricted during the bird breeding season from mid-May until mid-July.

Bamburgh:

 Toilets
There are toilets available in the village.

 Food
There is a café and hotel in the village, and ice-cream vans on or near the beach.

 Seaside activities
Swimming, surfing, windsurfing, diving, sailing and fishing.

 Wet weather alternatives
Castle, Grace Darling Museum and her grave in the village.

Seahouses:

 Toilets
Available in the village.

 Food
Food is available in the village.

 Seaside activities
Swimming, golf course, amusements.

 Wet weather alternatives
Marine Life Centre.

Track record

Bamburgh	✓✓✓✓✓✓✓
Seahouses	✓✓✓✓✓✓✓✓

RATING	NAME	TRACK RECORD	SEWAGE OUTLET	REMARKS
	LINCOLNSHIRE			
⌒⌒⌒	**Ingoldmells** - EU TF574685	✓✗✓✓✓✓✓✓	Macerated/screened, 116,000, LSO.	Sandy. Not featured due to adjacent sewage outfall.
⌒⌒⌒	**Chapel St Leonards** - EU TF564722	✓✗✓✓✓✓✓✓		Sandy. Beach cleaned regularly. Not featured due to insufficient information.
⌒⌒	**Anderby Beach** - EU TF553762	✓✓✓✓✓✓✓✓		Sandy.
⌒⌒⌒⌒	**Moggs Eye** (Huttoft) - EU TF550776	✓✓✓✓✓✓✓✓		Sand and shingle backed by dunes. Not featured due to insufficient information.
⌒⌒	**Mablethorpe** - EU TF508854	✓✗✓✗✓✓✓✓	Secondary, 28,000, to inland drain. Improvements planned for mid 1995.	Sandy.
	HUMBERSIDE			
f	**Cleethorpes** - EU TA310086	✗✗✗✗✗✗✗✗	Screened/macerated, 100,000, just above LWM. Improvements planned for mid 1995.	Sand. Beach cleaned regularly.
⌒⌒	**Withernsea** - EU TA344281	✗✗✓✓✗✓✓✓	Primary, 12,000, LSO.	Sand and shingle.
⌒⌒⌒⌒	**Tunstall** - EU TA322312	✓✓✓✓✓✓✓✓		Sand and pebbles. Not featured due to insufficient information.
⌒⌒	**Hornsea** - EU TA210478	✓✓✓✓✓✓✓✓	Screened/macerated, 10,500, LSO.	Sandy with some shingle.
⌒⌒⌒	**Skipsea Sands** - EU TA177572	✓✓✓✓✗✓✓✓		Sandy. Not featured on advice of local tourist authority.
⌒⌒⌒⌒	**Barmston** - EU TA172594	✓✓✓✓✓✓✓✓		Sand and shingle. Beach cleaned regularly. Not featured on advice of local tourist authority.
f	**Earls Dyke** - EU TA170615	✓✓✓✓✓✓✓✗		Sandy and tidal. Beach cleaned regularly.
⌒	**Fraisthorpe** - EU TA171629	✓✓✓✓✓✓✓✓		Sandy and tidal. Beach cleaned regularly.
⌒	**Willsthorpe** - EU TA172640	✓✓✓✓✓✓✓✓		Sandy. Beach cleaned regularly.
⌒	**Bridlington South** - EU TA181661	✓✓✓✓✓✓✓✓	Screened, 56,000, LSO (stormwater also).	Sandy. Beach cleaned regularly.
⌒	**Bridlington North** - EU TA190672	✓✓✓✓✓✓✓✓		Sandy. Beach cleaned regularly.
	Flamborough			
⌒⌒	South Landing - EU TA231692	✗✓✗✗✗✗✓✓	Primary, 2,176, LSO.	Beach cleaned as required.
⌒	North Landing - EU TA238722	✓✓✓✓✓✗✓✓		Sandy. Beach cleaned regularly.
–	**Thornwick Bay**		Primary, 300, at LWM.	Rocky. Bathing very dangerous.

RATING	NAME	TRACK RECORD	SEWAGE OUTLET	REMARKS
	YORKSHIRE			
⌒	**Reighton Sands** - EU TA144763	✓✓✓✓✓✓✓✓✓		Sand and boulders.
⌒	**Filey** - EU TA120806	✓✓✓✓✓✓✓✓✓	Stormwater only, 200 below LWM.	Golden sand. Beach cleaned regularly.
⌒	**Cayton Bay** - EU TA067845	✓✓✓✓✓✓✓✗✓		Sandy. Beware of incoming tide.
	Scarborough			
f	South Beach - EU TA046886	✗✗✓✓✗✓✓✓✗		Sandy.
⌒⌒	North Beach - EU TA037900	✓✗✓✗✓✓✓✓✓	Screened, 105,000, LSO.	Sandy.
⌒⌒	**Robin Hood's Bay** - EU NZ959045	✓✓✓✓✓✓✓✓✓	1, 5,500, at LWM.	Rocky. Swimming dangerous.
⌒⌒⌒	**Whitby** - EU NZ897117	✓✓✓✓✓✓✓✓✓	Raw, 20,000, at LWM.	Sandy. Not featured due to nearby sewage outfall.
⌒	**Sandsend** - EU NZ864126	✓✓✓✗✓✓✓✓✓	Raw, 450, at LWM.	Sand and shingle.
⌒	**Runswick Bay** - EU NZ811159	✓✓✓✓✓✓✓✓✓	Raw, 480, at LWM.	Sand and shingle.
f	**Staithes** - EU NZ787190	✓✓✗✗✗✗✓✗	Raw, 4,000, at LWM.	Sand and rocks.
	CLEVELAND			
⌒⌒	**Skinningrove** (Cattersty Sands)	✗✓✗	Raw, 9,000, at LWM.	Sandy. Beach cleaned regularly.
⌒⌒	**Saltburn-by-Sea** (Pier) - EU NZ660217	✗✗✗✓✓✓✗✗✓		
	Saltburn Gill	✗✗✗	2, raw, 13,850 and 6,800, at LWM, 2 stormwater overflows also. Improvements planned for mid 1995.	Sand and pebbles. Beach cleaned regularly.
–	**Skelton Beck** Beach	✗✗✗		
–	Footbridge	✗✗✗		
⌒⌒	**Marske-by-the-Sea** - EU NZ639229	✗✓✓✓	2, stormwater only, 25m below and at LWM.	Sandy. Beach cleaned regularly.
	Redcar			
⌒⌒	Stray - EU NZ625238	✓✓✓	Screened, 78,000, LSO. Improvements planned.	
⌒⌒	Granville - EU NZ613251	✗✓✗✓✓	Screened stormwater only, at LWM.	
⌒⌒	Lifeboat station - EU NZ606255	✗✓✓✓	Screened stormwater only, at LWM.	Sand and rocks.
⌒⌒	Coatham Sands - EU NZ592257	✓✓✓✓	2, screened stormwater only, at LWM.	Sandy. Beach cleaned regularly.
	Seaton Carew			
⌒⌒	North Gare - EU NZ540286	✗✗✓✓		Sandy.
⌒⌒	Centre - EU NZ531296	✗✗✗✗✗✗✗✗	1 stormwater only and 1 screened, 60,000, 300 below LWM and LSO. Improvements planned.	Sandy, some pebbles. Beach cleaned regularly.
⌒	North - EU NZ525305	✗✗✓✓	Improvements planned.	Sandy.

RATING	NAME	TRACK RECORD	SEWAGE OUTLET	REMARKS
f	**Hartlepool, North Sands**		3, 1 screened and 2 raw, 30,000, 4,300 and 3,600, 30 below LWM and 2 at LWM.	Sandy.
	DURHAM			
f	**Crimdon Park** - EU NZ485373	✗✗✗ ✗✗✗✗✗		Sandy.
–	**Crimdon South**	☐☐☐☐ ✗✗✗	Stormwater only.	Sandy.
–	**Blackhall**		Stormwater only, at LWM.	Sand and pebbles.
–	**Denemouth South**	☐☐☐☐ ✗✗☐	Screened, 33,000, at LWM. Improvements planned.	Sand with stones and coal waste.
–	**Horden**		2, raw, 6,900 and 11,500, above LWM.	Sand with coal waste.
–	**Easington**		Raw, 8,300, 50 below LWM. Improvements planned.	Sand with stones and coal waste.
–	**Dalton Burn**	☐☐☐☐ ✗✗✗	Improvements planned.	Coastal stream.
f	**Seaham** Remand Home - EU NZ424508	☐☐☐ ✗✗✗✗	Stormwater overflow. Improvements planned.	
f	**Seaham** Beach - EU NZ424508	✗✗✗✗✗✗✓✗✗	Improvements planned for 2000.	Sandy.
–	**Featherbed Rocks**	☐☐☐☐ ✗✓✗		Rocky area adjacent to mouth of Dalton Beck.
	TYNE AND WEAR			
–	**The City of Sunderland:** Ryhope South	☐☐☐☐ ✗✗✗	2, stormwater only, at LWM.	Sandy.
–	Hendon South	☐☐☐☐ ✓✓✓		
–	Sunderland		2, tidal tank and screened, 500 and 175,000, at LWM and 300 below LWM.	Rocky outfalls situated south of Wear Estuary.
⌒⌒	**Roker/Whitburn** South - EU NZ407593	✓✗✗✗✓✓✓✓✓		Sandy with small pebbles. Beach cleaned regularly.
–	**Roker/Blockhouse**	☐☐☐☐ ✗✗✗	Screened, 25 below LWM, within the Wear Estuary.	Sandy.
f	**Whitburn** (North) - EU NZ407605	☐☐ ✓✗✗✗✗✗	Stormwater only, at LWM.	Sandy.
⌒⌒	**Marsden Bay** - EU NZ400650	✓✗✗✓✓✓✗✓	Raw and stormwater. The sewage discharged at this beach is from the public toilet only.	Sandy.
⌒⌒⌒	**South Shields** Sandhaven - EU NZ379674	✗✗✓✓✗✓✓✓		Not featured due to insufficient information.
–	Inner Harbour	☐☐☐☐ ✗✗✗	2, raw and stormwater only, at LWM, within the Tyne Estuary.	Sandy.
⌒	**Tynemouth** King Edward's Bay - EU NZ373696	☐☐☐☐ ✓✓✓	Stormwater only, at LWM.	Sandy.

RATING	NAME	TRACK RECORD	SEWAGE OUTLET	REMARKS
⌒	Long Sands South - EU NZ369702	□□□□□✓✓✓		Sandy.
⌒	Long Sands North - EU NZ366708	□□□□□✓✓✓	Stormwater only, at LWM.	Sandy.
⌒⌒	Cullercoats - EU NZ365713	□□✗✓✓✗✓✓		Sandy. Beach cleaned regularly.
f	**Whitley Bay - EU** NZ353734	✓✓✗✗✓✓✓✓✗	10, raw and stormwater, at LWM. Improvements planned for mid 1995.	Long sandy beach with rocky shoals.
⌒⌒⌒	**Seaton Sluice - EU** NZ334771	✗✓✗✗✓✗✗✗✓	Screened stormwater only, 43,000, 60 below LWM.	Sandy. Beach cleaned regularly. Not featured because of adjacent stormwater outlet.
	NORTHUMBERLAND			
	Blyth:			
⌒⌒	South Beach - EU NZ322795	□✓✓✓✓✓✗✗✓		Sandy with dunes. Beach cleaned regularly.
–	**Cambois** South	□□□□□✗✗✗	Raw, 26,000, 50 below LWM. Improvements planned.	
–	North	□□□□□✗✗✗□		
⌒⌒	**Newbiggin** South - EU NZ311873	✗✗✗✗✗✗✗✓✓	Sandy.	
⌒	North - EU NZ313878	□□□□□✗✗✓✓	Screened, at LWM, emergency only.	Sandy.
–	**Cresswell**		1, 1,800 summer, 200 winter, at LWM.	Sandy.
⌒⌒⌒⌒	**Amble (Links) - EU** NU276044	□□□□□✓✓✓✓	Screened/macerated, 8,000, 250 below LWM.	Rocky. Not featured due to insufficient information.
⌒⌒⌒⌒	**Warkworth - EU**	✓✓✓✓✓✓✓✓✓		Sandy. Beach cleaned regularly. Not featured due to insufficient information.
⌒⌒⌒⌒	**Alnmouth - EU** NU253107	✓✗✓✓✓✓✓✓✓		Sandy. Not featured due to dangerous bathing conditions.
–	**Longhoughton Steel**		Raw, 1,200 summer, 200 winter, at LWM.	Sandy cove.
–	**Craster**		2, raw and stormwater, 400, 30 below LWM.	
–	**Embleton Bay**			Sandy.
–	**Holy Island**		Macerated/tidal tank, 500 summer, 200 winter, at LWM.	Pebbles.
–	**Cocklawburn Beach**		Raw, 15, 20 above LWM north of beach.	Sand and rocks.
⌒	**Spittal - EU** NU008515	✗✗✗✓✗✗✗✗✓		Sandy. Beware of ebbing tide.
–	Spittal Quay	□□□□□✗✗✗	Improvements planned.	Sandy.
–	**Berwick-upon-Tweed**	□□□□□✗✗✗	Raw, at LWM.	Sandy. Swim only between rocks and beach.

North-West England and the Isle of Man

From Skinburness in Cumbria down to West Kirby on the Wirral and including the Isle of Man, the north-west coast of England is the region that pioneered the seaside resort and the seaside holiday. It should, therefore, be a source of national shame that no beaches in this area are good enough to be featured in the Good Beach Guide and that only two have water quality of three- and four-dolphin standard.

•

It's not that there aren't many beautiful stretches of coastline along the North-West. The huge expanse of Morecambe Bay, for example, with its panoramic view over to the Lake District; Southport, its long beach and elegant buildings lending it a distinctly Victorian character; and the extensive dune system at Ainsdale National Nature Reserve, a habitat for rare natterjack toads and sand lizards, which has over 10 kilometres of clearly marked footpaths through dunes and pine woods down to National Trust land at Formby Point.

In the middle of the Irish Sea lies the Isle of Man, a fascinating destination often described as an island lost in time. It has an incredible variety of coastal scenery for such a small island, its fiercely rugged coastline contrasting with the delicate beauty of the Manx Glens. In the summer huge and gentle basking sharks are to be seen offshore feeding on plankton.

But the sad truth is that the entire region is badly affected by pollution, indelibly tainting its underlying beauty. The Irish Sea is now more chemically contaminated than the North Sea and, perhaps more insidiously, is affected by radioactive waste. The Mersey Estuary and Liverpool Bay have suffered particularly, not only from oil spills and incidents of accidental pollution, but from the deliberate and unacceptable discharges of mercury, cadmium and lead released into Liverpool Bay each day. As if the pollution from industrial sources and contaminated sewage outfalls to the Mersey and its tributaries weren't enough, at least 1.52 million tonnes of sewage sludge and 3.56 million tonnes of dredged spoil (sediments dredged from the estuary usually contaminated with heavy metals and other persistent toxic chemicals) are dumped into Liverpool Bay each year. This contaminated sea washes the shores of some of the most popular resorts in Britain, and as a result their beaches are among the most polluted in the whole of the country. Unhappily, visitors must expect to witness this pollution in some of its most distressing forms: sewage-related debris on beaches and illegally dumped refuse washed up on the shore.

Despite plans for significant new investment in sewage treatment in the near future, the legacy of under-investment means that no great improvement has been apparent in the North-West over the past year, although one sampling point at Blackpool has achieved minimum legal standards for the first time. North-West Water, in a move welcomed by the Marine Conservation Society, has just started work on a system for Blackpool that will provide full sewage treatment but the scheme will not be finished for several years and bathing is still not advisable at most beaches in this area.

The Isle of Man's beaches fare little better: although not as badly affected by industrial discharges as those on the mainland coast, they do have a problem with sewage. The island's sewage is discharged directly to sea via short sea outfalls, most with absolutely no treatment: unsurprisingly, the beaches are badly contaminated. The EC Bathing Water Directive does not apply to the Isle of Man, but in March 1990 the Manx Government decided that the EC standards should be adopted as a target. In 1994, however, only one bathing water passed the minimum requirements when tested.

This situation should change drastically with the coming on stream of the IRIS project – an ambitious scheme that aims to achieve Integrated Recycling of the Island's Sewage. Although still some way from completion, the scheme should make the Isle of Man's beaches some of the cleanest in the UK, and perfectly illustrates how a lamentable situation can be radically improved with a little imagination and the will to change.

Formby Point, Cumbria, a National Trust property and home to a red squirrel reserve.

RATING	NAME	TRACK RECORD	SEWAGE OUTLET	REMARKS
	CUMBRIA			
⌢	**Skinburness** (Silloth) - EU NY126565	☐✗✗ ✗✗✗✓✓		
⌢⌢	**Silloth** (Lees Scar) - EU NY094528	✗✓✗✓✗✗✓✓✓	Screened, 3,000, 60 below LWM. Improvements planned for 1995.	Sand and shingle.
f	**Allonby South** - EU NY078424	☐✗✗✗✗✗✗✗✗	Screened/tidal tank, 300, 50 below LWM. Improvements planned for 1995.	Sand and rock, slightly muddy. Popular beach.
⌢	West Winds - EU	✗✗✗✓✗✗✓✓		
–	**Maryport** NY028356		Raw, 11,500, above LWM. Improvements planned for 1995.	Sand, shingle. Fishing port.
–	**Flimby** NY018334		3, raw, 100, 1,500 and and 50, all 150 above LWM. Improvements planned for 1995.	Sand and shingle.
–	**Siddick** NY001316		2, both raw, 3,500 and 50, above and below LWM. Improvements planned for 1995.	
–	**Workington** NX983296		4, all raw, 2,500, 6,000, 12,000 and 5,500, at LWM, 10 and 20 above and below LWM. Improvements planned for 1995.	Shingle and slag. Low amenity.
–	**Harrington**			Shingle and slag.
–	**Parton**		Screened and macerated, 200 + industry, 800 below LWM. Improvements planned.	Shingle and sand. Low amenity.
–	**Whitehaven**		3, all raw, 500, 1,000 and 25,500, above HWM, above LWM and at LWM. Improvements planned.	Shingle and black sand. Cliffs. Little used. Industrial pollution from nearby works.
⌢⌢	**St Bees** - EU NX959117	✗☐ ✓✓✓✗✓✓	Primary/tidal tank 2,000, above LWM. Improvements 1995.	Sand and shingle. Strong tank currents.
–	**Nethertown**		Raw, 500, at LWM Improvements planned.	Sand and shingle.
–	**Braystones**		Raw, 9,000, 50 below LWM. Improvements planned.	Sand and shingle.
f	**Seascale** NY034010	✗✗✗✗✗✗✗✗✗	Raw, 2,200, below LWM. Improvements planned for 1995.	Sand, shingle and rocks.
–	**Ravenglass**		Primary, 250 + heavy tourist trade, to Esk at LWM.	Shingle and mud.
⌢⌢	**Silecroft** - EU SD120812	✗✓✓✓✓✓✓✓		Sand and shingle.
⌢⌢	**Haverigg** - EU SD157766	✗✗✗✗✗✗✗✗✓		Sand dunes. High amenity.

RATING	NAME	TRACK RECORD	SEWAGE OUTLET	REMARKS
–	**Millom**		Secondary, 7,500, at LWM.	Sand and shingle.
⌒	**Askam-in-Furness** - EU SD200788	✗ ☐ ✗✗✗✗✓	Secondary, 2,350, to Duddon Channel. Improvements planned for 1995.	Sand. Bathing safe inshore. Pollution in Duddon Estuary.
–	**Barrow-in-Furness**		32, raw/other, 73,000, all discharge to Walney Channel. Improvements planned for 1996.	
f	**Roan Head** - EU SD187769	✗✗✗✓✗✓✗✓✗		Some minor littering reported.
f	**Walney Island** West Shore - EU SD199857	✗✗✗✓✗✓✓✓✗		Beaches to the west of the island have sand dunes and normal bathing facilities.
⌒	Biggar Bank - EU SD208825	✓✓✓✗✓✓✓✓✓		
⌒⌒⌒⌒	Sandy Gap - EU SD208831	✓✗✓✗✓✓✓✓✓		Not featured due to adjacent sewage outfalls.
⌒	**Newbiggin** - EU SD314679	☐✗✗ ☐✗✗✗✗✓		Sandy.
⌒	**Aldingham** - EU SD320697	☐✗✗ ☐✗✗✓✗✓		Sandy.
⌒	**Bardsea** - EU SD326739	✗✗✗✓✓✗✗✗✓		Sandy. Country park.
–	**Grange-Over-Sands & Kents Bank**		3, secondary, 11,500, to Wyke Beck.	Mud, shingle and sand.
–	**Arnside**		Tidal tank, 2,000.	Mud, shingle and sand.
	LANCASHIRE			
–	**Hest Bank**		2, secondary, 2,850, one above HWM and one below HWM.	Mud flats, sea retreats 6.5km. No bathing.
f	**Morecambe** Morecambe North - EU SD397658	✗ ☐✗✗✗✗✗✗✗		
⌒	Morecambe South - EU SD393653	✗ ☐✗✗✗✗✗✗✓	Screened, 31,000, at LWM. Improvements planned for 1996.	North beach mud and shingle, south beach sandy.
⌒⌒	**Heysham** - EU SD382633	☐✗✗✗✓✗✗✗✗		Sand. Popular beach.
–	**Pilling Sands**			Mud flats and salt marsh.
–	**Knott End-on-Sea**			Sand and mud flats.
f	**Fleetwood** (Pier) - EU SD342487	✗✗✗✗✗✗✗✗✗	Tidal tank, 31,000, at LWM, stormwater also. Improvements planned for 1996.	Sand.
⌒	**Cleveleys** - EU SD312433	✗✗✗✗✗✗✗✗✓	1, 81,000. Improvements planned for 1996.	
⌒	**Bispham** - EU SD307397	☐✗✗ ☐✗✗✗✗✓		

RATING	NAME	TRACK RECORD	SEWAGE OUTLET	REMARKS
	Blackpool		3, screened, 105,000, below LWM. Improvements planned for 1995.	This area is very badly polluted and remains highly unsuitable for bathing. Discharges of stormwater occur directly on to the beach once or twice a year.
↷	North Pier - EU SD305364	XXXXXXX✓		
f	Lost Children's Post - EU SD306356	XXXXXXXX		
f	South Pier - EU SD304338	XXXXXXXX		
f	**St. Anne's North** - EU SD304305	XXXXXXXX		
f	**Lytham St Anne's** - EU SD318283	XXXXXXXX	Screened, 42,000, at LWM into the Ribble Estuary. Improvements planned for 1995.	Sand. Beach cleaned daily.
↷	**Southport** - EU SD322179	XXXXXXX✓	4, primary, 91,500, to Crossens Pool, 3 stormwaters. Improvements planned for 1995.	Sandy beaches. Lifeguard and first aid service in operation between Easter and October.
↷	**Ainsdale** - EU SD297129	XXX✓✓X✓X✓	Secondary, 12,000, to inland waterway.	Sandy. Lifeguard and first aid service in season.
↷↷	**Formby** - EU SD277100	✓✓X✓✓X✓X✓	Secondary, 18,000, to River Alt.	Sandy.
–	**Hightown**		Stormwater.	Sand and some mud.
–	**Blundell Sands**		2, 48,100. Improvements under construction.	Sandy.
↷↷	**New Brighton** - EU (Harrison Drive) SJ287937	X✓✓X✓✓XX✓		Sand and shingle.
↷↷↷↷	**Moreton** - EU SJ257918	✓✓✓✓✓✓✓✓	Macerated, 65,000, LSO.	Not featured due to adjacent sewage outfall.
↷	**West Kirby** - EU SJ210868	☐☐☐☐☐ XX✓		Sandy.
↷↷	**Meols** - EU SJ230906	XX✓XXXX✓✓		Sandy.
	THE ISLE OF MAN			
–	**Douglas** Summerhill	☐☐☐☐ ✓X✓X	3, all raw, 31,000, 2 at LWM and 1 600 below LWM.	A 2km sand, shingle and rock beach runs northwards from the river mouth and the island's main harbour.
–	Palace	☐☐☐☐ ✓X✓X		
–	Broadway	☐☐☐☐ ✓✓✓X		
–	**Laxey**	☐☐☐ ✓✓✓XX	Raw, 1,500, below LWM.	Sandy below half tide, shingle above.
–	**Ramsey**	☐☐☐ X✓XXX	Raw, 6,500, below LWM.	Two sandy beaches either side of old working harbour.
–	**Peel**	☐☐☐ XXXXX	Raw, 3,800, 50 below LWM.	Sandy beach. Old working harbour and Peel castle.
–	**Port Erin**	☐☐☐ ✓✓XXX	Raw, 3,000, tidal tank below LWM, rarely uncovered.	Sandy beach in sheltered bay on south of island.
–	**Port St Mary**	☐☐☐ XXX	2, raw, 2,000, at LWM.	Sandy beach at Chapel Bay; outer beach also sandy.

RATING	NAME	TRACK RECORD	SEWAGE OUTLET	REMARKS
–	**Castletown**	▢▢▢▢▢▢✓✗	2, raw domestic and industrial sewage 3,200, at LWM.	Sheltered area, sand, shingle and rock beach. Used extensively for watersports.
–	**Derbyhaven**	▢▢▢▢▢▢✓✓	Pumped tidal discharge, 150, below LWM.	Sheltered inner shingle area used for mooring boats, outer bay sandy.
–	**Gansey Bay** (Bay Ny Carrickey)			Sand and shingle beach. Watersports centre available.
–	**Kirk Michael**	▢▢▢▢▢▢✗	Screened and primary settlement, 1, 200, below LWM.	Narrow, exposed shingle and sand beach. Not extensively used for bathing.
–	**Jurby**		Primary settlement, 700, below LWM.	Bathing not advised due to currents.

Bradda Head, Isle of Man.

The dramatic stacks and cliffs of Duncansby Head are typical of the Highland coast of Scotland.

SCOTLAND

SCOTLAND HAS SOME OF THE MOST SPECTACULAR COASTAL SCENERY IN THE WORLD, FROM THE LONG SAND DUNES OF THE EAST COAST TO THE ROCKY SHORES OF FIFE WITH ITS SERIES OF PICTURESQUE FISHING VILLAGES. THIS CHAPTER COVERS THE COAST OF MAINLAND SCOTLAND: BEACHES THAT ARE RELATIVELY EASY TO REACH FOR A DAY AT THE SEA, OR AS A STARTING POINT TO EXPLORE THE DELIGHTS OF THIS COASTLINE FURTHER. INFORMATION ON THE HEBRIDES, ORKNEY AND SHETLAND HAS NOT BEEN INCLUDED AS BATHING WATER QUALITY DATA FOR THESE AREAS IS NOT AVAILABLE. BEACHES ABOUND ON THE OUTER ISLANDS, HOWEVER, AND MANY OF THEM ARE PRISTINE.

•

From the cliffs and stacks of Caithness to the west coast Highlands and Islands, with sea lochs and towering mountains in between, there are hundreds (if not thousands) of beaches and tiny sandy bays, mostly remote, deserted and beautiful. Many can only be reached by the keen walker, but the effort usually proves well worth while. If what you seek is peace and solitude combined with traditional hospitality, then Scotland may be the place for you.

That is not to say that Scotland does not have problems around its coast. Many Scottish beaches have failed to meet the minimum EC bathing water quality standard. Sea-borne rubbish is washed up on shore; sewage sludge and dredged spoil are dumped off the Clyde, Forth and Tay Estuaries; industrial waste is discharged into coastal waters, particularly around the Clyde and the Forth. Nuclear installations at Chapelcross, Hunterston, Torness and Dounreay contribute to pollution of the sea by discharging warm water and contaminants from antifouling treatments of the cooling water intake pipes.

The rapid development of the coastline has, seemingly inevitably, destroyed once scenic areas. The sea lochs of the west coast are studded with the floating cages of the fish farming business. The North Sea oil and gas industry has spawned the growth of massive onshore terminals and the view along the Cromarty Firth is dominated by a string of platforms. The recent discovery of a large oilfield off the west coast of Scotland is a cause for concern since its exploitation will lead to increased shipping and increased risk of accidents in an area of outstanding natural beauty, and of international importance for birds, seals and fish. Any future development of this oilfield must be carefully controlled and management must ensure that the risk of accidents and pollution is kept to a minimum.

THORNTONLOCH
Lothian
OS Ref: NT753746

Almost hidden behind the rocky outcrops of Torness Point and within sight of the nuclear power station, this beautiful sandy beach runs south for about 400m, backed along its length by shallow dunes. To the south are spectacular views of the Berwickshire cliffs, and the coastline is the main feature of a well marked Geology Trail which points out the features and fossils of the local limestone.

Water quality
No sewage is discharged in the vicinity of this beach.

Bathing safety
A strong undertow means swimmers should exercise extreme caution. There are no lifeguards on duty.

Litter
The beach is cleaned weekly throughout the summer.

Access
The beach is on an unclassified road off the A1, south of the entrance to Torness Nuclear Power Station, and is a short walk from the car park.

Parking
There is space for about 40 cars a short walk from the beach, near the caravan site.

Toilets
There are toilets on the caravan site adjacent.

Food
Available on the caravan site adjacent.

Seaside activities
Swimming, windsurfing and fishing.

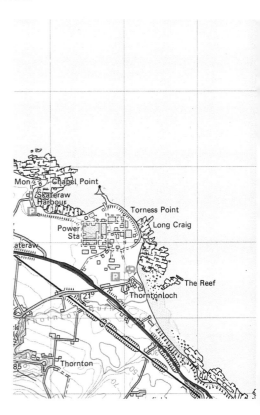

Wet weather alternatives
Dunbar Tourist Information has details of local attractions.

Wildlife and walks
There is a birdwatching centre at Barns Ness, 3 km to the north; the Geology Trail starts in the car park at White Sands Bay.

Track record ✓✓✓✓✓✓✓
Not EU designated.

*Torness nuclear power station makes an unusual
backdrop for the beach at Thorntonloch.*

WHITE SANDS BAY
Lothian
OS Ref: NT710773

An attractive, compact beach with fine golden sand bounded by a rocky shore and backed by low coastal grassland spotted with picnic tables, White Sands is an ideal place for an early-morning swim. There are pleasant views to be had along the coast towards the old Borders town of Dunbar.

Water quality
No sewage is discharged in the vicinity of this beach.

Litter
The beach is cleaned weekly during the summer season.

Bathing safety
Safe in all but the most extreme weather conditions. There is no lifeguard cover.

Access
Signposted off the A1 approximately five kilometres south of Dunbar.

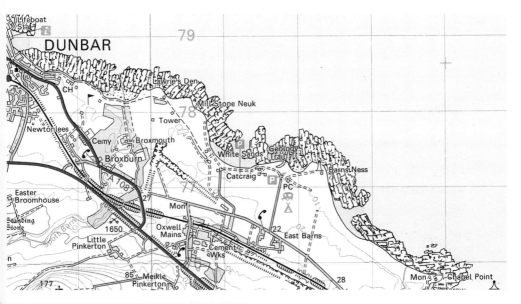

Parking
Ample space on grassland.

Public transport
Nearest rail station is Dunbar; a bus runs from the town to the cement works a short walk from the beach.

Seaside activities
Swimming.

Wildlife and walks
The Geology Trail starts and ends at the car park and this is a good base for easy coastal walks and rambles. There is excellent birdwatching and local pools and bushes attract a wide range of species especially at migration time.

Track record ✓✓✓✓✓✓✓✓
Not EU designated.

Wild flowers abound in the grasslands backing the beach and the rockpools are rich in marine life.

135

BELHAVEN BEACH
Lothian
OS Ref: NT658786

Nestling to the west of Dunbar, Belhaven Bay is an extensive sandy beach that forms part of the John Muir Country Park, noted for its rich variety of coastal habitats. The bay itself is fringed by low sand dunes, saltmarsh and coastal grassland.

Water quality
One screened storm water outlet at the beach.

Bathing safety
Hazardous for all but the strongest swimmers, especially at the northern end adjacent to the mouth of the River Tyne. There is no lifeguard cover, so extra care should be taken at all times.

Litter
The beach is cleaned regularly by the council.

Access
John Muir Country Park signposted from the A1 trunk road. A level footpath leads from the Linkfield car park.

Parking
Ample space at the Linkfield, an extensive grassland car park, and at the Shore Road car park.

Public transport
The beach is within walking distance of Dunbar rail station and bus routes.

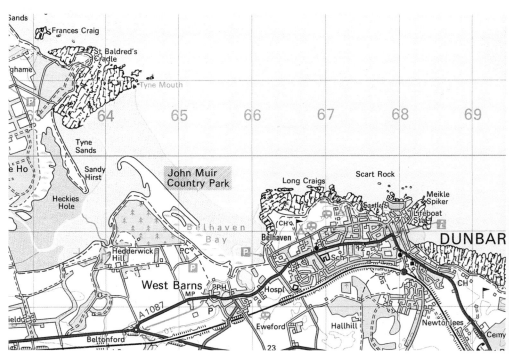

Beautiful but dangerous: bathing is not recommended at Belhaven because of strong currents.

 Toilets
There are toilets in both car parks.

 Food
Various kiosks and cafés in town.

 Seaside activities
Sunbathing, paddling, beach games.

Wildlife and walks
A ranger service arranges guided walks in the John Muir Country Park, a haven for families seeking an enjoyable day in the open air. The natural history enthusiast will find plenty to see: the Tyninghame (Tyne Estuary) has mud and sand flats, saltmarsh, dunes, parkland, pools and rocky shore providing habitats for a wide range of wildlife throughout the year. Access points at NT626808; NT615781; NT607801; NT662787.

Track record ✓✓✓✓✓✓✓✓

SILVERSANDS, ABERDOUR
Fife
OS Ref: NT203856

This fine sandy beach is popular with weekend visitors in the summer, attracted by the sheltered beach, safe bathing and the quaint little harbour with its views out over Inchcolm Island. A major improvement scheme started in September 1994 with tree planting and other projects to improve the local environment.

Water quality
One outfall serving 3,300 people discharges primary treated sewage 900 metres below LWM.

Bathing safety
Swimming is safe, with lifeguard and first aid cover seven days a week in summer, and first aid over the weekend in winter.

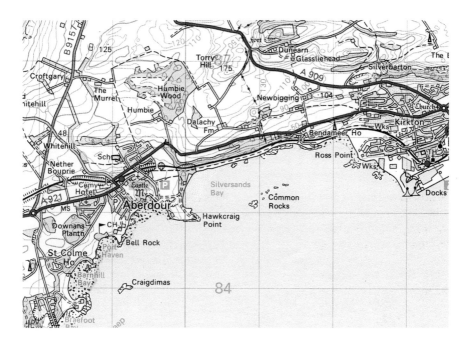

 Litter
The beach is cleaned daily by hand and three to four times a week by machine in season.

 Access
The beach is located off the A921 Aberdour to Burntisland road.

 Parking
Parking for coaches and cars 100 metres from the beach, and on the beach for disabled visitors.

 Public transport
Aberdour rail station is about one kilometre away; there are no buses.

 Toilets
Toilets available including facilities for disabled visitors.

A favourite haunt of weekend visitors from Edinburgh, Silversands has something to offer every member of the family.

 Food
Fast food and ice cream vans visit the beach, and a restaurant is open all year round.

 Seaside activities
Swimming, sailing, water-skiing. Next to the beach is a putting green, trampolines, and a play area for children. There is varied entertainment in the summer season.

 Wet weather alternatives
The 14th-century Aberdour Castle, now a ruin, has exquisite formal gardens with many well established specimen plants. The medieval St Fillans church stands next to the castle.

 Wildlife and walks
There is a Site of Special Scientific Interest near the harbour, and a coastal walk that gives view points all along the bay.

Track record ✓✓✓✓✗✗✗✓✓

SHELL BAY, EARLSFERRY
Fife
OS Ref: NO462003

A sandy beach in a well sheltered cove on the western outskirts of Earlsferry, Shell Bay is bordered by large sand hills and is popular with families and walkers. The beach is easily accessible from the adjacent caravan park.

Water quality
One outlet serving 100 people discharges primary treated sewage at LWM. Improvements planned for 2000.

Bathing safety
Safe with the usual precautions; no lifeguard cover.

Litter
The beach is regularly cleaned by machine, but marine and sewage-related debris are sometimes a problem.

Access
The A915 west from Kirkcaldy becomes the A917 to Fife Ness. Shell Bay caravan park is on the right, 1.5 kilometres before the port of Elie.

Parking
Visitors may park on the caravan site for a small charge.

Toilets
On the caravan site.

Food
There is a café and bar on the caravan site.

Seaside activities
Swimming, surfing, fishing, shell collecting; there are numerous golf courses nearby.

Wet weather alternatives
Kellie Castle, Scottish fisheries museum in Anstruther, recreation centre in Anstruther, coastal fishing villages of Elie and St Monance. St Andrews, the spiritual home of golf, is 19 kilometres away.

The desolate beauty of Shell Bay in winter is typical of many unspoilt Scottish beaches.

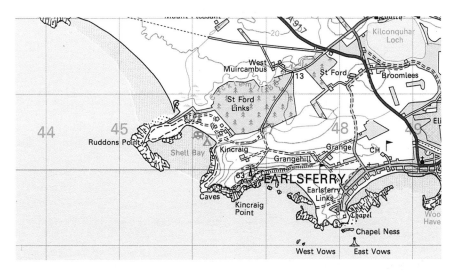

Wildlife and walks

There are spectacular coastal walks in both directions from Shell Bay. This is a popular area for birdwatching and trips to the Isle of May Nature Reserve run from Anstruther Harbour.

Track record ✓✓✗✗✓✓✓✗✓

Not EU designated.

WEST SANDS, ST ANDREWS
Fife
OS Ref: NO503175

Home to the oldest university in Scotland, the pretty town of St Andrews is a major tourist attraction, although the non-golfer may find it all slightly overwhelming. Essentially an overgrown medieval village, it has a turbulent history and suffered greatly in religious wars. Today it is chiefly famous as the home of the Royal and Ancient Golf Club, the supreme world authority in golfing matters.

Water quality
There is one stormwater outfall at this beach.

Bathing safety
Generally safe, but beware of offshore currents.

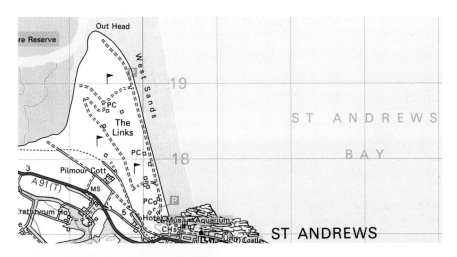

 Access
Direct from the town.

 Parking
Ample parking in St Andrews.

 Seaside activities
Swimming, sailing.

Wet weather alternatives
St Andrews has much to offer including a Sea Life Centre, Crawfor's Art Centre and the British Golf Museum.

Wildlife and walks
The flat West Sands are favoured by oystercatchers and sanderlings, which may be glimpsed at the water's edge. The Eden Estuary Nature Reserve (NO452188) at Guardbridge is but a short trip up the A91 where there is a large lay-by in which to park. Fife Bird Club has a hide on the shore.

Track record ✓✓✓✓✓✓✓✓

The vast, flat West Sands stretch to the north of St Andrews towards Out Head.

TENTSMUIR SANDS
Fife
OS Ref: NO5024

This extensive area of sand dunes north of the Eden Estuary has been stabilised by conifers planted in the early 1920s by the Forestry Commission. The coastline can still be reached along roads which cut through the forest giving access to parking and picnic areas behind the dunes. This is a wild and remote spot with a wide, flat, sandy beach backed by high dunes which are continually moving seawards.

Water quality
No sewage is discharged in the vicinity of this beach.

Bathing safety
Generally safe, but beware of offshore currents.

Access
A turning off the road north-east of Leuchars leads into the forest. The car park can be found near the eastern edge, just before the beach itself. There are paths to the beach from the car park.

Parking
There is a Forestry Commission car park behind the dunes.

 Toilets
At the car park.

 Food
None available.

Seaside activities
Swimming.

The rich vegetation around Tentsmuir attracts abundant wildlife; the area is a feeding ground for numerous waders and wildfowl.

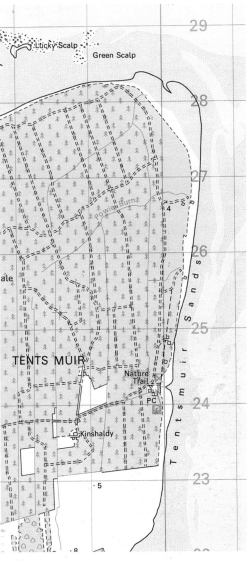

Wildlife and walks
A large area of the shore, including dunes and developing scrub woodland, is a National Nature Reserve. There is a ranger service based at the car park where a nature trail commences. This is an excellent spot for walking with views across the offshore sandbanks and away to the Tayside coast.

Track record ☐☐☐ ✓✓✓✓
Not EU designated.

LUNAN BAY

Tayside
OS Ref: NO6951

An east-facing bay north of Dundee, Lunan's beach is a broad sweep of sand stretching for eight kilometres from Boddin Point in the north to Ethie Haven in the south and divided almost exactly in the middle by Lunan Water. On a hilltop at the mouth of the stream stands the ruin of Red Castle, once owned by Robert Bruce.

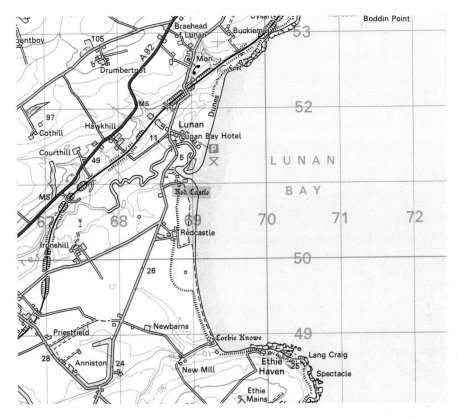

Water quality

 Bathing safety
Generally safe, except at the mouth of the river.

 Litter
Occasionally cleaned by hand in the summer.

 Access
Lunan is signposted off the A92, and the beach is a short walk from the village.

Swimmers at Lunan Bay may be fortunate enough to catch sight of a school of common porpoises offshore; grey seals are frequent visitors.

 Parking
Parking is limited; a car park at Boddin Point has a view point.

 Seaside activities
Swimming.

 Wet weather alternatives
None available at the beach.

 Wildlife and walks
St Cyrus National Nature Reserve to the north is rich in wild flowers, butterflies and moths. Montrose Basin is an Angus District Council and Scottish Wildlife Trust Reserve; observation hides give views across the tidal mud which fills at low water, best for autumn and winter watching.

Track record ☐☐☐ ✗ ✓ ✓ ✓ ✓
Not EU designated.

MONTROSE
Tayside
OS Ref: NO728579

Extending for approximately seven kilometres north of the town of Montrose between the estuaries of the North and South Esk rivers, this fine sandy beach is backed by high dunes which in turn form a backdrop to the Medal and Broomfield golf courses.

Water quality

Two outfalls serving 6,300 and 6,000 people discharge macerated and fine screened sewage 10m below LWM. Four outfalls at Rossie Island and Ferryden serving 800 people discharge untreated sewage at LWM. A waste water treatment plant is to be provided by 2000.

Bathing safety

A good bathing beach with a designated area for swimming and beach wardens in attendance. Bathing is dangerous near the rivermouths.

Litter

The beach is cleaned regularly by hand, although the north end is occasionally affected by marine debris.

Access

Direct from the town off the A92, with entrances from the car park, road or golf course.

Parking

There is a large car park at Trail Pavilion.

Public transport
The town is served by the East Coast bus and rail route to Dundee and Aberdeen; there is no public transport from the town to the beach.

 Toilets
At Trail Pavilion and including facilities for disabled visitors.

 Food
A beach café is adjacent to the Trail Pavilion and there are various facilities in the town.

 Seaside activities
Swimming and windsurfing.

Wet weather alternatives
Amusement arcade, sports centre, indoor swimming pool, playscheme, picture gallery, House of Dun, William Lamb Memorial studio, Sunnyside Museum and Montrose Basin Visitor Centre.

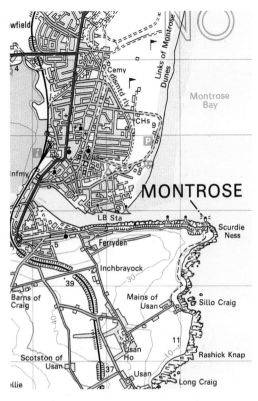

Wildlife and walks
Montrose Basin is tidal and has now become a protected environment for wildlife of many species, with a visitor centre opening in June 1995. St Cyrus Nature Reserve, where more than 300 varieties of wild flowers have been recorded, is just north of Montrose.

Track record ✓✓✓✓✓✓✓✓

A vast expanse of sandy beach stretches away from the Links of Montrose to the South Esk Estuary and the lighthouse at Scurdie Ness.

BALMEDIE
Grampian
OS Ref: NJ9818

Just north of Aberdeen lies one of Britain's longest sandy beaches, extending from the River Don on the city's northern outskirts to the mouth of the River Ythan 16 kilometres to the north. The beach is backed by extensive dunes, and the fine sand shifts continuously. Shell spotters will find an abundance of fine specimens, both common and exotic, at the tideline. Towards the southern end of the beach a rifle range at Blackdog flies red flags when the range is in use. The sheer size of the beach means it is seldom crowded and makes it possible to find a quiet spot at any time of year.

Water quality
One outfall in the vicinity discharges secondary treated sewage through a long sea outfall via pumped diffusers.

Bathing safety
Swimming is generally safe along the whole of the beach, and lifeguards patrol a marked section near Balmedie.

Litter

Occasionally severely affected by deposits of marine debris.

Access

The main point of access is at Balmedie, signposted from the A92.

Parking

There are several car parks at Balmedie.

Seaside activities

Swimming.

The constantly shifting sands of Balmedie have created Sahara-like landscapes where majestic dunes sometimes reach 50 metres in height.

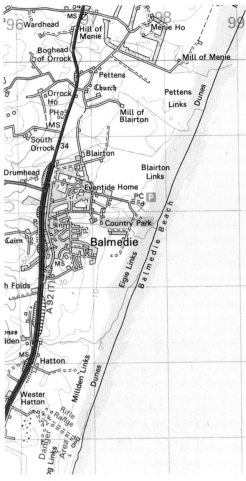

Wet weather alternatives

Old Slains Castle to the north; Crathes Castle and Gardens to the west; several museums in Aberdeen to the south.

Wildlife and walks

The Sands of Forvie Nature Reserve at the northern end of Balmedie beach, which includes the Ythan Estuary, is home to kittiwakes, terns, geese and ducks, and contains the largest colony of eider ducks in Britain. Access is via a car park on the A975 road north of Newburgh.

Track record ✓ ✓ ✓ ✓ ✓ ✓

Not EU designated.

ST COMBS
Grampian
OS Ref: NK056632

Extensive sandy beaches are a feature of this part of the coast, with superb dunes extending 14 kilometres south to Peterhead. North of the dune system the attractive coastal village of St Combs, which takes its name from St Colomba, is characterised by rows of 18th-century fishermen's cottages, usually set gable-end to the sea for protection.

Water quality
No sewage is discharged in the vicinity of this beach.

Litter
The beach is cleaned regularly between April and September.

Bathing safety
Safe with the usual precautions; no lifeguard cover.

Access
Off the B9033 six kilometres south-east of Fraserburgh.

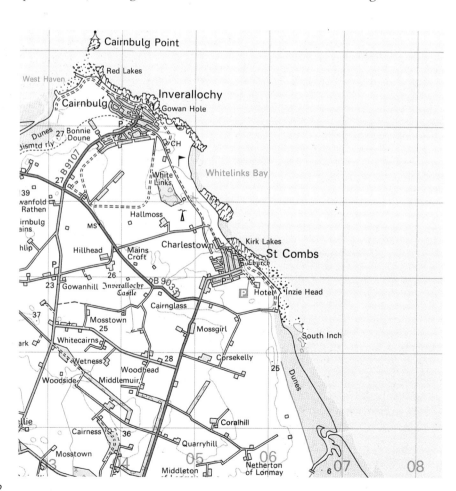

Seemingly endless stretches of sand, backed by extensive dunes, are a feature of this stretch of the coast.

 Parking
In the village.

 Food
Cafés and pubs in the village.

 Wet weather alternatives
Museums, leisure centre, shops and sports facilities in Fraserburgh.

 Wildlife and walks
The extensive dune system plays host to a wide range of flora and fauna. To the north, the Loch of Strathbeg is an important wintering ground and migration staging post for wildfowl and the 2,300-acre RSPB Reserve attracts over 40,000 geese, ducks and swans between September and April. In summer many rare and unusual birds visit and over 180 species have been recorded in the area. Because access is across Ministry of Defence property from the A952 road at Crimond, visitors must obtain a permit from the RSPB in advance.

Track record ☐ ☐ ☐ ✗ ✓ ✓ ✓ ✓
Not EU designated.

NAIRN CENTRAL
Highland
OS Ref: NH883572

Situated on the western side of the pretty Highland town of Nairn, with its narrow rows of fishermen's cottages and fine ornamental gardens, this is a mainly sandy beach with rockpools at low tide and a fully serviced 100-berth leisure marina at its eastern extreme. Dogs are banned from the beach between May and September.

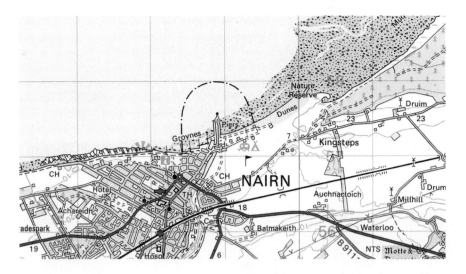

Water quality

One sewage outlet serving 180 people discharges seven metres above LWM.

Bathing safety

Bathing is safe, with first aid available between 10am and 6pm during July and August.

Litter

The beach is cleaned daily by street sweeper and fortnightly by rake sweeper.

Access

There are numerous points of access along the entire length of the beach from the A49 Aberdeen to Inverness road.

Parking

In the Links car park by the leisure centre.

A beautiful sheltered beach with safe bathing and fine local amenities make Nairn a focal point for this stretch of the Moray Firth.

Public transport

All buses and trains on the Inverness to Aberdeen route stop at Nairn.

Toilets

A new block of toilets was completed in 1994, with facilities for disabled visitors.

Food

There is a Links tearoom.

Seaside activities

Swimming, boating, fishing; two 18-hole golf courses. During July and August the Links summer centre stages activities including beach Olympics for 8–15 year olds.

Wet weather alternatives

Swimming pool, amusement arcade and museums.

Wildlife and walks

Attractive walks are to be had on both sides of the River Nairn; details are obtainable from the Tourist Information Office.

Track record ✓✓✓✓✓✓✓✓

Not EU designated.

DORNOCH
Highland
OS Ref: NH805890

The excellent Royal Dornoch Links attracts golfers from around the world, but Dornoch's wide, sandy beach remains quiet and uncommercialised. The approach is unassuming; the low-lying lands do not permit any view of the beach until you cross the dunes. To the south is Dornoch Point and the entrance to the Firth which stretches almost 32 kilometres inland, while to the north of the town the beach narrows towards Loch Fleet.

Rockpools exposed at low tide teem with marine flora and fauna.

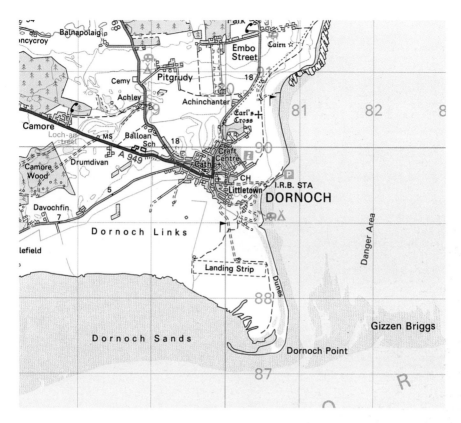

Water quality
No sewage is discharged in the vicinity of this beach.

Bathing safety
Bathing is safe in the central area of the bay, but beware of currents at the northern and southern ends.

Access
From the Main Square in Dornoch a road leads to the shore and golf courses; another goes north to the village of Embo from where it is a short walk across the dunes to the sand.

Parking
Limited space at the beach.

Toilets
One toilet block.

Food
None available at the beach.

Seaside activities
Swimming, golf, Highland Games in August.

Wet weather activities
Dornoch Cathedral and the old Post Office; Dornoch social club is open during the season.

Wildlife and walks
Loch Fleet is the last of the Firth indents into this coastline going north. The loch and the alderwoods behind the mound are nature reserves and the Scottish Wildlife Trust Warden runs guided walks in summer.

Track record ✓✓
Not EU designated.

RATING	NAME	TRACK RECORD	SEWAGE OUTLET	REMARKS
	BORDERS			
∩	**Eyemouth** NT945640	✓✓✗✓✗✗✓✓	2, raw, 2,500, and 850, remote from the beach. Improvements planned.	Rocks and sand. Bathing can be unsafe due to currents.
∩∩	**Coldingham Bay** NT918666	✓✓✓✓✓✓✓✓	Raw, 50, 12 above LWM. Improvements planned.	Sandy.
∩∩	**Pease Sands** - EU NT794710	✓✓✓✓✓✓✓✓	Secondary, 1,000, above LWM.	Red cliffs and sand.
	LOTHIAN			
∩	**Dunglass** NT774724	✓✓✓		Coarse sand and rocks.
∩	**Dunbar East** NT686786	✗✗✗✓	Screened stormwater, at LWM.	Sand and rocks. Beach cleaned regularly.
∩∩∩∩	**Peffersands** NT622829	✓✓✓✓✓✓✓✓		Sandy with dunes. Not featured due to insufficient information.
∩∩∩∩	**Seacliff** NT605846	✓✓✓✓		Sandy sheltered bay. Not featured due to insufficient information.
∩	**Milsey Bay** - EU NT565853	✓✓✗✓✓✓✓✓	Screened stormwater, at LWM.	Sandy and rock outcrops. Beach cleaned regularly.
∩	**North Berwick Bay** NT553855	✓✓✗✗✗✗✓✗✓	Stormwater only.	Sandy and rock outcrops. Beach cleaned regularly.
∩∩	**Yellowcraig** (Broad Sands Bay) - EU NT515859	✓✓✓✓✗✓✗✓✓	Raw, 300, at LWM.	Sandy, some rocks. Beach cleaned regularly.
∩∩	**Gullane** - EU NT476834			Sandy, backed by dunes. Beach cleaned regularly.
–	**Gosford Sands** NT449787	✓✓✓✗✗✓✓✓	Raw, at LWM.	Sandy with rocky upper shore.
∩	**Longniddry** NT438776	✓✗✗✗	Secondary, at LWM.	Sand and rocks. Beach cleaned regularly.
–	**Seton Sands** NT411759	✗✗✓ ✗✓✗✓	Raw, 3,700, at LWM. Improvements planned.	Sand and rocks.
–	**Fisherrow** NT323731	✓✓✗		Sandy. Beach cleaned regularly.
f	**Portobello** NT304745	✗✗✗✓✗✗✗✗	Screened stormwater only, at LWM beyond the rocks at Juppa.	Mostly sand. There are dangerous old wooden stands, visible at low tide.
–	**Silverknowes** NT204722	✗✓✓		Sand and mud.
∩∩	**Cramond** NT192771	✓✗✓✓	Raw and macerated. Improvements planned.	Sandy.
	FIFE			
–	**Dalgety**		Primary, 7,740, at LWM. Improvements planned.	Sand and rocks.
f	**Aberdour Harbour** NT194850	✓✓✓✗	Primary, 700, 10 below LWM. Improvements planned for 1996.	Sand and rocks.

RATING	NAME	TRACK RECORD	SEWAGE OUTLET	REMARKS
f	**Burntisland** NT239858	✓✓✓ ✓✗✗✓✗	Raw, 20, above LWM. Improvements planned for 1995/6.	Sandy. Beach cleaned regularly.
⌒⌒	**Pettycur** - EU NT264862	✗✗✓ ✓✗✗✓✓	Septic tank, 1,000, 500 below LWM.	Sandy. Beach cleaned regularly.
f	**Kinghorn** NT272868	✗✗✗✗✗✗✗✓✗	Primary, 2,400, LSO.	Sandy. Beach cleaned regularly.
f	**Kirkcaldy Linktown** NT281904	✗✗ ✗✗✗✓✗		Sandy.
⌒⌒	**Pathhead Sands** (Kirkcaldy Harbour) NT292923	✓✓✓✓	Fine screened, 49,570, 500 below LWM. Improvements planned.	Sand and coal spoil.
–	**Leven West** NO386005	✗✗✗	Screened, 92,180, 50 below LWM. Improvements planned.	Sand and rocks.
f	**Leven East** NO396014	✓✓✓ ✗✗✗✓✗	Improvements planned.	Sandy. Beach cleaned regularly.
–	**Lundin Links** NO410022	✓✓✓✓✗✓✗✓	Primary, 1,090, 200 below LWM. Improvements planned.	Sandy to west rocks.
f	**Lower Largo** NO417022	✓✓✓✓✓✓✓✗	Primary, 1,400, 240 below LWM. Improvements planned.	Sandy.
⌒	**Upper Largo** NO427025	✗✗✓✓	Improvements planned.	Sandy.
⌒	**Elie/Earlsferry** NT489998	✓✓✓✗✗✓✓✓✓	Stormwater/septic tank, 1,500 summer and 890 winter, 270 below LWM.	Sandy.
–	**Pittenweem** NO550022	✓✓✓ ✗✗✗✓	Stormwater, at LWM.	Rocky fishing port.
⌒⌒	**Anstruther** NO564031	✓✓✓✓✓✓✓✓	Raw, 1,700, at LWM. Improvements planned for 1995.	Sand and rocks.
⌒	**Roome Bay, Crail** NO618078	✓✓✓✓✓✓✗✓✓	Raw, 230, at LWM. Improvements planned for 1995.	Sand and rocks.
f	**St Andrews East** NO518164	✓✓✗✗✗✓✓✗	Primary and disinfection, 12,970, above LWM. Improvements planned.	Shingle and rocks.
f	**Tayport** NO463306	✗✗✗✗	Fine screened, 3,280, above LWM. Improvement planned to give primary by 2000.	Sandy.
	TAYSIDE			
f	**Broughty Ferry** NO469306	✗✗✗ ✗✗✓✗	Fine screened, 70,000, LSO. 3, stormwater only. Improvements planned for 1996.	Sandy.
⌒⌒	**Monifieth** NO500320	✗✗✗ ✗✗✗✓	Sewage information as above.	Sandy.
⌒⌒	**Carnoustie** - EU NO565343	✓✓✓✗✗✗✓✗✓	Fine screened, 10,300, above LWM. Improvements planned.	Sandy.

RATING	NAME	TRACK RECORD	SEWAGE OUTLET	REMARKS
⌒⌒	**Arbroath** - EU NO630400	✓✓✗✗✗✗✓✓✓	2, fine screened and stormwater only, 23,000 and 900m below LWM, SSO. Improvements planned.	Red sands.
⌒⌒⌒	Victoria Park NO651410	□□□□✗✗✓✓		Sandy. Not featured due to insufficient information.
f	**Westhaven** NO574347	□□□□✓✗✓✗		Sandy. Regular problems with sewage-related debris.
	GRAMPIAN			
⌒	**St Cyrus** NO757648	□□□✓✗✗✗✗✓	Macerated, 820 at LWM.	Sand and saltmarsh.
⌒⌒	**Stonehaven** NO891877	✓✓✓✓✓✓✓✓✓	2, macerated/primary, 9,000, LSO.	
–	**Muchalls**			Pebbles and rock. Bathing unsafe.
⌒	**Aberdeen** - EU NJ955072	✓✓✓✓✓✓✓✓✓	2, raw, 8,000, into harbour in tidal river. Improvements planned for 1996.	Beach cleaned daily by hand.
⌒⌒⌒⌒	Aberdeen/Footdee NJ958060	□□□□□✓✓✓✓		Sandy. All beach details as above, located at the southern point of Aberdeen beach itself. Not featured due to adjacent sewage outfall.
⌒⌒	**Collieston** NK040285	□□□□✓✓✓✓✓	Macerated, 200, at LWM.	Old fishing port.
f	**Cruden Bay** NK090356	□□□✓✓✗✓✓✓✗	Macerated, 2,200, at LWM.	Sand and dunes.
⌒⌒	**Lido Peterhead** NK123451	□□□✓✓✓✓✓✓✓	Screened and primary, 20,100, LSO.	Sandy sheltered beach. Beach cleaned regularly.
⌒⌒	**Fraserburgh** - EU NK005661	✓✓✗✓✓✓✓✓✓	12, raw, 15,690, Improvement scheme under way.	Sand and dunes. Beach cleaned regularly.
⌒⌒⌒⌒	**Rosehearty** NJ933675	□□□□✓✓✓✓✓	Raw, 1,250,	Sandy. Beach cleaned regularly. Not featured due to adjacent sewage outfall.
–	**Banff Bridge**	□□✗✗✗✗✓□□	2, raw, 4,180, 143 & 55 below LWM. Improvements planned for 1995.	Sandy.
⌒⌒	**Inverboyndie** NJ671646	□□□□□□✓✓✓		Sandy. Beach cleaned regularly.
⌒	**Sandend Bay** NJ557662	□□□□□✓✓✓✓✓	Primary, 280.	Sandy.
⌒⌒⌒⌒	**Cullen** - EU NJ448671		2, raw, 1,500, LWM.	Red sand. Beach cleaned regularly. Not featured due to adjacent sewage outfall.
–	**Findochty**		2, raw and macerated, 1,050, 1 at and 1 below LWM.	Sandy cove overlooking rock stacks and caves. Beach cleaned regularly. Swimmers take care to avoid rocky outcrops.

RATING	NAME	TRACK RECORD	SEWAGE OUTLET	REMARKS
–	**Strathlene, Buckie** NJ448671	☐☐☐☐☐☐☐✓	3, all raw, 240, 175 and 450, 58m, 71m and 95m below LWM. Improvements planned.	Sandy. Beach cleaned regularly.
⌒⌒	**Lossiemouth East** NJ240705	✗✗✗✓✓✗✓✓	Screens, 42,700, LSO.	Sandy with dunes. Bathing dangerous. Beach cleaned regularly.
–	**Lossiemouth West** NJ212712	✓✓✓✓✓✓✓✓		Sandy. Beach cleaned regularly.
–	**Hopeman** NJ144697		Primary, 1,800, 280 below LWM. Improvements planned.	Sandy. Beach cleaned regularly. Dangerous rocks just under the water on either side of bay.
–	**Burghead**		Macerated, 1,440, LSO.	A long stretch of sand and pebble. Beach cleaned regularly.
	HIGHLAND			
⌒⌒	**Nairn East** - EU NH891574	✓✓✗✓ ✓✓✓✓	Primary, 8,200, below LWM at east of beach. Improvements planned.	Sandy. Beach cleaned regularly.
–	**Rosemarkie** NH7357	☐☐☐☐☐☐☐✓		Sand, gravel and shingle.
–	**Cromarty** NH7867		Raw, 200, below LWM Improvements planned.	Sandy.
–	**Nigg Bay**			Sandy.
–	**Portmahomack** NH915844		Secondary, 450, below LWM.	Sand and dunes.
–	**Sinclairs Bay,** near Wick ND3455		5, 3 primary, 2 raw, 777, at LWM by gravity. Improvements planned for 1996.	Sandy.
–	**Duncansby Head** ND4073			Sandy.
–	**Dunnet Bay/Murkle Bay** ND2170		2, macerated & primary, 965, 170, at and below LWM.	Sand and dunes.
–	**Thurso** ND1168	☐☐☐☐☐☐☐✓	Macerated, 9,200, LWM. Improvements planned.	Sandy.
–	**Sandside Bay** NC9665		Macerated, 340, below LWM.	Dunes, rocky outcrops.
–	**Coldbackie** NC6060			Sand and dunes.
–	**Sango Bay/Balnakeil Bay** NC4068		Primary, 200, at LWM.	Sandy bay with extensive dunes.
–	**Sandwood Bay** NC2165			Sand and dunes.
–	**Scourie** NC1544		2, primary, 200, at LWM.	Sandy.
	Clashnessie Bay NC0531			Sandy.
–	**Clachtoll** NC0327			Sandy.
	Achmelvich NC0524			Sandy.

RATING	NAME	TRACK RECORD	SEWAGE OUTLET	REMARKS
–	**Achnahaird** NC0113			Sandy.
	Achiltibuie NC0109			Shingle.
–	**Gruinard Bay** NG9490			Pink sand.
–	**Gairloch** NG7977	☑	4, primary, all below LWM by gravity. Improvements planned.	Sandy.
	Applecross NG7145			Sandy.
–	**Coral Beaches** NG2254			Sand and shells.
	Morar NM6792		2, primary, 100 below LWM.	Sandy.
–	**Camusdarrach** NM6691			Sand and dunes.
–	**Traigh, Arisaig** NM6387			Sand and dunes.
–	**Sanna Bay** NM4469			Sandy.
	STRATHCLYDE			
–	**Calgary Bay**			Sand and dunes.
–	**Erraid**			Sand and dunes.
–	**Kilchattan Bay**		Raw, 170, at LWM.	Sandy.
–	**Kames Bay**		Several, raw, 550.	Sand and pebbles.
–	**Dunoon** (West Bay)		Unknown, raw, below LWM.	Sand and pebbles.
–	**Ganavan**		Septic tank, 100, below LWM.	Sand and rocky outcrops.
–	**Macrihanish**		Raw, 200, at LWM.	Sandy.
–	**Carradale**		2, raw, 480, at LWM.	
–	**Helensburgh**		Macerated, 13,200.	Sand and pebbles.
–	**Portkil/Meikleross**		2, raw, <100, below LWM and <100, above LWM.	Sand and rocks.
–	**Gourock** (West Bay)		4, raw, 2,600, below LWM. Improvements planned.	Shingle and rocks.
–	**Lunderston Bay**		Septic tank, above LWM.	Shingle and sand.
–	**Wemyss Bay**		3, 2 unknown, 100, above LWM, 1 macerated, 11,000, below LWM. Improvements planned.	Sand and shingle.
–	**Largs**		Raw, 12,000, below LWM.	Sandy with rocky outcrops. Beach cleaned regularly.
–	**Fairlie**		2, raw, 1,000, below LWM and 500, at LWM. Improvements under construction.	Sand and rocks.
–	**Millport**		11, primary, 2,700, at LWM.	Sand and rocks.

RATING	NAME	TRACK RECORD	SEWAGE OUTLET	REMARKS
–	**Seamill**		3, raw, 4,500, all at LWM. Improvements due.	Sandy with rocky outcrops.
–	**Ardrossan** (Boydston)			Sand and rocks.
f	**Saltcoats** - EU NS236420	✓✓✗✗✗✓✗✗✗		Sandy bay. Beach cleaned regularly.
–	**Stevenston**		Screens, 41,000, LSO.	Sandy.
f	**Irvine** (Beach Park) - EU NS306377	✗✗✗✗✗✗✗✗		Sandy. Beach cleaned regularly.
–	**Gailes**		Screens, 100,000, LSO	Sandy.
–	**Brodick Bay**		2, raw, 1,300, 1 below LWM/1 above LWM.	Rocks and sand.
–	**Lamlash Bay**		6, raw, 950, all at LWM.	Rocks and sand.
–	**Whiting Bay**		2, raw, 800, below LWM.	Sand and shingle.
–	**Blackwaterfoot**		4, discharges of septic tank effluent, 200.	Sand and shingle.
–	**Troon** North			Sandy.
⌐	South - EU NS321307	✓✓✓✓✓✓✓✓✓		Sandy.
f	**Prestwick** - EU NS345262	✓✓✓✗✗✗✗✗✗		Sandy.
f	**Ayr** - EU NS331219	✗✗✗✗✗✗✗✗✗	Screens, 16,200, 140 below LWM. Improvements planned.	Sandy.
–	**Doonfoot**		Macerated, 8,000, 220 below LWM. Improvements planned.	Sand and rocks.
–	**Butlins** (Heads of Ayr)		Secondary, 8,500, below LWM.	Sandy.
–	**Maidens**		Primary, 600, at LWM. Improvements planned.	Sandy and rocks.
f	**Turnberry** - EU NS199058	✓✓✗ ✗✗✗✗	Primary, beyond LWM.	Sand and rocks.
f	**Girvan** - EU NX182974	✗✗✗✓✗✓✗✓✗	3, screened/macerated, 4,000, 10 below LWM; tidal tank, 500, at LWM; tidal tank, 2,500, at LWM. Improvements under construction.	Sandy.
	DUMFRIES AND GALLOWAY			
f	**Stranraer** Marine Lake NX053615	✗✗✓✗	Primary, 10,000, 10 below LWM. Improvements planned.	Area affected by silt and effluent from local creamery.
f	Cockle Shore NX080620	✗✗✗✗	Creamery effluent discharged to beach.	Fine sand and silt.
⌐⌐	**Portpatrick Outer Harbour** NW997541	✓✓✓✓	Primary, 600, above LWM in rocks.	Rocky.
–	**Portlogan Bay**		Primary, 75, 200 below HWM.	Sandy.
f	**Drummore** NX135369	✓✓✓✗	2, primary, 280, 50.	Sandy.
–	**Ardwell Bay**		Primary, 75, 75 below HWM.	Sand and shingle.

RATING	NAME	TRACK RECORD	SEWAGE OUTLET	REMARKS
⌒⌒	**Sandhead** NX103501	✗✓✓✓	Primary, 250, discharge to river.	Sandy.
⌒⌒	**Monreith** NX368392	✓✓✓		Sandy.
⌒⌒	**Mossyard** NX552518	✓✓✓✓		Sandy.
⌒⌒	**Carrick Shore** NX575498	✓✓✓✓		Sandy.
⌒⌒	**Brighouse Bay** NX636455	✓✓✓✓	Secondary, 400, 30 below LWM.	Sandy.
⌒⌒	**Dhoon** NX657486	✓✓✓✓	2, primary, 6,000, 200.	Fine sand and silt.
⌒⌒	**Rockcliffe** NX847537	✗✗✓✓	2, secondary, 200, 300.	Sandy.
f	**Sandyhills - EU** NX892551	✓✓✓✗✓✓✓✗	Secondary, 220.	Sandy.
⌒⌒	**Southerness**	✓✓	Primary, 3,500, 500 above.	Sand and rock.
f	**Powfoot** NY147654	✓✗✗✗	Primary, 400.	Silty.
f	**Annan** NY198649	✗✗✗✗	Primary, 7,900, above LWM. Improvements planned for 2000.	Mud. Unsuitable for bathing, due to deep channel and nearby sewage outfall.

Scotland is full of charming, small fishing ports like Keiss Harbour, north of Wick.

WALES

THE SAND DUNES OF ANGLESEY, THE POUNDING OF SURF ON THE LLEYN, ENDLESS KILOMETRES OF SAND, THE CLIFFS AND SECLUDED COVES OF DYFED, THE MEANDERING ESTUARIES, THE BEAUTIFUL GOWER PENINSULA – THIS IS THE COAST OF WALES. THIS CHAPTER COVERS ALL THE BATHING WATERS IN WALES IDENTIFIED UNDER THE EC BATHING WATER DIRECTIVE, AND INCLUDES MANY BEACHES NOT IDENTIFIED UNDER THE TERMS OF THE DIRECTIVE.

•

There are beaches in Wales which compare with the best anywhere in the country, and which often have the added advantage of being relatively uncrowded. Sadly, a number of individual beaches throughout the region have failed to meet even the minimum EC standard for bathing water through contamination by sewage. The problem has been recognised and is being addressed: Dwr Cymru (Welsh Water), the private company responsible for sewerage in Wales, is alone among the water companies in having pledged to treat all its sewage discharges to at least secondary level, with tertiary treatment where necessary. This work will take a long time to complete, and until then there will undoubtedly be pollution blackspots around the Welsh coast; it is, however, a major step forward and the other water companies would do well to follow this lead.

Encouraging though it is, even this will not solve all Wales' pollution problems: the north and south coasts suffer from industrial effluent as well as sewage contamination. Swansea, Cardiff, Port Talbot and Newport all play a part in polluting the south coast with discharges of domestic and industrial waste. The north coast is directly affected by discharges from Merseyside and the Wirral, while Milford Haven has suffered oil pollution from the terminals and refineries that line its shore, and has also had to put up with the harmful effects of antifoulants used on oil tankers. The best beaches are to be found farther west, away from the centres of population. Clean and unspoilt, and often wild and romantic, many are worth exploring at leisure.

RHOSNEIGR (TRAETH CRIGYLL)
Gwynedd
OS Ref: SH323722

One of Anglesey's best-known resorts, set on slightly raised ground among dunes which stretch back from the sandy beach, Rhosneigr is a year round centre for windsurfing – reefs shelter the bay from the Irish Sea's winter storms. Situated in the centre of nearly five kilometres of sandy beaches, the scattered fishing village has fine views in both directions.

Water quality
One outfall serving 1,532 people discharges raw sewage 150 metres below LWM in the rocks. Enhanced treatment is to be provided by 1995 subject to planning approval.

Bathing safety
Swimming is safe; lifebuoys are provided.

Litter
The beach is cleaned daily.

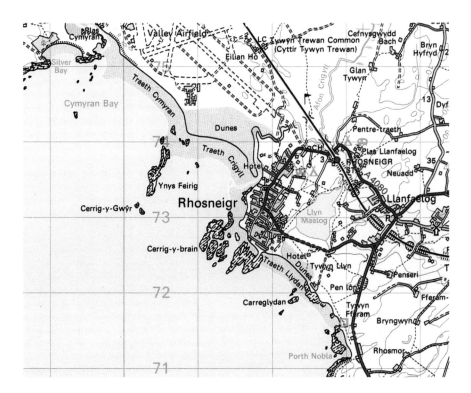

 Access
On the A4080 six kilometres south-west of the A5 at Bryngwran. There are a number of access points to the beach.

 Parking
Several car parks in Rhosneigr.

 Public transport
Nearest rail station is at Ty Croes; also served by local buses.

 Toilets
Existing toilets to be adapted for disabled visitors during 1995.

 Food
Pubs and cafés in Rhosneigr.

Sailing dinghies and fishing boats now crowd the waters at Rhosneigr where once wreckers lured ships to their doom.

 Seaside activities
Windsurfing all year round, swimming, sea or freshwater fishing, sand yachts, golf, tennis and crown green bowling.

 Wet weather alternatives
Anglesey Heritage Gallery: an introduction to the island's history, folklore and culture; Anglesey Sea Zoo; the National Trust mansion at Plas Newydd; Pili Palas (butterfly palace); Beaumauris Gaol, a model prison from Victorian times.

Wildlife and walks
Llyn Maelog lake and the dunes are ideal for birdwatching. The minor road from Llanfaelog to Bryngwran passes Ty Newydd burial chamber, where remains have been found from both the Bronze and the Stone Ages.

Track record ☐☐ ✓ ✓ ✓ ✓ ✓

LLANDDWYN BEACH
Niwbwrch, Anglesey, Gwynedd
OS Ref: SH403634

With its long ribbon of sand backed by forest and five kilometres of high dunes, and its spectacular views across to the mountains of the Llyn Peninsula dipping into the horizon, Llanddwyn is acknowledged as one of the finest beaches in Britain. A path leads through the grassy hills from the beach to the nature reserve at Llanddwyn Island.

Water quality
No sewage is discharged in the vicinity of this beach.

Bathing safety
Safe, except near Abermenai Point. Lifebuoys are provided and there is a phone in the car park.

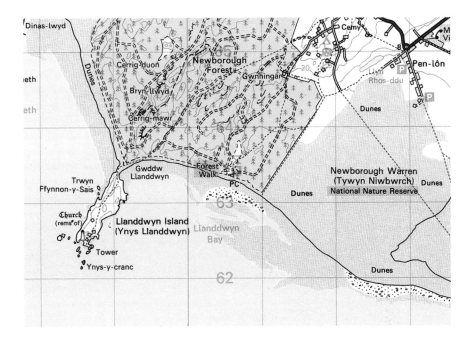

 Litter
The beach is cleaned daily.

 Access
Signposted off the A4080 in Niwbwrch (Newborough); a forestry commission toll road leads to the beach.

 Parking
There is a large car park and picnic area.

 Public transport
Nearest rail stations are Bodorgan and Llanfairpwll; there are buses to Niwbwrch.

 Toilets
There are toilets including facilities for disabled visitors.

 Food
Food stores, pubs and cafés in Niwbwrch.

 Seaside activities
Swimming, canoeing, beachcombing, birdwatching.

 Wet weather alternatives
See Rhosneigr (previous page).

 Wildlife and walks
Newborough Warren National Nature Reserve is just behind the beach and covers 1,565 acres. It can be reached via the A4080 which crosses the River Cefni at Malltraeth Pool; approach the reserve through Niwbwrch village just after the junction with the B4421.

Llanddwyn Island and its distinctive stone lighthouse; nearby is the cannon once used to raise the Newborough lifeboat.

Track record ☐☐☐☐☐☐☑☑
Not EU designated.

ABERDARON BEACH
Gwynedd
OS Ref: SH174263

Over two kilometres of fine sandy beach fringe this lovely remote village of tiny whitewashed cottages nestling in rugged coastline on the tip of the Lleyn Peninsula. The beach is sheltered from all winds except from the south and south-west, and when these blow they can create ideal surfing conditions. This is a designated Area of Outstanding Natural Beauty and Heritage Coast which looks across the sound to Bardsey Island (Ynys Enlli).

Aberdaron Church was built on a site well inland; in the intervening centuries, the receding coastline has brought it to the water's edge.

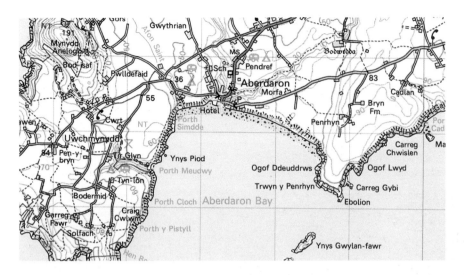

Water quality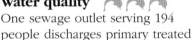

One sewage outlet serving 194 people discharges primary treated sewage into the River Daron.

Bathing safety

There is safe unrestricted bathing but no lifeguard cover.

Litter

The beach is cleaned regularly between Easter and September. There are restrictions on dogs to the right of the main access but not to the left side.

Access

Follow the A497 out of Pwllheli then the A499 towards Abersoch. At Llanbedrog turn left and follow the B4413 until you reach Aberdaron. There is a slipway/walkway to the beach from the village centre.

Parking

Car parks in the village a few minutes walk from the beach.

Public transport

The nearest rail station is at Pwllheli.

Toilets

The toilets are close to the car park.

Food

There are shops and cafés in the village.

Seaside activities

Swimming, surfing; boat trips around Bardsey Island and for offshore fishing.

Wet weather alternatives

Several riding centres; Llanbedrog shooting school. Leisure centre and Starcoast World at Pwllheli. Bodvell Hall Adventure Park and a National Trust mansion at Plas yn Rhiw.

Wildlife and walks

There are many superb walks in this area, both around the coasts and inland; details are available from the Tourist Information Centre at Pwllheli.

Track record ☐☐☐☐ ✓ ✓ ✓

Not EU designated.

PORTH NEIGWL BEACH
Gwynedd
OS Ref: SH284263

Known in English as 'Hell's Mouth', this south-west facing bay presented a formidable obstacle to sailing ships unlucky enough to be blown inshore along its length. Today, precisely the same conditions attract surfers in droves. Over six kilometres of sand edged by steep cliffs are reached via a steep path.

Water quality
No sewage is discharged in the vicinity of this beach.

Bathing safety
Safe in calm weather, but bathers should beware of the surf. There is no lifeguard cover.

Access
The main access point is from the village of Llanengan via a path which needs care in wet weather.

Parking
At the main access point close to the village of Llanengan.

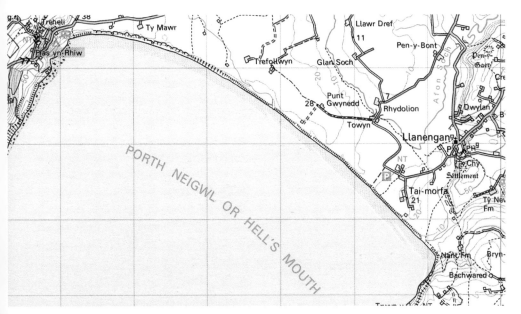

Public transport
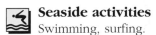
Pwllheli is the nearest rail station; from there the beach is served by buses.

Food
The nearest shops and cafés are at Llanengan and Abersoch.

Seaside activities
Swimming, surfing.

Wet weather alternatives
See Aberdaron (previous page).

Wildlife and walks
See Aberdaron (previous page).

Track record ⬜⬜⬜⬜⬜⬜✔✔✔
Not EU designated.

Spectacular breakers offer some of the country's best surfing conditions at Porth Neigwl.

ABERSOCH
Gwynedd
OS Ref: SH316277

Two extensive sandy beaches, the southernmost of which is backed by massive dunes and a golf course, are separated by a rocky headland and small harbour. This popular resort has in the last years become a major sailing and powerboating centre, and somewhat at odds with its undeveloped surroundings on the Lleyn Peninsula.

Water quality
One sewage outfall serving 1,356 people discharges secondary treated sewage 100 metres below LWM.

Bathing safety
Swimming is safe and a patrol operates on the beach.

The east-facing beaches, away from the prevailing winds, offer sheltered conditions and safe bathing at Abersoch.

Litter
The beach is cleaned regularly between Easter and September. There are dog restrictions by the two main access points.

Access
From Pwllheli take the A499 road to Abersoch.

Parking
Car parks close to the two main access points.

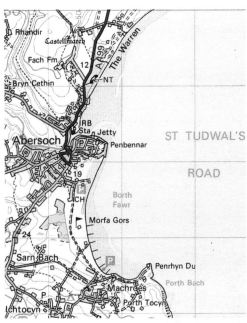

Public transport
Pwllheli is the nearest rail station; from there the beach is served by buses.

Food
There are a number of stores in the village centre and close to the beach.

Seaside activities
Swimming, sailing and fishing.

Wet weather alternatives
Several riding centres; Llanbedrog shooting school. Leisure centre and Starcoast World at Pwllheli. Bodvell Hall Adventure Park and a National Trust mansion at Plas yn Rhiw.

Wildlife and walks
Boat trips around Bardsey Island leave from Pwllheli, but landing on the island is not encouraged.

Track record ✓✓✗✓✓✓✓✓

BARMOUTH
Gwynedd
OS Ref: SH608159

Over three kilometres of firm golden sands sweep around this little resort town at the mouth of the Mawddach, whose warm beaches attract families and watersports enthusiasts in equal numbers. Dogs are banned from parts of the beach in the season.

Water quality
One sewage outlet serving 2,200 people discharges screened sewage through a long sea outfall.

Litter
The beach is cleaned regularly by the local District Council.

Bathing safety
Safe, except in the harbour and estuary areas. The beach is patrolled in season and safety equipment is available.

Access
Barmouth Beach is signposted off the A496 coastal route. There are slipways and paths from the promenade down to the beach.

Majestic mountains plunge down to the sea, forming a magnificent backdrop to this popular family resort.

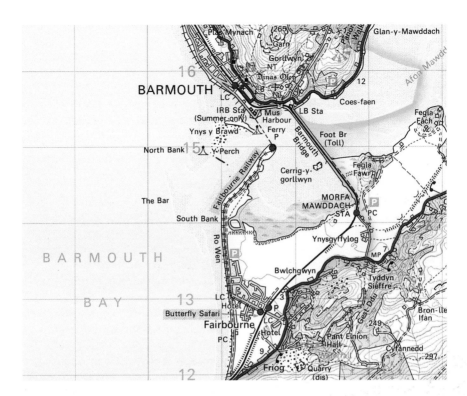

Parking
In a large pay-and-display car park on the promenade.

Public transport
Barmouth rail station and regular buses.

Toilets
Excellent toilet facilities are adjacent to the beach, including facilities for disabled visitors and mother-and-baby rooms.

Food
Numerous cafés and restaurants within easy walking distance of the beach and refreshment kiosks on the promenade itself.

Seaside activities
Everything one would expect of a typical 'bucket and spade' beach, including donkey rides, trampolines and a miniature train. There is a colourful funfair near to the beach.

Wet weather alternatives
Leisure centre on the promenade; nearby recreation ground with bowls, putting, tennis and children's play area. Excellent shopping facilities, Ddraig Goch theatre, Ty Gwyn Museum and the Welsh Gold Centre at nearby Dolgellau. The Maes Artro Craft Village and the famous Harlech Castle are both within easy reach.

Wildlife and walks
Cadair Idris National Nature Reserve. Numerous walks and climbs, including the well-signposted Panorama Walk to Cutiau and a footpath along the wooden railway bridge.

Track record ✓ ✓ ✓ ✓ ✓ ✓ ✓ ✓

FAIRBOURNE
Powys
OS Ref: SH611130 (for map see previous page)

Along, gently sloping sand and shingle beach at the mouth of the magnificent Mawddach Estuary, with spectacular views of Cardigan Bay and north to the Lleyn Peninsula. The beach is close by the quiet Victorian seaside village of Fairbourne.

Water quality
One sewage outlet serving 474 people discharges 400 metres below LWM.

Bathing safety
Safe, with beach patrols for eight weeks over the summer season and safety equipment available.

Litter
The beach is cleaned regularly by the local District Council.

Access
Fairbourne is signposted off the A493 between Dolgellau and Tywyn. Access to the beach is via paths and slipways from the embankment.

Parking
Two pay-and-display car parks adjacent to the beach.

Public transport
To Fairbourne rail station.

Toilets
Adjacent to the beach.

Food
A number of cafés and shops are within walking distance of the beach.

Seaside activities
Swimming, windsurfing.

Wet weather alternatives
Fairbourne narrow-gauge railway runs alongside the beach. Excellent pony trekking is available nearby. There is a leisure centre at nearby Dolgellau and a cinema at Tywyn.

Wildlife and walks
The well documented Morfa Mawddach walk from Marby Arthog to Penmaenpool along the disused railway line gives spectacular views of the Mawddach Estuary; nearby mountain walks on the Cader Idris range and around the wonderful Crogonaan lakes; popular walk from Fairbourne across the Barmouth railway bridge footpath.

Track record ✓✓✓✓✓✓✓✓

The village of Fairbourne nestles in the coastal plain between the mountains and the peninsula of Morfa Mawddach.

BORTH
Dyfed
OS Ref: SN608901

The village of Borth boasts nearly five kilometres of unbroken sands divided by wooden groynes. The water is shallow and is therefore extremely popular with visitors and locals. There are facilities for sea- and sand-based activities with the slipway near the lifeboat station providing access for small sailing craft.

Borth straddles a narrow strip of dry land between the sea and the Cors Fochno marshes.

Water quality

No sewage is discharged in the vicinity of this beach.

Bathing safety

Safe, except near the estuary. A beach officer patrols during the peak holiday season and lifebuoys are provided at regular intervals.

Litter

The beach is cleaned daily by hand throughout the bathing season. Dogs are banned from May to September between the slipway at the lifeboat station and the slipway at Cambrian Terrace.

Access

From the A487, turn off on to the B4572 for Borth.

Parking

Roadside parking and car parks within easy walking distance of the beach.

Public transport

The nearest rail station is Borth; buses run from Aberystwyth (numbers 511, 512, 520 and 524).

Toilets

Toilets are available at both ends of the beach, and include facilities for disabled visitors. RADAR keys are available from the Tourist Information Centre.

Food

A variety of shops, cafés and restaurants within walking distance.

Seaside activities

Surfing, windsurfing, sand yachting, sailing and swimming.

Wet weather alternatives

Borth Animalarium; Ynyslas

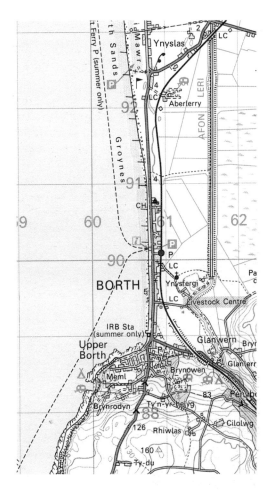

Nature Reserve; local folk museum at Tre'r Ddol; Dyfi Furnace (CADW); RSPB Yny-Hir Reserve; Clarach Golf Driving Range.

Wildlife and walks

The Ceredigion Heritage Coast Unit provides a system of guardianship which covers all Ceredigion beaches. The unit organises a programme of educational guided walks and talks on a variety of subjects relating to the coastline. There is a coastal walk from Borth to Clarach. Ynyslas Nature Reserve and the RSPB Ynys-Hir Reserve are nearby.

Track record ✓✓✓✓✓✓✓✓

LLANRHYSTUD SOUTH
Dyfed
OS Ref: SN524692

Situated on the edge of the fertile coastal plain, and extending inland along the banks of the River Wyre, Llanrhystud village has long been a focal point of agricultural activity in the area. More recently, the coast has attracted visitors with the two beaches providing a range of scenery and ample space.

Water quality
One sewage outlet serving 500 people discharges primary treated sewage.

Bathing safety
Generally safe; lifebuoys are provided at various points along the beach.

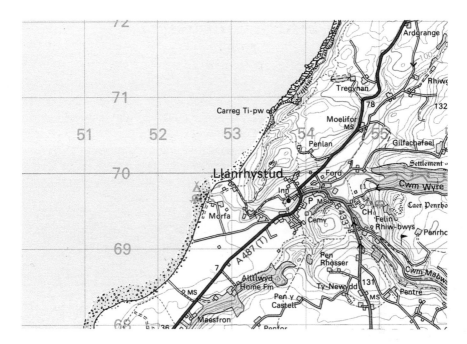

Litter
The beach is cleaned as required during the year.

Access
Follow the A487 south from Aberystwyth for 14 kilometres; the beach is signposted from the village.

Parking
A parking area is available at the beach.

Public transport
A bus service runs from Aberystwyth to Llanrhystud (numbers 550/551A).

Food
A shop and a restaurant in the village.

Wet weather alternatives
Clos Pencarreq Craft Centre, Sea Aquarium, Aerial Ferry, Honey Bee Exhibition, Derwen Welsh Cob Centre, Ffynnonlas vineyard.

Wildlife and walks
Ceredigion's Heritage Coast Unit provides a system of guardianship which covers all beaches along the Ceredigion coast and organises a programme of guided walks and talks on a wide variety of subjects relating to the coastline. Contact Aberaeron Tourism Office for details of inland walks.

Track record ☐☐☐☐☐ ✓✓✓✓
Not EU designated.

Llanrhystud boasts two superb beaches, one on either side of the river.

MWNT, CARDIGAN
Dyfed
OS Ref: SN193519

The 300 metres of gently sloping sands at Mwnt Beach are fringed by folded and faulted shale and mudstone cliffs and shadowed by the imposing form of Foel-y-Mwnt, a conical hill on the headland. The tiny whitewashed church of the Holy Cross nestles in a hollow at its foot. The only other obvious sign of man is the remnant of a lime kiln adjacent to the path down to the beach; limestone was landed in the bay and fired ready for use by the local farmers.

Water quality
No sewage is discharged in the vicinity of this beach.

Bathing safety
Bathing is safe inshore, but care is required as surface currents arising from waves breaking on the headland deflect across the bay. There is an emergency phone on the cliff path.

Litter
Dogs are banned between May and September.

Access
Mwnt is signposted from the B4548 north of Cardigan. Lanes lead to the car park above the beach. Steps and a steep path lead down the cliff to the beach.

Parking
There is a National Trust car park with 250 spaces.

Toilets
There are toilets at the head of the steps to the beach, with facilities for disabled visitors.

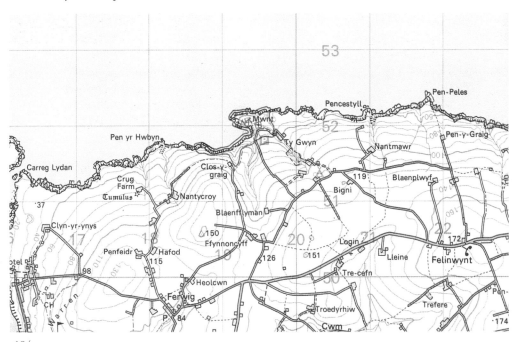

 Food
Refreshments are available from Easter to October.

 Seaside activities
Swimming.

 Wet weather activities
Cardigan is the nearest centre.

Wildlife and walks
Superb National Trust cliff-top walks; a pack detailing these and other walks in the Cardigan area is available from local Tourist Information Centres. Foel-y-Mwnt hill provides good views of the bay

A natural suntrap surrounded by National Trust land, this undeveloped sandy beach is easily accessible and can be very popular in summer.

south to Cardigan Island and the narrow rocky inlet to the north. The Teifi Estuary and marshes (Dyfed Wildlife Trust) can be viewed from the B4546 at St Dogmaels – hide at SN182458. There is a wildlife centre open on the Reserve which can be reached from Cilgerran.

Track record ☐☐☐☐☐✔✔✔
Not EU designated.

ABEREIDDY BAY (AT SLIPWAY)
Dyfed
OS Ref: SM796312

Pebbles and sand made of pounded grey slate form this rural beach, and the same slate gives a brilliant deep blue colour to the water in the extraordinarily beautiful little harbour – a breached quarry – just to the north of the beach. This is a fine starting point for a coastal walk: surrounded by National Trust land there is magnificent cliff scenery at every turn and the evening sunsets are marvellously romantic.

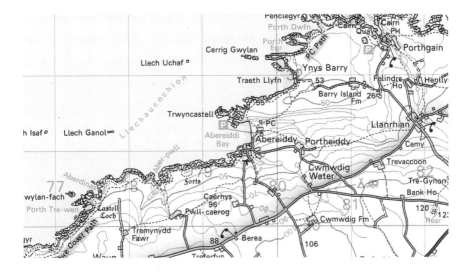

Water quality

No sewage is discharged in the vicinity of this beach.

Bathing safety

Swimming is not advised: this beach faces west and swells and waves can develop unexpectedly, with dangerous undercurrents and undertows. Lifesaving equipment and an emergency telephone are provided; there is no lifeguard cover.

Litter

The beach is cleaned daily in the summer.

Access

From the A487 follow the lanes from Croesgoch to Abereiddy; a slipway leads down to the beach.

P Parking

Near the beach.

Public transport

Buses stop at Croesgoch.

Known locally as the Blue Lagoon, the harbour provides ideal anchorage for small boats.

Toilets

There are toilets behind the beach.

Food

A mobile kiosk, selling ices and teas, visits the car park.

Seaside activities

Boating, windsurfing, canoeing. Care should be taken, as heavy surf can develop within 20 minutes.

Wet weather alternatives

Tregwynt Woollen Mill with café at St Nicholas. Llangloftan cheese factory with café near Mathry. There is a woodturner and craft shop at Mathry.

Wildlife and walks

Spectacular cliff scenery and walks from Abereiddy to Porthgain: this land is owned by the National Trust and one walk explores an old industrial quarry site at Porthgain where stone was shipped to make the roads in Bristol.

Track record

Not EU designated.

WHITESANDS BAY, ST DAVID'S
Dyfed
OS Ref: SM733270

This wide expanse of fine white sand curving north towards the remote rocky headland of St David's is one of the best surfing beaches in the country. Open fields slope down to the shore from the imposing craggy hill Carn Llidi, which provides good walking with excellent sea views of the group of islands known as the Bishops and Clerks: the South Bishop can be identified on the far horizon by its lighthouse.

Water quality
No sewage is discharged in the vicinity of this beach.

Bathing safety
Warning signs indicate where to bathe and flags indicate when it is safe: there are dangerous and unpredictable currents off parts of the beach and at some states of the tide. Lifeguards patrol the beach during the summer and first aid is available at the lifeguard centre.

Litter
The beach is cleaned regularly; dogs are banned from May to September.

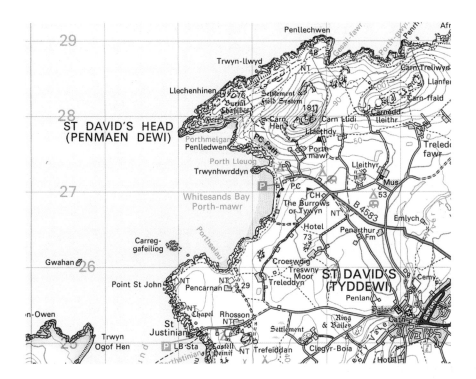

Access
From the A487 north of St David's, signposted for Whitesands. This beach is suitable for wheelchair users and people with mobility difficulties.

Parking
There is a car park behind the beach with approximately 400 spaces.

Toilets
There are toilets at the car park including facilities for disabled visitors.

Food
There is a café and shop at the car park.

Gorgeous sunsets framed in the wide arc of Whitesand Bay are an added attraction of this lovely beach.

Seaside activities
Swimming, surfing and canoeing, with zoning of activities when the beach is busy.

Wildlife and walks
The coast path north provides an interesting circular walk, taking in St David's Head with the remains of a fort and a burial chamber, and returning around Carn Llidi Hill. A guide describing the route is published by the Pembrokeshire Coast National Park and can be obtained at information offices locally. Ramsey Island lies just south of the bay, and boat trips from Whitesands (in 12-person inflatables, May–September) or St Justinians (daily) take you around the island to view the seabird colonies. This area is excellent for chough, raven and peregrine.

Track record ✓✓✓✓✓✓✓
Not EU designated.

MARLOES SANDS, MARLOES
Dyfed
OS Ref: SM7908

Two kilometres of wide flat golden sands stretch from the imposing bulk of Gateholm Island in the north to Red Cliff and Hooper's Point in the south, backed by steep cliffs. Beds of rock laid flat on a sea bed long ago are tilted and seem to be pushing up through the sands; their jagged outlines point skywards along the length of this glorious bay. The barnacle and seaweed covered rocky outcrops testify to the fact that the whole beach disappears at high water, and with only one access point where a tiny stream flows through a narrow valley, visitors should take care not to get cut off at the extremities of the beach by the incoming tide.

Water quality
No sewage is discharged in the vicinity of this beach.

Bathing safety
Beware of currents and submerged rocks; some lifesaving equipment is available.

Access
From Marloes take the lane signposted Marloes Sands.

Parking
A National Trust car park has about 50 spaces.

Toilets
None.

Seaside activities
Swimming, surfing and fishing.

Wildlife and walks
A three-kilometre nature trail starts from the car park. To the south-west, the coast path leads to West Dale Bay and a series of secluded beaches around the Dale Peninsula that can only be reached on foot. To the north-east, the path heads to Albion Beach and Martin's Haven. Boat trips run from here to Skomer Island, a Marine Nature Reserve renowned for its seabirds, wild flowers and seal colonies.

Track record ☐☐☐☐☐ ✓✓✓
Not EU designated.

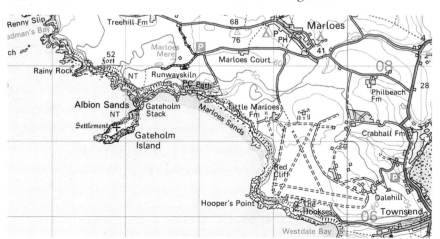

*The coast path that follows the cliff top around the bay is covered in
wild flowers and provides excellent views of the sands.*

FRESHWATER WEST
Dyfed
OS Ref: SS895000

A beautiful open sandy beach edged by rocks and backed by extensive dunes. Seaweed used to be collected on this shore for making laver bread, a local delicacy, and a small hut once used for drying the seaweed before it was boiled still stands on the southern headland. This beach is particularly popular with surfers but is not recommended for swimming.

Water quality

Bathing safety
Strong offshore currents and undertows make bathing dangerous at this beach, despite its popularity with surfers. Two Perry buoys are available.

Litter
The beach is cleaned regularly by the District Council.

Access
Via the B4320 or the B4319 from Pembroke. There is a walkway to the beach.

Parking
There is a car park at the beach.

Public transport
Pembroke is the nearest rail station; the beach is served by a bus.

Toilets
Available at the car park.

Food
An ice-cream van parks at the car park.

Seaside activities
Surfing, cliff-walking, windsurfing and canoeing.

Wet weather alternatives
Pembroke Castle, Museum of the Home and Visitor Centre.

Wildlife and walks
Freshwater West is situated in the Pembrokeshire Coast National Park, over 320 square kilometres of spectacular coastal scenery with many fine walks in the surrounding area.

Track record ☑
Not EU designated.

The dunes behind the beach at Freshwater West are studded with Stone Age and Bronze Age burial sites.

FRESHWATER EAST
Dyfed
OS Ref: SS019979

A large sandy beach protected from prevailing winds by extensive sand dunes is accessible from a steep road giving fine views across the bay. The beach is overlooked by a holiday park and several properties dotting the coastline. Local fishermen launch regularly from the beach.

Water quality
One sewage outlet serving 600 people discharges raw sewage at LWM.

Bathing safety
Generally safe. Two Perry buoys are situated on the beach.

Litter
The District Council cleans the beach daily in the holiday season.

Access
From Pembroke take the A4139 to Lamphey, then the B4584. There is a walkway and a slipway on to the beach.

Parking
One car park at the beach.

Public transport
The nearest rail station is Pembroke; a bus from Lamphey goes to Freshwater East.

Toilets
At the beach.

Food
There is a small shop at the beach.

Seaside activities
Swimming, windsurfing and surfing.

Wet weather alternatives
Pembroke town, Pembroke Castle.

Wildlife and walks
Freshwater East is situated in the Pembrokeshire Coast National Park, over 320 square kilometres of spectacular coastal scenery with many fine walks in the surrounding area.

Track record
Not EU designated.

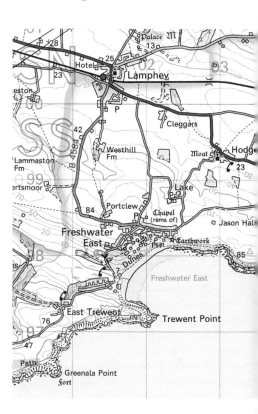

MANORBIER BEACH
Dyfed
OS Ref: SS061974

Manorbier has been described as the most delectable spot in Wales, and perhaps this description is not too far off the mark. The village itself is picturesque and the beach extremely popular with bathers and surfers, the water getting crowded when surf conditions are good. Although mainly sandy, there is a pebble bank at the high tide line.

Water quality
One outfall serving 520 people discharges secondary treated sewage.

Bathing safety
Care is needed as rough weather can produce a dangerous undertow. Basic lifesaving equipment is provided at the beach.

Litter
The beach is cleaned as required.

Access
Signposted from the village of Manorbier, off the B4585.

Parking
The National Trust runs a pay-and-display car park.

Toilets
At the car park.

Food
There are shops and pubs in the village.

Seaside activities
Swimming and surfing.

Wildlife and walks
The area around Manorbier is steeped in history and is well worth exploring: the castle and church date from the 12th century and overlook the beach. To the south is the King's Quoit, a 5000-year-old burial chamber. A circular walk can be taken on Old Castle Head.

Track record
Not EU designated.

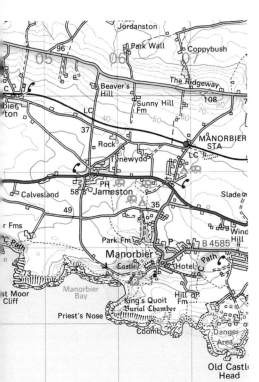

RHOSSILI BAY, RHOSSILI
West Glamorgan
OS Ref: SS413884

A spectacular five-kilometre sweep of golden sands fringes Rhossili Bay, from Worms Head to Burry Holms in the north, the sands overlooked by Rhossili Down whose grass slopes rise 200 metres above the beach. At its southern end, the beach is ringed by steep cliffs which fall away northwards as the down is replaced by sand dunes. Worms Head, contrary to its name, is in fact an island, linked to the mainland only at low tide. The beach and the adjacent down are owned by the National Trust.

Water quality
One outfall serving 380 people discharges primary treated sewage.

Bathing safety
Usually safe for bathing, but beware of rip currents in bad weather.

Reliable air currents and a network of paths providing easy access to potential launch sites on the downs make Rhossili a popular destination for hang- and paragliding enthusiasts.

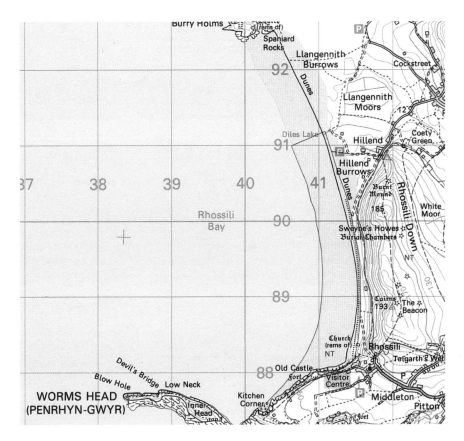

 Litter
Considerable quantities of marine litter are washed up on the beach.

Access
The B4247 leads to Rhossili village, from where a good path leads down the cliffs to the beach. A slipway makes access easier for wheelchair users and people with mobility difficulties.

Parking
There is a car park in village.

Toilets
There are toilets including facilities for disabled visitors at the car park.

Food
Food is available in the village.

Seaside activities
Swimming, surfing (extremely popular), canoeing, hang-gliding and fishing.

Wildlife and walks
Worms Head island and the adjacent stretch of coast are a National Nature Reserve. The limestone cliffs are rich in flora, and nesting birds can be seen on the nature trail. Cliffs and grassy summits lead eastwards towards coastal dunes and marshes. This is also an excellent vantage point for seawatching.

Track record ✗ ✓ ✓ ✓ ✓ ✓ ✓ ✓

PORT EYNON
West Glamorgan
OS Ref: SS475855

A sandy cove sheltered by the rocky headland to the south, with wide, flat sands backed by high dunes. High cliffs rise on either side of the bay with rocky outcrops at their base. At the eastern end stand the newly excavated remains of a salt house and workings. The wide, gently sloping sands are safe for bathing, and an ideal spot for building sand castles or playing cricket. A dog restriction byelaw is being considered.

Water quality

One outfall serving 1,200 people discharges primary and secondary treated sewage at LWM off Overton Mere, east of Port Eynon Point.

Bathing safety

Warning notices indicate where it is safe to bathe. The beach is patrolled by lifeguards from May until August.

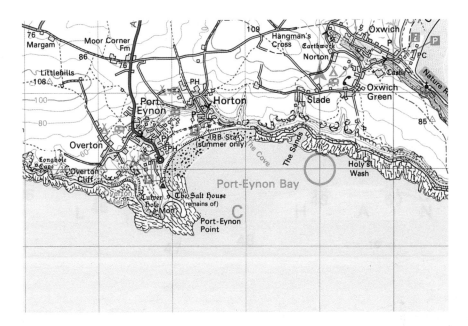

Litter

The beach is cleaned daily in the summer and twice weekly in the winter.

Access
From the village Post Office a road leads down to the shore where a short section of newly built promenade gives access to the beach. A slipway makes access to the beach easier for wheelchair users and people with mobility difficulties.

Parking
There is a car park behind dunes with 500 spaces.

Toilets
There are toilets including facilities for disabled visitors at the beach entry point.

The pretty village of Port Eynon is surrounded by chalk downland with a wide range of limestone flora.

Food
There is a shop and café at the beach entrance.

Seaside activities
Swimming, surfing, windsurfing, diving, canoeing and fishing. A boat ramp leads from the car park to the tidal sand, providing easy access to the beach for boats.

Wildlife and walks
The South Gower Coast Nature Reserve stretches from Port Eynon to Worms Head at Rhossili, comprising ten kilometres of rocky shore with faulted and folded grey limestone cliffs. The limestone rocky shore of the Gower is one of the best examples in Britain. A footpath on to Port Eynon Point climbs the cliff from the eastern end of the beach, leading to the Culver Hole, a deep cleft in the cliff which has been sealed off with a wall.

Track record ✓ ✓ ✓ ✓ ✓ ✓ ✓ ✓

RATING	NAME	TRACK RECORD	SEWAGE OUTLET	REMARKS
	CLWYD			
⌒⌒	**Point of Ayr Lighthouse** SJ121859	✓✗ ✓		
f	**Prestatyn Central** - EU SS054839	✗✓✓✓✗✗✓✓✗	Screened/macerated, 16,246, LSO. Improvements planned for 2000.	Sandy.
–	**Ffrith**			Sandy.
⌒	**Rhyl** - EU SJ002826		Primary, 22,600, LSO.	Sandy. Bathing unsafe at river mouth.
⌒⌒	**Kinmel Bay** - EU Sandy Cove SH978866	✗✗✗✗✗✗✗✓✓		Sandy flats, shingle spit and dunes. Bathing unsafe at river mouth.
–	**Abergele** Towyn	✗✓✓	Screened, macerated and tidal tank, 4,237, 100 above LWM.	Sand and shingle.
⌒⌒	Pensam	✓	Screened, macerated and tidal tank, 7,487, 100 above LWM.	Sandy at low tide.
⌒⌒	**Llanddulas**	✓✓✗ ✓	Screened, macerated and tidal tank, 1,550, 75 below LWM.	Sand and shingle.
⌒	**Colwyn Bay** - EU SH858791	✓✓✓✓✓✓✗✓		Sandy.
⌒⌒	End of Cayley Prom	✗✓✗✓		Sandy.
⌒⌒	Opposite Rhos Abbey Hotel	✓✓✓✓	Screened, macerated and tidal tank, 25,800, LSO. Improvements planned for 2000.	Sandy.
	GWYNEDD			
f	**Penrhyn Bay**	✗✗✗✗✗	Screened, macerated and tidal tank, 3,500, 100 above LWM.	Sand and shingle.
⌒⌒	**Llandudno** North Shore - EU SH791822	✓✓✓✓✗✓✗✗✓		Sandy.
f	West Shore - EU SH765816	✗✗✗✗✗✗✗✗✗	Screened, macerated, tidal tank, 34,000, LSO.	Sand and shingle. Beach cleaned regularly.
f	**Deganwy** (North) SH775794	✗✗	Stormwater only. Improvements planned.	Shingle.
⌒⌒	**Penmaenmawr** (Conwy Bay)	✗✓ ✓✓	1 macerated, 3,700, 200 above LWM, 2, raw, 160, 200 above LWM. Improvements planned.	Sand and shingle.
⌒⌒	**Llanfairfechan**	✗✓		Sandy. Dangerous tidal currents.
	ANGLESEY			
–	**Beaumaris**		Raw, 4,005, 200 below LWM. Improvements planned for 1995.	Shingle and sand. Bathing dangerous.
–	**Red Wharf Bay**			Sandy. Bathing unsafe at ebb tide. Beach cleaned regularly.

RATING	NAME	TRACK RECORD	SEWAGE OUTLET	REMARKS
⌒	**Benllech** - EU SH526825	✓✗✓✓✗✗✓✓		Sandy.
–	**Craig Dwllan** (Benllech)		Raw, 2,284, 200 below LWM. Improvements planned for 1995.	Sandy.
–	**Moelfre** (Treath Lligwy)		Raw, 894, 100 below LWM.	Shingle beach.
–	**Amlwch** (Bull Bay)		Raw, 4,200, 50 below LWM. Improvements planned.	Sandy.
–	**Cemaes Bay**		Macerated/tidal tank, 1,000, 70 below LWM.	Sandy.
–	**Newry Beach**, Holyhead		5, raw, 11,000, all above LWM.	Docks area.
⌒	**Trearddur Bay** - EU SH255789	✗✗✓✓✓✓✓✓	Screened and disinfection.	Sandy and rocky cove. Beach cleaned regularly.
–	**Traeth Llydan** (Broad Beach)			Dunes.
–	**Aberffraw Bay**		Screened/macerated, 534, at HWM.	Sandy with extensive dune system.
–	**St George's Pier**, Menai Bridge	✗✓		
	GWYNEDD			
⌒⌒	**Menai Straits** Porth Dinorwic Sailing Club	✗✗ ✓	There are 19 outfalls discharging into the Menai Straits, most untreated. Improvements planned for 1996.	
⌒⌒	Plas Menai	✓✓ ✓		
⌒⌒⌒⌒	**Dinas Dinlle** - EU SH434566	✓✓✓✓✓✓		Sandy. Beach cleaned regularly. Not featured due to insufficient information.
–	**Pontllyfni**	✓		Sandy.
–	**Trefor**	✓	Secondary, 582, at LWM.	Sand and shingle.
⌒⌒	**Porth Nefyn**	✓ ✓	Macerated, 2,800, HWM.	Sandy.
–	**Morfa Nefyn**	✓✓✓	Macerated, 2,100 LWM.	Sand and rocks.
–	**Porth Dinllaen**	✗✓✓✓		Sand and rocks.
–	**Rhos-y-Llan**		Primary, 420.	Sandy.
–	**Traeth Penllech**		1	Sandy.
–	**Porth Colman**	✓✓		Rockpools.
–	**Porth Iago**	✓✓✓		Sandy.
–	**Porthor**	✓✓✓	Primary, from public toilets.	Sandy cove surrounded by rocky promontories.
f	**Llanbedrog**	✗✗✗✓ ✗	Macerated/tidal tank, 672, 50 below LWM.	Sandy.
⌒⌒⌒⌒	**Pwllheli** - EU SH371340	✓✓✓✓✓✓✓✓	Macerated/tidal tank, 4,107, at harbour mouth. Improvements planned for 2000.	Sandy. Fast currents. Not featured due to insufficient information.
⌒⌒⌒⌒	**Morfa Aberech**	✓		Sandy. Not featured due to insufficient information.
–	**Afon Wen**		1, macerated/tidal tank, 46, at LWM.	Sand and shingle.

RATING	NAME	TRACK RECORD	SEWAGE OUTLET	REMARKS
f	**Criccieth Beach** (East) - EU SH503387	✓✗✓✗✗✓✗✓✗	Tidal tank, 800, 50 below LWM. Improvements planned for 1995.	Sand and shingle.
f	**Black Rock Sands** - EU SH542359	☐☐☐☐☐✓✗✓✗	Macerated, LSO.	Sandy.
–	**Morfa Bychan**	✗✗✓✓✓✓✓☐☐	Macerated, 800, LSO.	Sandy. Beach cleaned regularly. Do not bathe at south-east end.
⌒⌒	**Harlech** - EU SH567314	✓✓✓✓✓✓✓✓✓	Primary, 1,291, at LWM. Improvements planned.	Sandy.
⌒⌒	**Llandanwg** - EU SH566281	✓✓✓✓✓✓✓✓✓	Primary, 258, at LWM.	Sand and rock. Bathing unsafe at low tide.
–	**Tal-y-Bont**	☐☐☐☐☐☐✓✓✓		Sandy with dunes.
–	**Llanaber** (Dyffryn)	☐☐☐☐☐☐☐✓✓		
–	**Llwyngwril**	☐☐☐☐☐✗✗☐☐	Raw, 370, at LWM.	Sand and shingle.
⌒⌒	**Tywyn** - EU SH576003	✗✓✓✓✓✓✓✓✓	Macerated/tidal tank, 2,811, above LWM. Improvements planned.	Sandy.
⌒	**Aberdyfi** - EU SN607958	☐☐☐✗✗✓✗✗✓	Primary/tidal tank, 6,000, at LWM in estuary.	Sandy.
	DYFED			
⌒⌒⌒⌒	**Ynyslas** North	☐☐☐☐☐☐✓☐✓		Sandy. Not featured due to insufficient information.
⌒⌒	**East Tywyni, Ynyslas**	☐☐☐☐☐☐✓☐✓		Sandy.
f	**Clarach Bay** South of river	✓✗✗✗✗✗✗✗		Sand and shingle. Beach cleaned regularly.
f	North of River	☐☐☐☐☐✗✗✗		Sand and shingle.
⌒⌒	**Aberystwyth** North - EU SN583822	✓✓✓✓✓✓✓✓✓		Sand and shingle. Beach cleaned regularly.
f	Harbour	☐☐☐☐☐✗✗✗✗		
f	South - EU SN579814	✗✗✓✗✗✓✗✗✗	Screened, 9,100. Improvements planned.	Sand and shingle.
f	Tanybwlch Beach,	☐☐☐☐☐✓✓✓✗		Shingle.
⌒	**Morfa Bychan** slipway	☐☐☐☐☐✓✓✓✓		Rocky.
⌒⌒	**Llansantffraid**	☐☐☐☐☐✓✓✓✓	Primary, 1,160, at LWM.	Sand and shingle.
⌒	**Llanon Slipway**	☐☐☐☐☐✓✓✓✓		Shingle.
⌒⌒	**Aberarth**	☐☐☐☐☐✓✓✓✓	Primary, 470, at LWM.	Shingle beach.
f	**Aberaeron** Northern Groyne	☐☐☐☐☐☐✗✗✗		Pebbles with sand at low tide.
f	Fourth Groyne (North Harbour)	☐☐☐☐☐✓✓✓✗	Raw, 5,000, at LWM. Improvements planned.	Sand and shingle.
f	Central Groyne	☐☐☐☐✓✓✓✓✗		Sandy.
⌒	**New Quay** Harbour	☐☐☐☐☐✓✗✓✓		
⌒⌒	South	☐☐☐☐☐☐✓✓✓		Sandy.
f	Traeth Gwyn - EU SN398597	✓✓✓✓✓✓✓✓✗	Primary, 6,000, LSO off Llanina Point.	Golden sand. Beach cleaned regularly.
⌒	**Cwmtydu**	☐☐☐☐☐✓✓✓✓		Shingle and sand cove. Toilet and parking facilities.

RATING	NAME	TRACK RECORD	SEWAGE OUTLET	REMARKS
f	**Llangrannog**	✗✗✓✓✗	Primary, 400, 75 below LWM.	Sand and shingle. Beach cleaned regularly.
–	**Penbryn**	✗✓✓		Sandy. Beach is cleaned regularly.
⌒	**Tresaith**	✓✗✗✓✓✓	Macerated, 180, 75 below LWM. Improvements planned.	Sandy. Beach cleaned regularly.
f	**Aberporth** Traeth y Dyffryn	✗✗✓✓✗		Sandy.
f	Slip	✗✗✓✗	Macerated, 1,842, 75 below LWM. Improvements planned.	Sandy with rockpools at low tide.
f	**Gwbert-on-Sea at Craig y Gwert**	✗✗ ✗	Affected by discharges from caravan park & private properties.	Shingle.
⌒	**Poppit Sands** West SN152489	✓✓		Sandy, backed by dunes. Bathing dangerous in river.
⌒	East SN156492	✓✓	Secondary.	Sand and shingle. Bathing only safe where there are lifeguard indicators.
f	**Newport Sands** North - EU SN053407	✓✓✓✓✓✓✗✗		Sandy.
⌒⌒⌒⌒	**Newport Sands** South SN052405	✓✓	Macerated, 1,400, 700 below LWM.	Sand and shingle. Bathing safe in centre of beach. Not featured due to insufficient information.
f	**Pwllgwaelod** SN003399	✓✗	Secondary, 880, at LWM.	Grey sand.
⌒	**Goodwick Harbour** (South) SM948381	✓ ✓✓		Sandy.
f	**Goodwick Beach** SM949379	✓✓ ✓✗	Raw, 2,710, at LWM. Improvements planned.	Ferry terminal. Sandy.
⌒⌒	**Caerfai Bay**	✓✓✓✓		Cliffs are unstable and should be treated with caution.
⌒	**Newgale Sands** - EU SM846217	✗✓✓✓✓✓✓✓		Sand backed by pebble bank. Swimmers beware of unpredictable currents.
f	**Broad Haven** - EU SM861138	✗✓✓✓✓✓✓✗	Secondary, 2,200, at HWM.	Sandy.
–	**St Brides Haven**	✓		Many rockpools.
–	**Musselwick Sands**			Cliff-backed cove - possible to get cut off by the rising tide.
⌒⌒⌒⌒	**Dale**	✓✓ ✓	Macerated/tidal tank, 600, above LWM.	Shingle and sand. Not featured due to adjacent sewage outfall.
–	**Sandy Haven**		Secondary, 1,360, LWM.	Red sand.
–	**Milford Beach**			Sandy. Near refinery town.
–	**Neyland Slip**			Shingle bank.
–	**Angle Bay** SM852033		Secondary, 500, at LWM.	Shingle and muddy sand.
⌒	**Barafundle Bay**	✓✓✓		Sandy beach backed by high dunes and steep limestone cliffs on either side.
⌒⌒	**Lydstep Haven** SS0998	✓✓		Sand and pebble beach, backed by wooded cliffs.

RATING	NAME	TRACK RECORD	SEWAGE OUTLET	REMARKS
⌢	**Tenby** North - EU SN134008	✓✗✓✓✓✓✓✓		Sandy. Beach cleaned regularly.
⌢⌢	South SS132998	✗✗✓✓✓✓✓✓	Screened/macerated, 25,000, LSO.	Sandy with dunes. Beach cleaned regularly.
f	**Saundersfoot** Beach - EU SN141047	✓✗✓✓✓✗✓✗	Primary, 11,000, 50 below LWM. Improvements planned.	Sand and shingle beach. Beach cleaned daily.
⌢⌢	Amroth - EU SN167068	✗✗✓✓✓✓✓✓		Sand and shingle. Beach cleaned regularly.
⌢	**Pendine Sands** - EU SN238074	✓✓✓✓✓✓✓✓		Sand and dunes.
⌢	**Pembrey Beach** (Cefn Sidan) - EU SS400998	✓✓✓✓✓✓✓✓	Secondary, 2,500.	Sand edged by a belt of sand dunes.
f	**Burry Port Beach East** SN446002	☐☐☐☐☐✓✓✓✗	Secondary, 6,000, below LWM. Improvements planned.	Industrial and muddy. Bathing unsafe.
f	**Llanelli Beach** (fourth groyne) SS496995	☐☐☐☐✗✗✗✗	See above for treatment.	Sandy.
	WEST GLAMORGAN			
f	**Broughton Bay** SS419930	☐☐☐☐☐☐✓✓✗		Sandy bay fringed by dunes. Bathing unsafe at LWM and on ebbing tide due to currents.
–	**Fall Bay**	☐☐☐☐☐✓☐☐	Primary.	Sandy.
–	**Mewslade**		Primary, 270, below LWM.	Sandy.
⌢⌢⌢⌢	**Oxwich Bay** - EU SS507862			Sandy, backed by dunes. Not recommended because of adverse reports. Under investigation at time of going to print.
–	**Three Cliffs Bay** SS535876			Sandy.
–	**Southgate** (Pobbles Bay)		Secondary, 500, below LWM.	Rocky.
–	**Brandy Cove**	☐☐☐☐☐✓☐☐	Secondary, 2,000, below LWM.	Sandy, with rocks and pebbles.
⌢	**Caswell Bay** - EU SS591874	✓✗✓✓✓✗✓✓		Sandy. Beach cleaned regularly.
⌢⌢	**Langland Bay** West - EU SS606871	✗✓✓✗✓✓✓✗✓		Sandy.
f	**Limeslade Bay** - EU SS625870	✗✗✓✗✓✓✓✓✗		A rock cove with some sand.
⌢⌢	**Bracelet Bay** - EU SS630871	✓✓✓✓✓✓✓✓		Pebbles and rock pools.
⌢	**Swansea Bay** The Mumbles - EU SS644921	✗✗✗✗✗✓✗✗✓		Sandy.
⌢	Knapp Rock SS625878	☐☐☐☐☐✗✓✓✓		Sandy.
f	Opposite Black Pill Rock SS632898	☐☐☐☐☐✓✓✗✗		Sandy.

RATING	NAME	TRACK RECORD	SEWAGE OUTLET	REMARKS
⌐	Mumbles Head Pier SS632874	✗✗✗✓	Screened/tidal tank, 170,000, below LWM. Improvements planned.	Sandy.
–	**Jersey Marine,** nr Swansea SS704925	✓✓✓		
–	**Baglan** (Neath)		Screened, 60,000, LSO. Improvements planned.	Sandy.
–	**Afan** (Port Talbot)		Screened, 60,000, LSO. Improvements planned.	Sandy.
⌐	**Aberafan** - EU SS739896	✗✓✓✗✓✓✓		
⌐	East SS744889	✓✓		
–	Margam Sands (opposite steel works)	✓✓		Sandy.
	MID GLAMORGAN			
⌐⌐	**Porthcawl** Rest Bay - EU SS800779	✗✓✓✓✓✓✓		Sand and rocks.
⌐⌐	Sandy Bay - EU SS824765	✗✗✗✓✗✓✓✓		Sand and rocks. Bathing prohibited either side of beach.
⌐⌐	Trecco Bay - EU SS831763	✗✗✓✗✓✓✓✓		Sand and rocks.
f	**Newton Bay** (Newton Point) SS838766	✗ ✗		Sand and rocks. Bathing prohibited at Newton Point.
–	**Ogmore-by-Sea**	✗✗✗✓	Secondary/other, 140,000, LSO.	Sand and rocks. Bathing prohibited near estuary.
⌐	**Southerndown** (Dunraven Bay) - EU	✗✓✗✓✓✓✓✓		Sand and rocks. Bathing prohibited off headland.
	SOUTH GLAMORGAN			
–	**Nash Point**			Rocky. Bathing unsafe.
–	**Tresilian Bay**		Macerated, 8,000, LWM.	Rocky. Bathing unsafe.
⌐⌐	**Llantwit Major Beach** SS955673	✗✓✓✓		Sand and shingle.
⌐⌐	**Limpert Bay**	✓ ✓	Macerated, 4,500, LWM.	Rocks, shingle and sand.
⌐⌐	**Font-y-Gary Bay** (Rhoose)	✓✗✓✓✓		Rocky. Difficult current.
f	**Barry** Watch House Bay	✓✓✓✗		Shingle.
–	Little Island Bay	✓✓✓		Shingle.
⌐	**Cold Knap Beach** - EU ST096664	✗✗✗✓✗✓✓✓	Screened, 23,000, LSO.	Pebbles and sand.
f	**Whitmore Bay Central** - EU ST114662	✓✗✓✗	2, macerated, 21,000, 1.8 km, raw, 23,000, at LWM. Improvements planned.	Sand, shingle and mud.
f	**Jacksons Bay** - EU ST122665	✗✗✗✗✗✗✗✓✗		Sandy, unstable rocks at the back of the beach.
f	**St Mary's Well Bay**	✗✗✗✓✗		Shingle and rocks.
f	**Penarth** ST189708	✗✗✗✗	4	Shingle and rocks. Bathing dangerous.

The Giant's Causeway, near Portrush in County Antrim, draws thousands of visitors every year.

Northern Ireland

THE NORTHERN IRISH COASTLINE REMAINS A WELL KEPT SECRET TO THOSE OUTSIDE THE PROVINCE: IT IS BEAUTIFUL AND VARIED BEYOND IMAGINATION, RANGING FROM CLIFFS POUNDED BY THE ATLANTIC ON THE NORTH COAST OF ANTRIM TO THE SOFT, WOODED SHORES OF CARLINGFORD LOUGH IN THE SOUTH.

•

Its most famous feature, the Giant's Causeway, is one of the wonders of the natural world, consisting of huge polygonal basalt columns that disappear into the waves like a stairway to the depths. Legend has it that the Causeway was built by the giant Finn MacCool to speed his path to Scotland, and sure enough a similar rock formation juts out of the sea off the Scottish island of Staffa. Its actual origins are a little more mundane, the result of the slow cooling of volcanic outpourings of basalt to form the regular crystalline structure we see today. Since 1987 the Giant's Causeway has been listed as a World Heritage Site.

The whole coast has a rich and varied geology with a succession of bays and rugged headlands. The high plateau of Antrim is broken by steep glens and coastal cliffs with spectacular views to Scotland and the Isles, while further south the Irish Sea bites deep into the gentle hills of County Down. The beaches, too, span the range of variation, from the long sandy strands of County Londonderry with their popular holiday resorts, to the nine glens of Antrim, each with a little beach nestling at its mouth, providing a quieter alternative.

Both Belfast's sea loughs, Strangford and Carlingford, are rich in wildlife and scenery; the former is particularly beautiful, with hundreds of kilometres of coastline and over 120 islands. In early summer seals come to Strangford to give birth to their young, and a wide variety of birdlife is found there all year round. Visitors to Northern Ireland will find their own reward in the dramatic seascapes and lovely beaches, still largely undiscovered and some with excellent water quality.

MAGILLIGAN STRAND, BENONE, LIMAVADY
Co. Londonderry
OS Ref:C723362

One of the most impressive stretches of beach in the country: 11 kilometres of firm, flat, golden sand reaching south-east from Magilligan Point at the entrance to Lough Foyle to the cliffs at Downhill, with dunes fringing the wide, curving beach (most of which disappears at high tide) and sand hills covering the peninsula. The eastern end is backed by 225 metre cliffs, themselves shadowed by a heather-clad plateau and the Binevenagh Mountains. A new leisure complex provides excellent facilities close to the beach. (Note that half of the beach is used by the Ministry of Defence as a firing range and is thus out of bounds to the public.)

Should you prefer to get away from the sandcastles and games, miles of sand offer solitude with only the sea and sky for company.

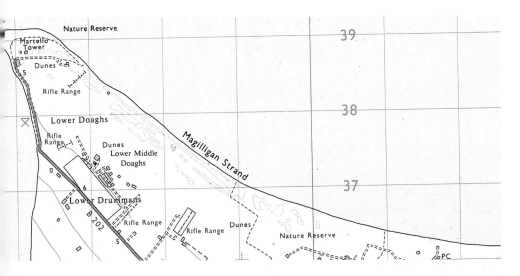

Water quality

No sewage is discharged in the vicinity of this beach.

Bathing safety

Bathing unsafe in some areas due to currents; notices indicate where not to bathe. The beach is patrolled by lifeguards from June to September.

Litter

Dogs must be on a lead.

Access

Off the A2 Limavady to Castlerock road. It is a short walk from the car park to the beach.

Parking

One car park behind the dunes has 300 spaces. Parking is also permitted on the sands but should be avoided on any beach.

Toilets

Public toilets at the beach and also facilities at the leisure complex.

Food

Refreshments available at the leisure complex.

Seaside activities

Swimming, surfing, windsurfing, sailing and fishing from the beach. Golf course, tennis and a children's activity area are available at the leisure complex. A concrete ramp to the beach allows access to launch boats.

Wet weather alternatives

Benone Tourist Complex.

Wildlife and walks

It is claimed that up to 120 different species of shell have been found on Benone Beach in one day, and an outdoor field studies recreation centre at Magilligan reflects the local interest in flora and fauna. 57 hectares of the sand dune system around the Martello Tower on Magilligan Point form a nature reserve and access is restricted to protect this fragile environment. Inland, the Binevenagh mountains provide excellent hill walking and good views of the coast.

Track record ✓ ✓ ✓ ✓ ✓ ✓ ✓

THE STRAND, PORTSTEWART
Co. Londonderry
OS Ref: C808367

Smaller and more restrained than its near neighbour Portrush, but no less beautiful for it, this Edwardian resort located around its harbour on a promontory has an air of old-fashioned charm. To the west are three kilometres of beautiful sandy beach, backed by 75 hectares of dunes owned by the National Trust. Fine cliff scenery extends east towards Portrush, and the superb North Antrim Coast Path follows the cliff top.

Portstewart's flat sands are safe for swimming and good for fishing.

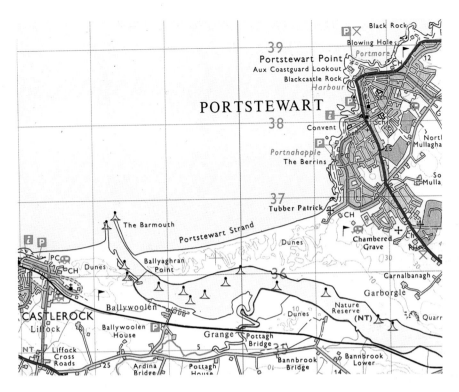

Water quality

One sewage outlet serving 6,040 people discharges macerated sewage at LWM.

Bathing safety

Safe, but beware of currents around the rivermouth. The beach is patrolled by lifeguards during July and August.

Litter

The beach is cleaned regularly.

Access

Direct from the road.

Parking

On the beach at low tide but motorcycles are not permitted.

Food

One confectionery shop at the beach entrance.

Seaside activities

Swimming, surfing, windsurfing, sailing, diving and fishing. Two golf courses. Boat trips from the harbour along the causeway.

Wildlife and walks

The dunes support a wide variety of fauna and flora, and offer attractive walks through the dunes from the beach to the estuarine shore of the River Bann. Barmouth, on the Castlerock shore at the mouth of the Bann, is a good birdwatching area noted for unusual passage migrants. The hide will accommodate wheelchair-users.

Track record ✓ ✓ ✓ ✓ ✓ ✓ ✓

MILL STRAND and CURRAN STRAND, PORTRUSH,
Co. Antrim
OS Ref: C856406 and C865406

Portrush is the largest and most popular seaside holiday centre in Northern Ireland. A Victorian and Edwardian resort located on rocky Ramore Head, it has all the facilities and amusements that might be expected of a traditional holiday town, and two excellent beaches on either side of the promontory. From its elevated position there are excellent views across Lough Foyle to Donegal in the west and out towards Rathlin Island in the east. A low sea wall bounds the soft sands of the West or Mill Strand which curves gently south from the small harbour. The promenade which runs along the sea wall is on two levels separated by grassy banks. The larger East or Curran Strand is also backed by a sea wall but this gives way to dunes and a links golf course.

**Water quality
(Mill Strand)**
One outfall serving 5,000 people discharges macerated sewage at LWM.
(Curran Strand)
No sewage is discharged in the vicinity of this beach.

Bathing safety
Generally safe, but beware of currents; unsafe areas are marked.

Litter
The beaches are cleaned daily; dogs are banned in July and August.

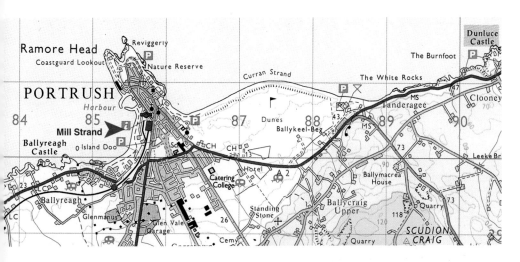

Access

Steps and a ramp from the promenade.

Parking

150–200 spaces at West Strand, 250–300 at East Strand.

Toilets

At each end of West Strand and on East Strand.

Food

Many places to eat and drink nearby.

Seaside activities

Swimming, surfing, windsurfing, sailing, diving and fishing. Boat trips from the harbour.

Wet weather alternatives

Water World alongside the old harbour has a swimming pool complete with flumes and jacuzzis. Its facilities include an aquarium and light entertainments. Amusements.

Wildlife and walks

A section of the rocky shore on the eastern side of Ramore Head between the Portandoo Harbour and Bath Road is a Nature Reserve noted for its fossil ammonites. Adjacent to the reserve is the Portrush Countryside Centre, an interpretative centre which can provide further information about the reserve and surrounding area. East of Portrush there is superb cliff scenery, including towering limestone cliffs eroded by the waves to form arches and caves. The white cliffs are replaced by the brown basalt which forms the famous Giant's Causeway further east; leaflets about the area are available from the National Trust. The coastal path follows the clifftop to the picturesque ruin of Dunluce Castle (the castle is closed on Sunday mornings and on Mondays during the winter).

Track record ✓✓✓✓✓✓✓✓
(both beaches)

Miles of sandy beach sweep east from the White Rocks to Portrush's Curran Strand.

CRAWFORDSBURN, BANGOR
Co. Down
OS Ref: J467826

The 500-metre sandy beach at Crawfordsburn is divided in two by the stream that flows from the glen behind the sands. Both the beach and the glen fall within the Crawfordsburn Country Park: on the right bank of the stream stands the house of the Scottish family who settled here in the 17th century and gave the bay their name. Crawfordsburn and Helen's Bay are both within easy reach of Belfast, and as a result they can become crowded in summer. Under these circumstances you might try Swineley Bay to the east, which tends to be more secluded.

Water quality
One sewage outfall serving 1,200 people discharges secondary treated sewage to the stream.

Bathing safety
Safe bathing.

Access
By road along the A2, and also by train.

Parking
The Country Park car park is 400 metres from the beach.

Public Transport
Trains stop at Crawfordsburn Halt, one and a half kilometres from the beach along the road through the Country Park.

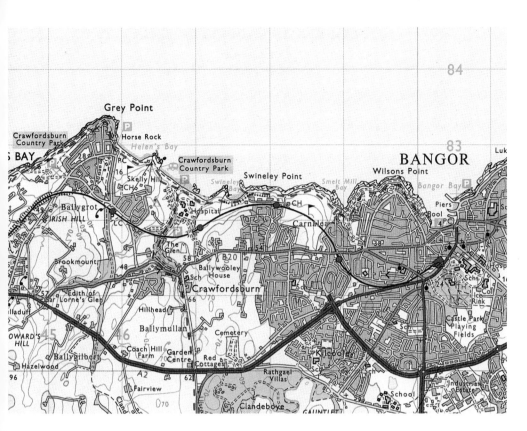

 Toilets
In the car park, and including facilities for disabled visitors.

 Food
Café/restaurant.

 Seaside activities
Swimming, golf. Orienteering courses held in the Country Park. Visitors' and Interpretative Centre.

Wildlife and walks
The stream from Crawfordsburn village flows through a steep-sided valley, wooded with some exotic species. Below the village, it descends to a waterfall and flows under one of the railway viaduct's 24 metre-high arches. Marked footpaths provide circular walks of varying lengths. Information about the park, including its walks and wildlife, is available from the interpretative centre. The beach is part of the North Down Coastal Path and also forms part of the Ulster Way; it follows the coast from Hollywood, passes through the glen to Clandeboye Estate and on to Newtownards.

Track record ✓✓✓✓✓✓✗✓

Crawfordsburn is a popular weekend destination for families from Belfast.

TYRELLA BEACH, CLOUGH
Co. Down
OS Ref: J456357

An enclosed beach/dune complex in Dundrum Bay comprising five kilometres of wide sandy beach backed by 25 hectares of mature dune conservation area. The clean, shallow water and safe bathing make this a very popular beach on sunny Sundays in the holiday season; at other times it is blissfully quiet. There are six golf courses within a 20-kilometre radius of the beach, including the excellent Royal County Down.

Water quality
No sewage is discharged in the vicinity of the beach.

Bathing safety
Safe, with a warden service between 9.00am and 10.00pm during the summer season, and at weekends from 9.00am to 5.00pm between Easter and September.

Litter
The beach is cleaned daily by hand and twice weekly by machine in summer, in winter as required. Some marine debris is washed up on shore.

Access
The beach is situated and signposted on the A2 Killough to Clough road, with access via the Council-controlled road.

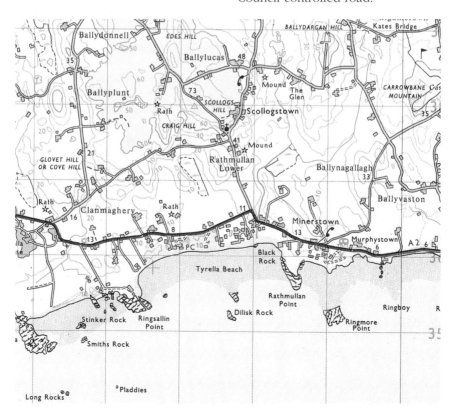

Parking
To the right of the access road; to the left is a car-free zone introduced in 1994.

Toilets
There is a new amenity block with facilities for disabled visitors and baby changing.

Food
Food vans visit the beach during the summer.

Seaside activities
Swimming, organised activities for children starting in 1995, beach games, guided walks and nature walks.

Wet weather alternatives
Down County Museum, Delamont County Park, Tropicana complex (Newcastle), Seaforde Butterfly house, Castleward House and gardens (NT). There is a tourist information and interpretation centre next to the toilets.

Shallow water means safe bathing for all the family at Tyrella Beach.

Wildlife and walks
Close by is the Murlough Nature Reserve, a dune system with plenty of interesting wildlife and vegetation, and organised walks open here in 1995. There are Forest Parks at Castlewellan and Newcastle. The area is dotted with signs of man's early habitation: forts, dolmens and some of the earliest Christian remains (St Patrick landed near here). The Ulster Way goes past the beach before threading its way through the beautiful Mourne Mountains to the south.

Track record ✓✓✓✓✓✓✓

217

NICHOLSON'S STRAND, KILKEEL
Co. Down
OS Ref: J282109

An Area of Outstanding Natural Beauty adjoining a Site of Special Scientific Interest, Nicholson's Strand stretches along the eastern shores of the entrance to Carlingford Lough. The south-facing sand and shingle beach is backed by dunes and has the magnificent Mourne Mountains as a backdrop. There are good views across the Lough to Ballagan Point and away down the coast beyond Dundalk Bay.

Water quality
No sewage is discharged in the vicinity of the beach.

Access
A road leads to the car park a short walk from the beach.

Bathing safety
Safe bathing.

Parking
Car park with 150 spaces.

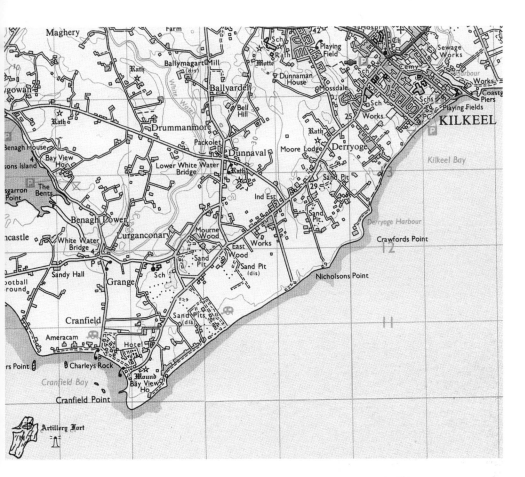

 Toilets
There are public conveniences.

 Food
Hotel, two cafés and three shops.

 Seaside activities
Swimming, windsurfing, diving, water-skiing and fishing. Beach entertainment and band concerts. Golf course.

 Wet weather alternatives
Analong Cornmill and Marine Park.

A south-facing sand and shingle beach attracts visitors throughout the season.

Wildlife and walks
The Mourne Mountains provide some of the best walking in Britain. The Silent Valley Reserve – a 14,000 million-litre reservoir set among the peaks with fine parkland on the approaches to the dam – is just north of Kilkeel. Slieve Donard, at 850m Northern Ireland's highest peak, rises just to the north-east.

Track record | | | | | | ✓ | ✓ | ✓ |

RATING	NAME	TRACK RECORD	SEWAGE OUTLET	REMARKS
	CO. LONDONDERRY			
⌃	**Castlerock** - EU C777364	□✗✓✓✓✓✓✓	Macerated, 1,060, at LWM.	Sandy.
	CO. ANTRIM			
⌃⌃⌃⌃	**Ballycastle** - EU D123412	✗✗✓✓✓✓✓	Macerated, 3,920, 30 below LWM.	Sandy. Beach cleaned regularly. Not featured due to insufficient information.
–	**White Park Bay**			Sandy, dunes.
⌃⌃	**Browns Bay** - EU D436028	✓✓✓✓✓✓✓		Sandy.
	CO. DOWN			
⌃	**Helen's Bay** - EU J460829	✓✓✓✓✓✓✓	Tidal tank, 1,600, at LWM.	Sandy. Beach cleaned regularly.
⌃⌃⌃	**Ballyholme** - EU J518824	✗✗✓✓✓✗✓✓		Sandy. Beach cleaned regularly. Not featured due to insufficient information.
⌃⌃⌃⌃	**Groomsport** - EU J450836	✓✗✓✓✓✓✓✓	Screened, 40,000, at LWM.	Sandy. Beach cleaned regularly. Not featured due to insufficient information.
⌃⌃	**Millisle** - EU J601755	✓✓✓✓✓✓✓	Primary, 1,000, at LWM.	Sandy.
–	**Murlough**			Sandy.
⌃⌃	**Newcastle** - EU J384318	✗✗✗✓✗✓✓✓	Secondary, 20,000, 285 below LWM.	Sandy.
f	**Cranfield Bay** - EU J268105	✓✓✓✓✓✓✓✗	Screened, 2,200, 410 below LWM.	Sandy. Beach cleaned regularly.

The Channel Islands

THE MOST SOUTHERLY LAND IN THE UNITED KINGDOM, LYING JUST 23 KILOMETRES OFF
THE COAST OF FRANCE, THE CHANNEL ISLANDS HAVE HAD CONTINUING POLITICAL LINKS
WITH BRITAIN SINCE THE TIME OF WILLIAM OF NORMANDY, WHO RULED OVER THEM
BEFORE HE CONQUERED ENGLAND. OF THE FIVE MAIN ISLANDS, ONLY JERSEY AND
GUERNSEY ARE COVERED IN THE *GUIDE*. ALDERNEY, SARK AND HERM ARE FABULOUS
PLACES TO VISIT, HOWEVER, EACH WITH ITS OWN DISTINCT WAY OF LIFE, AND CARING
LITTLE ABOUT THE OUTSIDE WORLD.

•

Sark is only 5 kilometres long and has been a feudal state governed by a Seigneur since 1565. Travel on the island is by bicycle, tractor or horse-drawn carriage – cars are not allowed. Herm is even smaller than Sark measuring only 2.5 kilometres long by 1 kilometre wide. Shell Beach at the north of Herm consists of millions of tiny shells, some from as far away as the Gulf of Mexico. There are, not surprisingly, no cars or roads on the island but Herm is home to around 100 of the famous Guernsey cows.

Guernsey itself is a picturesque island with spectacular cliffs and sandy beaches. Its capital, St Peter Port, is known as one of the finest harbour towns in Europe. The island has its own government, issues its own coins and stamps but is subject to the Crown, and although the islanders are English-speaking, French Patois can be widely heard. The island's turbulent history is reflected in its archaeology which ranges from neolithic remains to Royalist castles and concrete defences constructed by the occupying forces during the Second World War.

Sewage treatment on the island is less than ideal. There are three main outfalls and several minor discharges; there is, however, very little contamination from industrial sources in the island's sewage.

Jersey was established as an independent state over 700 years ago. When King John lost the island to France in 1204, the islanders chose to remain loyal and to this day they are subject to the Crown, although not governed by Parliament.

Jersey is famous for its coastline. It has an excellent record for water quality and has one of the most comprehensive sewage treatment programmes in Britain, which includes screening, settlement, activated sludge oxidation, secondary treatment and ultraviolet disinfection. Beaches on Jersey are cleaned daily by hand and by machine. Dogs are banned from the beaches in Jersey between 10.30am and 6pm from 1 May to 30 September, with fines for those not complying. Jersey takes real care of its beaches, and with 55 kilometres of coastline ranging from high cliffs to sweeping bays and bathing waters which meet the highest EC standards, it must count as a prime destination for the discerning beach lover.

PEMBROKE BAY

Guernsey

OS Ref: 340837

Pembroke Bay, also known as L'Ancresse Bay, is a large, almost unbroken expanse of sandy beach in a horseshoe-shaped gulf, sheltered from winds from most directions. It is ideal for serious sunbathers and for beach games. Dogs are banned from the beach between May and September.

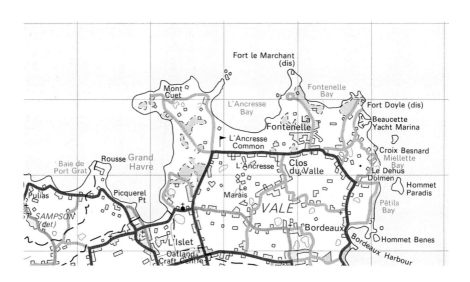

Water quality

No sewage is discharged in the vicinity of this beach.

Bathing safety

Bathing is safe at any state of the tide.

Litter

The beach is cleaned daily by hand during the summer and four days a week in winter. Dog litter bins are available in the car parks.

Access

There are two signposted access roads to the beach. A mixture of slipways and steps lead down to the beach.

Parking

Adequate parking immediately above the beach.

Public transport

Buses run regularly to and from St Peter Port, numbers J1, J2 and J3.

Toilets

There are toilets at both ends of the beach.

Food

Food is available from kiosks at both ends of the beach. Two adjacent hotels serve bar lunches and evening meals.

Seaside activities

Swimming, windsurfing. There is a windsurfing and Hobie Cat school and equipment is available for hire. Activities are zoned, and lifebuoys are provided at key access points to the beach. There is a golf course on L'Ancresse Common.

Wet weather alternatives

Oatlands Craft Centre and Koi fish farm.

Pembroke Bay boasts the best sunshine record in Guernsey.

Wildlife and walks

Immediately behind the beach, L'Ancresse Common is the site of a number of Neolithic burial chambers and Martello towers dating from Napoleonic times.

Track record ✓✓

Not EU designated.

223

HAVELET BAY
Guernsey
OS Ref: 341780

South of St Peter Port lies the town beach, Havelet Bay, the only beach on the island designated for water-skiing. The foreshore is shingle with sand at low tide and numerous rock pools. Dogs are allowed on this beach, but owners are required by law to pick up and dispose of their dog's litter.

Water quality
The Fort George sewage outlet is situated south of Havelet Bay, 30 metres offshore.

Bathing safety
Generally safe.

Litter
The beach is cleaned manually five days a week in summer and four times a week in winter.

Access
On foot or by car from St Peter Port. The beach is accessible via two slipways at either end.

Parking
Adequate parking along the beach front.

Public transport
The island's main bus terminus is situated about 5 minutes from the bay.

Toilets
Near the bus terminus including facilities for disabled visitors.

Food
A café overlooks the bay.

Seaside activities
Swimming, water-skiing. Tidal rock pools are very popular with families and there is a picnic area near by.

Wet weather alternatives
Aquarium, La Vallette underground military museum, Guernsey brewery, Victor Hugo's house, Castle Cornet and the town shopping centre. Above the aquarium are the ruins of an ancient fort.

Wildlife and walks
The footpaths of the east coast are accessible from here. Several cliff walks lead along shady paths to other bays along the coast.

Track record ☐☐☐☐☐✓✓
Not EU designated.

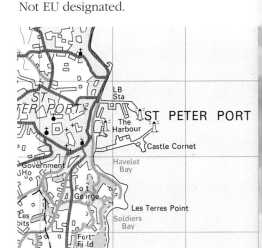

The receding tide exposes countless rock pools, teeming with life and just waiting to be explored.

FERMAIN
Guernsey
OS Ref: 339761

The most popular east coast beach, and one of the prettiest on the island, sheltered from all except east winds. A pebble bank at the top of the beach gives way to firm sand at low tide. The beach is reached via a steep winding road down a beautiful valley which is closed to all except essential traffic towards the end, or by following the cliff paths.

Water quality
One outlet discharges macerated sewage 30m from the beach.

Bathing safety
Safe at all times.

Litter
The beach is cleaned by hand daily in the summer and four times a week in the winter. Dogs are banned between May and September.

Access

Fermain Bay is situated off the Saumarez to St Martin's road towards La Favorita Hotel and is well signposted. Access is by foot from the Cholet Hotel car park or along the cliff path from St Peter Port.

Parking

Parking is at the top of the access road near the Cholet Hotel.

Trees cloak the steep cliffs and tumble almost to the water's edge at pretty Fermain Bay.

Public transport

Buses (numbers B and B1 from St Peter Port) run frequently along the Saumarez road and Fermain Bay is 10–15 minutes walk from the bus stop.

Toilets

At the top of the slipway near the kiosk.

Food

A café near the bay at the top of the slipway; both hotels at the top of the access road serve lunch.

Seaside activities

Good bathing.

Wet weather alternatives

Saumarez Manor, a stately home with large gardens and exhibitions open to the public.

Wildlife and walks

Fermain is two miles along the cliffs from St Peter Port and included in the largest nature conservation site on the island. Many walks crisscross the south and east coasts.

Track record ✓✓✓

Not EU designated.

PETIT BOT BAY
Guernsey
OS Ref: 305749

This popular bay lies at the foot of two beautiful wooded valleys. The beach is pebble at high tide but at low tide a large expanse of sand is exposed. Dogs are banned between May and September.

Water quality
One outlet serving 8,000 people discharges macerated and screened sewage three kilometres out to sea.

Bathing safety
Safe.

Litter
The beach is cleaned daily by hand in the summer and four times weekly in the winter.

Access
A clearly signposted road leads down to the beach just before the airport. A slipway makes the beach easily accessible.

P Parking
There are parking facilities at the top of the beach.

Public transport
Regular buses run to and from St Peter Port, numbers B1, C1 and C2.

WC Toilets
Well maintained toilets are located at the top of the beach.

Food
There is a kiosk immediately above the beach.

Seaside activities
Good bathing.

Petit Bot Bay offers safe swimming in all conditions.

☂ Wet weather alternatives

The Occupation Museum at Le Bourgs which houses artefacts and military memorabilia dating from the German occupation of Guernsey.

✿ Wildlife and walks

Petit Bot is situated halfway along the cliff path network (46 kilometres of footpath), and the valley has wooded footpaths stretching inland from the bay.

Track record ☐☐☐☐☐ ✓✓✓
Not EU designated.

L'EREE
Guernsey
OS Ref: 255780

Offering a large area of sand with good bathing, this beach is sheltered from the north-west wind and is therefore an excellent place to sunbathe. It is, however, prone to deposits of seaweed. Dogs are banned between May and October.

Stunning sunsets are an added attraction of this beautiful west-facing bay.

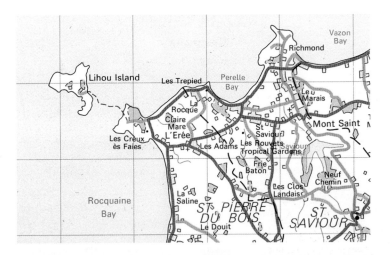

Water quality

No sewage is discharged in the vicinity of this beach.

Bathing safety

Generally safe; lifebuoys are provided at key access points to the beach.

Litter

Cleaned by hand daily during the summer and four times weekly in the winter.

Access

Via the Plaisanoe road or along the west coast road. Steps lead to the beach and slipways at either end give access for disabled visitors.

Parking

There is plenty of parking directly above the beach.

Public transport

Regular buses run to and from St Peter Port, numbers O1, O2, D, D1 and E.

Toilets

Well maintained toilets are located at the top of the beach.

Food

Two cafés opposite the beach and ice cream vans in the car park. The L'Erée Hotel serves bar meals.

Seaside activities

Good bathing.

Wet weather alternatives

Tropical gardens and copper craft centre.

Wildlife and walks

At low water spring tides you can walk across the causeway to Lihou Island. Nearby is Saumarez Pebbles Bank, a conservation site of national importance. It is jointly managed by La Societé Guemesiaise and the Board of Administration. The bay forms part of the Catioroc nature trail.

Track record

Not EU designated.

VAZON BEACH
Guernsey
OS Ref: 285798

This wide crescent of lovely clean sand gets the sun from early morning until sunset. It is exposed to the wind from most directions, which is bad news for sunbathers but often creates excellent conditions for surfers. Dogs are banned from the beach between May and September.

Water quality
There is no sewage discharged in the vicinity of this beach.

Bathing safety
Generally safe bathing, but observe the warning flags. Lifebuoys are provided at key access points.

Litter

The beach is cleaned by hand daily in the summer season and four times a week in winter.

Access

Situated on the west coast near Fort Hommet Headland, the beach is reached via flights of steps, with slipways at either end providing access for disabled visitors.

Fishing boats lie at anchor just off Vazon.

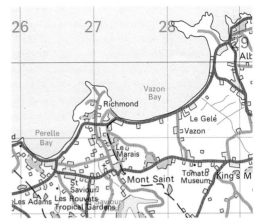

Parking

Plenty of space at two large car parks to the north end of the bay.

Toilets

Well maintained toilets are located at both ends of the beach, with facilities for disabled visitors at the north end of the bay near the terminus car park.

Food

There are two beach kiosks and a number of restaurants and hotels in the area.

Seaside activities

Swimming, surfing, windsurfing and canoeing. All activities are strictly zoned.

Wet weather alternatives

Guernsey Tomato Museum.

Wildlife and walks

The Fort Hommet headland at the northern end of the beach is a Nature Conservation Area of considerable interest, both historically and for its wildlife, with ten rare plant species found here.

Track Record ☐☐☐☐☐☐ ✓✓✓

Not EU designated.

233

PORT SOIF BAY, WEST COAST
Guernsey
OS Ref: 305819

Port Soif is an almost entirely circular bay which offers shelter from virtually any wind. It has a foreshore area of wonderful fine, dry sand. Dogs are banned between May and September.

Water quality
No sewage is discharged in the vicinity of this beach.

Bathing safety
Generally safe, with lifebuoys at the key access points and a trained first-aider in attendance.

Litter

The beach is cleaned daily by hand and four times a week in the winter.

Access

Located on the coast road in the north-west of the island. Four access points consist of steps and a slipway for disabled visitors.

Wild flowers thrive in the dunes behind the beach at Port Soif.

Parking

There is plenty of parking immediately above the beach.

Public transport

Regular buses from St Peter Port, numbers F1, G and G1, run to within a five-minute walk of the beach; H2 goes all the way.

Toilets

Well maintained toilets are available.

Food

There is a kiosk at the top of the beach.

Seaside activities

Swimming.

Wildlife and walks

The Port Soif Nature Trail lies just behind the beach, with a leaflet available from the tourist office. Port Soif Common is a Site of Nature Conservation Interest.

Track record ✓ ✓ ✓

Not EU designated.

ST OUEN'S BAY
Jersey
OS Ref: 565514

St Ouen, the longest beach in Jersey spanning nearly the full length of the island's west coast, is locally referred to as 'the five mile road', for obvious reasons. It is a superb surfing beach and has been the venue for international surfing competitions. The vast sandy beach is backed by Les Mielles conservation area. Situated to the south of the bay is La Rocco Tower which can be visited at low tide but is cut off at mid to high tide.

Water quality

Bathing safety
The same conditions which make this beach popular with surfers can also make it dangerous for all but the strongest swimmers: observe the safety flags at all times. There is safety cover from the island's main beach guard headquarters between late April and the end of September, to which emergency telephones at seven locations are linked directly.

Litter

Litter bins are emptied daily between May and September; dog waste bins are provided.

Access

There are numerous points of access to the beach by means of slipways and steps.

Parking

There are many car parks along the length of the bay, some of which have been specially designed to blend in with the surrounding dune area by partially enclosed grass banks.

Public transport

Bus number 12a runs to St Ouen's Bay.

Toilets

There are toilets at numerous places along the bay with facilities for disabled visitors, who can gain access to cubicles across the island by obtaining a Radar key at the Town Hall.

Food

Cafés, beach kiosks and licensed restaurants.

Seaside activities

Surfing instruction and equipment hire; nine-hole municipal golf course at Les Mielles together with a driving range and crazy golf course.

Wet weather alternatives

Les Mielles interpretation centre.

Britain's first concrete lighthouse, built in 1874, stands in splendid isolation at the tip of Corbière Point at the southern end of St Ouen's Bay.

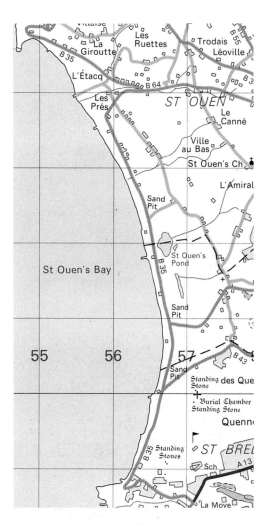

Wildlife and walks

La Mielle de Morville, adjacent to Kempt Tower, is a pleasant place to walk and the starting point for longer circular routes. The sand dunes support over 400 plant species. The Les Mielles conservation area is an area designated to conserve and protect the dune area together with surrounding flora and fauna. There are weekly guided walks around Les Mielles every Thursday afternoon between May and September.

Track record   ✓✓✓

Not EU designated.

BEAUPORT
Jersey
OS Ref: 579479

A beautiful and secluded sandy bay on Jersey's southern coast, with a beach sheltered by rocky headlands on either side.

Water quality
No sewage is discharged in the vicinity of this beach.

Litter
Bins at the beach are emptied regularly.

Bathing safety
There is no beach guard cover but bathing is relatively safe.

Parking
There is a small car park at the top of the path.

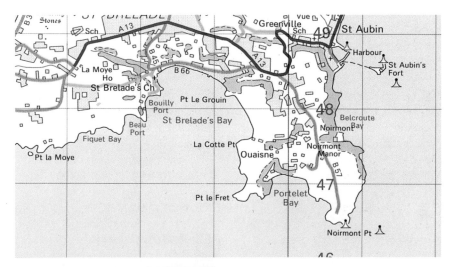

Public transport
The number 12 bus stops about 10 minutes' walk away.

Toilets
There are no toilet facilities at the beach.

Food
A refreshment van visits the car park occasionally.

Seaside activities
Swimming.

Wet weather alternatives
None at the beach.

Walks and wildlife
A path runs along the headland offering spectacular views of the bay. Beauport is home to the Dartford Warbler.

Track record
Not EU designated.

Beauport provides a quieter and more relaxing alternative to the much larger St Brelade's Bay next door.

ST BRELADE'S BAY
Jersey
OS Ref: 585483 (see map on p. 239)

The most popular family beach in Jersey with a large expanse of white sand, many beach activities and a landscaped promenade which is floodlit in the evenings. At the western end of the bay stands the picturesque St Brelade's parish church.

An attractive promenade with palm-fringed gardens and fountains backs the beach at St Brelade's Bay.

Water quality
No sewage is discharged in the vicinity of this beach.

Bathing safety
Safe, but observe the safety flags at all times. Beach guards patrol from Easter to September.

Access
Easy access to the beach from the promenade.

Parking
There are three main car parks with nearly 400 spaces.

Toilets
There are toilets at four different sites. These are clearly signposted and are suitable for disabled users.

Food
Several cafés and kiosks overlook the beach.

Seaside activities
Funboats, windsurfers, trampolines, deck chairs and loungers, changing tents, pedalos and canoes are for hire. Water-skiing is also available.

Track record
Not EU designated.

PORTELET
Jersey
OS Ref: 600470 (see map on p. 239)

This quiet, sandy beach in a sheltered bay on the south-west coast of the island is popular with the locals. Wooded hills rise steeply from the rocky foreshore and an islet in the bay is fully encircled at half to full tide.

Water quality

 Bathing safety
Generally safe. There is no beach guard cover.

 Litter
Litter bins are emptied daily May to September.

 Access
Access is via steep steps with bench seating at three points. This beach is not suitable for people with limited mobility.

P **Parking**
There is parking behind the beach.

Public transport
Bus number 12a.

 Food
A café sells food and beach goods. There is a newly refurbished bar and restaurant adjacent to the car park.

 Seaside activities
Deck chairs and windbreak hire. This is a particularly good area for exploring rockpools.

 Wet weather alternatives
St Aubin Harbour is a short drive away and has many attractive shops and restaurants.

Just offshore at Portelet lies the Ile au Guerdain, crowned by an 18th-century Martello tower.

Wildlife and walks
A path leads to Noirmont Point from where there are fine views of the bay and across to St Helier.

Track record | | | | | | ✓ | ✓ | ✓ |
Not EU designated.

GREEN ISLAND
Jersey
OS Ref: 673461

Just a ten-minute drive from the town of St Helier, Green Island is fine sandy beach with outcrops of rock, and very popular with the locals. Low tide reveals dozens of interesting rockpools and also permits access to the island across the sands. Don't get cut off when the tide comes in!

Water quality

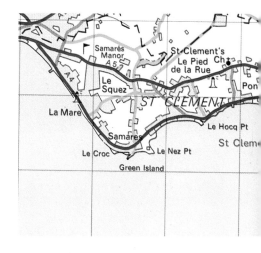

 Bathing safety
Generally safe; there is no beach guard cover.

 Litter
There are litter bins at the beach.

 Access
One main slipway to the beach.

 Parking
In St Clements.

 Public transport
Bus number 1.

 Toilets
There are toilets at the car park.

 Food
Cafés nearby.

 Seaside activities
Swimming.

 Wet weather alternatives
St Helier, the capital with shops and other facilities is nearby.

 Walks and wildlife
Green Island is too popular for shore birds to be in evidence, but a walk east towards Le Hocq Point reveals an excellent habitat.

Track record
Not available. Not EU designated.

More of a mound in the seabed than a real island, Green Island nevertheless gets cut off at high tide.

ARCHIRONDEL
Jersey
OS Ref: 712516

This is a quiet shingle beach situated on the east coast of the island, in an area often used by canoeing clubs. The beach is unspoilt and offers spectacular views of St Catherine's Breakwater.

Water quality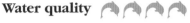

 Bathing Safety
Safe; there is no beach guard cover.

 Litter
Bins are provided and emptied daily between May and September.

P **Parking**
There is a small car park specifically for the beach and café.

Public transport
Bus Number 1 (check timetables as some do not go as far as Archirondel).

WC **Toilets**
There are no public toilets,

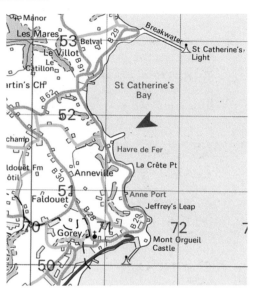

but the café proprietor allows beach users access to the toilets in the café.

 Food
There is a café next to the beach with indoor and outdoor seating, serving a range of food.

Seaside activities
Swimming and canoeing.

Wildlife and walks
There are barbecue and picnic areas close to Archirondel offering fine views of the breakwater.

Track record ☐☐☐☐☐☐✓✓✓
Not EU designated.

Superb bathing in a quiet, sheltered bay is the main attraction of Archirondel.

GREVE DE LECQ
Jersey
OS Ref: 582556

This sandy horseshoe-shaped bay has expanses of flat rocks exposed at low tide. The jetty at the end of the bay is used by the local fishermen. A sharp decline in water quality last year was thought to be due to pollution from agricultural run-off; this year's result is a huge improvement, and water quality is once again excellent.

Water quality
No sewage is discharged in the vicinity of this beach.

Grassy cliffs shelter Grève de Lecq beach.

Bathing safety
Generally safe, but observe the safety flags at all times. This beach is not patrolled by beach guards.

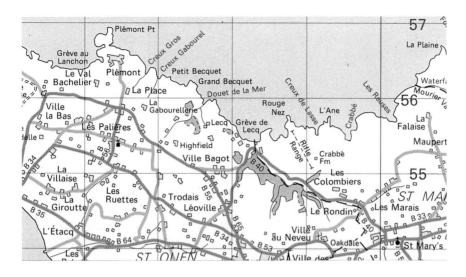

P **Parking**
There is adequate parking space.

WC **Toilets**
Public toilets are available.

Food
A kiosk on the beach and several cafés serving local seafood nearby.

Wet weather alternatives
None near the beach.

Wildlife and walks
There are cliff path signs from the main car park taking the walker all the way to the famous 'Devil's Hole' or to Plemont.

Track record
Not EU designated.

RATING	NAME	TRACK RECORD	SEWAGE OUTLET	REMARKS
	GUERNSEY			
–	**Grand Havre**	☐☐☐☐☐✓☐☐		Sandy edged by granite outcrops.
–	**Moulin Huet Bay**			Sandy beach with fascinating rock formations.
–	**Perelle Bay**			Sandy, surrounded by rocks. Not very good for swimming.
⌒	**Cobo Beach** 296809	☐☐☐☐☐✓✓✓		Cleaned regularly. Bathing unsafe in marked areas.
–	**Saline Bay** (Grandes Rocques)			Sand and shingle.
	JERSEY	☐☐☐☐☐☐✓✓✓		
⌒	**Grouville** 710501	☐☐☐☐☐☐✓✓✓		Sandy.
⌒⌒	**Plemont** 561566			Sandy.

BRITAIN'S COASTLINE UNDER THREAT

Sewage pollution is the reason this book was written and sewage is still a wide-spread problem in Britain. Of the hundreds of millions of gallons of sewage pumped into the sea around our coasts every day, most is either raw or simply screened. A mixture of domestic waste water, cleaning agents, industrial and trade effluent, solid litter and storm water, it will typically contain human wastes, sanitary protection, condoms, bathroom wastes, engine oils, fat balls from domestic and trade kitchens, and a range of heavy metal contaminants (mercury, lead, cadmium, arsenic, copper) from trade effluent, detergents and road surface run-off. It also contains viruses and bacteria that can cause disease in humans.

To catch a potentially fatal illness from sewage whilst bathing is rare, but many studies show that the chances of contracting other, less serious illnesses are quite considerable. It is entirely possible to contract an ear, nose and throat infection from the water, or to suffer diarrhoea and vomiting after swimming. Each year the Marine Conservation Society receives reports from people who have become ill after wind-surfing or diving in sewage-contaminated waters.

When you consider what sewage is, the harm it can do and how much of it we produce, comprehensive treatment would seem an essential step to protect our health and the marine environment. But very little sewage in this country receives adequate treatment, despite the fact that the technology exists to make sewage pollution a thing of the past.

Sewage Treatment – the Ideal and the Reality

Comprehensive sewage treatment has a number of stages. The first and most basic, PRELIMINARY TREATMENT, attempts to remove the larger solids – the plastics, nappies and all manner of debris that finds its way into the sewers – by a very coarse filtering process called SCREENING. The material screened out is largely unrecyclable and is disposed of in landfill sites or possibly incinerated. The treatment may also include a process called MACERATION, which is roughly equivalent to putting the sewage through a food blender. Preliminary treatment is a starting point for proper treatment of sewage, but in no sense adequate on its own. And yet around 40% of major coastal outfalls (those serving over 10,000 people) discharge sewage which has had only preliminary treatment, and a further 40% do not even receive that.

The sewage now contains 200–500 milligrams per litre of suspended solids, and the next stage, known as PRIMARY TREATMENT, allows these to settle out. Several hours of settlement before the effluent is passed on removes 50–60% of suspended solids and up to 50% of bacteria and viruses, and produces a large volume of sludge.

The effluent is then subjected to SECONDARY TREATMENT which stimulates biological activity and reduces the oxygen demand of the sewage; there are several ways of achieving this, all of which generate more sludge which has to be dealt with. Secondary treatment removes 90–95% of suspended solids, 80–90% of the oxygen demand, 75–99% of bacteria and viruses and about 50% of heavy metal contamination.

In some cases, though this is still rare in the UK, TERTIARY TREATMENT may be

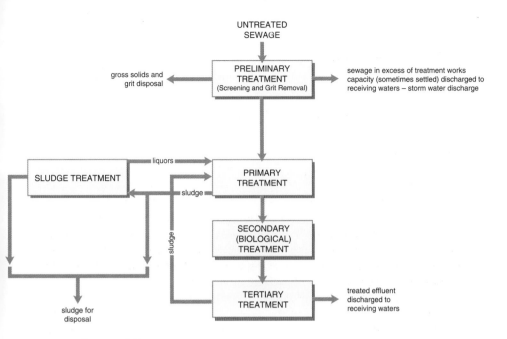

Figure showing full sewage treatment.

used to reduce the nitrogen and phosphorus levels in the effluent in order to lessen its fertiliser effect, in a process known as nutrient stripping. This is important since nutrients in sewage (like nitrogen and phosphorus) can severely disrupt marine ecosystems, causing algal blooms and the death of marine life. Inputs of nutrients from agricultural practices also contribute greatly to the problem of nutrient enrichment and pollution.

Sewage is discharged to sea via OUTFALL PIPES which vary widely in length. Many discharge a matter of a few metres below low water mark and some may even discharge above the level of low tide. In the past, the LONG SEA OUTFALL was seen as the solution to contaminated bathing waters, but discharging the sewage as far out to sea as possible is no longer regarded as a substitute for treating it. There are significant ecological problems with raw sewage wherever it is discharged. Sewage slicks from long sea outfalls may be washed back towards beaches by wind, waves and currents and result in unpleasant encounters for swimmers and sailors.

The SLUDGE generated by sewage treatment should not be regarded as a waste to be disposed of as quickly and as cheaply as possible, but as a resource to be exploited. There are many options: sludge can be used for the production of fertilisers, soil conditioners, peat substitutes, methane production for electricity generation and even oil production. An innovative scheme piloted in Britain by Wessex Water using the Swiss Combi process has shown that a commercial fertiliser can be made from sewage sludge.

At whatever stage the effluent is discharged to sea, whether raw or treated, CHEMICAL DISINFECTION may be applied. The chemicals used may include sodium hypochlorite, peracetic acid or ozone. None of these has been adequately tested to ensure their safety with regard to marine life and human health. There is also doubt about the efficacy of these methods in destroying the disease-causing agents in the effluent: the use of chemical disinfection may be lulling us into a false sense of security by removing the indicators of sewage pollution and leaving the problem behind.

It is widely agreed that chemical disinfection is no substitute for comprehensive sewage treatment. PHYSICAL DISINFECTION, using ultrafiltration methods or possibly ultraviolet light systems, appears to present no threat to the marine environment, since these treatments are non-additive.

In addition to the routinely discharging outfalls, OVERFLOW OUTFALLS come into use during storms and times of heavy rainfall – on average around 10 times a year as treatment works become overloaded and sewers fill up. These discharge completely untreated sewage, sometimes directly on to the beach above low water mark.

Sewage Pollution and the Law

There is no doubt that improvements are being made to sewage treatment systems, but progress is painfully slow. The water service companies have control over the vast majority of discharges (with the exception of a small number of privately operated sewage outfalls) and as such are directly responsible for this massive pollution of our seas. Although some companies are investing millions in long-term improvement projects, others appear to be doing only the absolute minimum required of them by law. There are three main pieces of legislation that refer directly to the discharge of sewage to the sea:

Under the Water Resources Act (1991) the National Rivers Authority (NRA) must give a consent to the water companies for each discharge to sea. These consents ought to protect the waters into which the sewage is being discharged, but in practice the system does not always work effectively and can be undermined by political considerations. Some coastal discharges regularly breach their consents and many simply do not have numerical consents, meaning that no limit is put on the volume of raw sewage that goes down the outfall pipe and straight into the sea. In Scotland, these aspects are regulated by the River Purification Boards under the Control of Pollution Act (1974).

Unfortunately sewage is not all that ends up in the sewers: a loophole allow industrial discharges – containing heavy metals, industrial detergents and dyes and oils – to be made to sewers without the need for a direct licence from the NRA. The NRA is soon to be merged with Her Majesty's Inspectorate for Pollution to form the new Environment Agency, and its duties will be transferred to this new body. There is widespread concern that the new agency's powers will not be as wide ranging as those of the NRA and that the water environment may suffer as a result.

A European law, the Urban Waste Water Treatment Directive (91/27/EEC), seeks to make secondary treatment the standard minimum level of treatment throughout the Union for all coastal sewage discharges serving populations of more than 10,000 and estuarine discharges serving populations of more than 2,000. Full implementation of the Directive will undoubtedly produce an improvement in the coastal waters around Britain, although the Directive itself is not entirely satisfactory, since numerous smaller outfalls are not covered and primary treatment will be considered adequate for large outfalls where coastal waters are declared less sensitive. The Government has already declared many areas of the British coast less sensitive, including the Severn and the Humber, two of the most polluted estuaries which ought to be treated as priorities for a long overdue clean-up. We appear to be as enthusiastic for the Urban Waste Water Treatment Directive as we were for the Bathing Water Directive: at that time the Government identified only 27 bathing waters in Britain, while land-locked Luxembourg declared 34! The Urban Waste Water Treatment Directive must be implemented and areas such as the Severn Estuary must be reclassified so they receive the full sewage treatment they require.

The Government is now considering the ratification of Annex IV of the International Agreement on the Prevention of Pollution from Ships (MARPOL). This makes it an offence to discharge without treatment sewage from ships and large boats and yachts. Holding tanks on ships are to be encouraged so that sewage can be discharged to land-based treatment works at ports and harbours, and reception facilities here will have to be upgraded to cope: there is no point in bringing raw sewage back to land if the land-based solution is simply to pump it back to sea via an outfall pipe. While it appears to be a step in the right direction, many countries with large shipping fleets do not recognise the MARPOL Agreement and continue to discharge raw sewage. Boat owners wanting guidance on how to deal with sewage should contact the Royal Yachting Association and ask for a copy of their code of conduct – the Clean Code for Boat Owners and Users.

Despite the ready availability of the technology for adequate treatment, and in the face of the legal framework designed to protect the seas, the simple fact is that much of the sewage from coastal populations is discharged without any form of treatment. As long as this is the case, those who use the sea will have to put up with sewage-related debris on the beach and will continue to fall ill from sewage-borne disease. We can all help reduce the problem of debris: it is a simple matter to dispose of sanitary items, condoms or cotton buds in the bin rather than down the lavatory pan. Simply bagging and binning waste products and using less plastic will help clean up beaches and bathing waters in the short term, as well as making the water companies' treatment of sewage easier. Less debris in the sewers would mean fewer blockages in the pipes and fewer breakdowns of the treatment machinery.

The Problem of Marine Litter

The dropping of litter in public places – which include beaches – was outlawed by the Environmental Protection Act (1990). Littering at sea is also illegal under Annex V of MARPOL which prohibits the dumping of plastics overboard from ships and boats. This is regulated in British waters under the Merchant Shipping (Prevention of Pollution by Garbage) Regulations (1988), but these appear to be less than adequately enforced, with only one prosecution to date. The *Reader's Digest* Beachwatch beach-cleaning campaign found that over 50% of all the debris collected was plastic. And as compliance with Annex V is voluntary and has been ratified by only 65% of the gross shipping tonnage of the world fleet, it is all too clear that many ships are still dumping rubbish over the side at sea.

We can all play a part in helping to reduce the amount of litter on our beaches by ensuring that we put our own rubbish in the bin or take it with us.

Other Forms of Marine Pollution

Catastrophic incidents of accidental pollution – the horrific oil spills in the Gulf, the Exxon Valdez incident in Alaska in 1989 and, closer to home, the Braer in 1993 – seem to occur with such regularity that one could be forgiven for thinking they were the main source of oil pollution. In fact accidents of this sort account for only around 10% of the oil that finds its way into the sea each year. The remainder comes from routine losses and controllable discharges. Continual chronic oil pollution is caused by the deliberate and illegal flushing of tanks at sea by the bulk oil carriers, by spills at on-shore and off-shore oil installations during the loading and unloading of tankers and by pipeline fractures which can allow tonnes of oil to escape into the seas each year: evidence of this can be seen in the form of the sticky tar found on many beaches in the UK. Oil has a clogging and smothering effect on marine life. About 60% of dead seabirds found around the UK are oiled; in the English Channel this figure rises to a shocking 75%. Marine life under the water is also at risk: under certain weather conditions the heavier fractions of an oil slick sink to the sea bed, forming an impenetrable barrier under which bottom-dwelling animals and plants may die.

How you can help

A visit to the beach should be a pleasant experience. If you encounter dirty water, sewage, litter or other dangerous items, then COMPLAIN ABOUT IT. If the authorities are unaware of the problem, or think that people don't care, the situation will not improve. There are various bodies – local and national government agencies, the water companies and others – to whom you should report pollution.

If you have a complaint about a beach you visit, please write to us at the Marine Conservation Society and tell us about it. Tell us all you can. We can advise you on what action to take with the relevant authorities, although we cannot act on individual cases. The more we know about the problems around our coast, the more we can do about them.

While local authorities in England and Wales are not responsible for sewage treatment, they are charged with keeping beaches free of litter and safe from dangerous items – chemical drums and canisters, for instance – that may be washed up. If you find something you think might be dangerous, call the Environmental Health Department straight away. On no account touch whatever it is you find. You should also register a complaint if you find the beach littered with drink cans, plastic bottles or discarded fishing nets. The local authority has a legal duty under the Environmental Protection Act (1990) to keep public places clean and free of litter. Tell the Environmental Health Department where the litter is and ask that they clear it up.

These departments are also responsible for publishing the results of bathing water monitoring at the EC designated beaches in line with government policy. The results should be displayed on posters in a clear, easy-to-understand form at the beaches themselves. If they are not, contact the Chief Environmental Health Officer to ask why. Ask that posters be displayed near the beach showing up-to-date water quality monitoring results.

Although tourism departments have no direct responsibility for pollution on the beach or at sea, they stand to lose out if a resort gets a bad name. They are usually quick to act, ensuring that the relevant agency addresses any complaints they receive.

The National Rivers Authority (NRA) is responsible for water quality and pollution incidents in England and Wales. The NRA also carries out the routine monitoring of bathing waters, from the results of which compliance with the EC Bathing Waters Directive is assessed. The River Purification Boards (RPBs) in Scotland and the Department of the Environment for Northern Ireland (DoE-NI) carry out broadly similar roles to those of the NRA.

If you come across an instance of severe sewage pollution in the water, or if there is evidence of other pollution, contact the local NRA or RPB office or call the NRA Emergency Hotline on 0800 807060. They should be able to investigate the pollution and may be able to track down and prosecute the polluter. The addresses and telephone numbers of the responsible bodies are given in the appendix.

The private water service companies are responsible for the operation of the coastal sewage works and outfall pipes around the coastline of England and Wales. In Scotland and Northern Ireland the water industry has not been privatised and sewage treatment is the responsibility of the water and sewerage departments of the Regional Councils and Local Authorities. The private water service companies in England and Wales are currently investing large sums of money in a range of improvement projects, but pressure must be maintained to ensure they do the job properly. Some areas can boast tremendous success stories but in others the improvements are taking place at a barely detectable rate. The implementation of the Urban Waste Water Treatment Directive will see a great deal of investment and a corresponding improvement in coastal sewage treatment. Some water companies, however, openly assert that they will do only the minimum required of them by the Directive and the NRA. Neither their interests nor ours are served by this short-sighted attitude. Not only is sewage pollution deeply unpleasant and potentially hazardous to people using the beach, it is also extremely costly: in the loss of revenue from tourism, in the drain on precious health service resources treating bathing-related illnesses, in legal settlements and fines arising from the increasing number of legal actions filed against the water companies and in the direct costs of picking up sewage-derived rubbish from our beaches.

If you come across an outfall pipe discharging raw sewage near a beach, write to your local water company. Ask whether they consider it acceptable to discharge raw sewage to sea, and whether they are aware of the damage caused by sewage pollution. Ask them also for information about the beaches you visit. How many outfall pipes are there and how many people do they serve? To what level is the sewage treated prior to discharge? Are the outfalls clearly marked with signs giving details of how much sewage is discharged and what sort of treatment it has received? If there is no treatment, why not? Ask for details of improvement schemes. What level of treatment will be provided by the improvement scheme and when will it be completed? Make sure that your local MP and MEP knows your views as well. It is important that they know there are votes in sewage.

If we ask no questions, we will get no answers. Those responsible for coastal water quality must be held to their promises of improvements. We must let the authorities know how we feel. They must understand that we value our precious coastal environment and want money spent on safeguarding it. The capacity of the sea is not infinite and we cannot continue to use it as a giant dustbin. International agreements and national legislation, often only enacted after campaigning pressure from groups like the Marine Conservation Society and private individuals such as yourself, must be enforced and rigorously policed. We still have a long way to go if we are to enter the next century with clean seas. Giving support to organisations such as the Marine Conservation Society is one way to voice your concern. It is the duty of us all to speak out, to report pollution where we see it and to complain about the degradation of a unique resource. The longer we remain silent, the worse it will become. We must act now to safeguard our coast for ourselves and for other creatures, and to ensure that it remains a fitting heritage for future generations.

THE MARINE CONSERVATION SOCIETY
9 Gloucester Road,
Ross-on-Wye,
Herefordshire HR9 5BU.
Tel: 01989 566017
Fax: 01989 567815

The Coastguard
The Coastguard is available to help anyone in danger at sea or on the beach. If you think someone needs help, DON'T HESITATE – dial 999 and ask for the Coastguard.

The National Rivers Authority (NRA)
England and Wales
NRA Pollution Hotline:
0800 807060

NRA Head Office
Rivers House,
Waterside Drive,
Aztec West, Almondsbury,
Bristol BS12 4UD.
Tel: 01454 624400
Fax: 01454 624409

London Office
Eastbury House,
30-34, Albert Embankment,
London SE1 7TL.
Tel: 0171 820 0101
Fax: 0171 820 1603

NRA Anglian Region
Kingfisher House,
Goldhay Way,
Orton Goldhay,
Peterborough PE2 0ZR.
Tel: 01733 371811
Fax: 01733 231840

NRA Northumbria and Yorkshire Region
21, Park Square South,
Leeds LS1 2QG.
Tel: 01132 440191
Fax: 01132 461889

Gosforth Office,
Eldon House, Regent Centre,
Gosforth,
Newcastle upon Tyne
NE3 3UD.

Tel: 0191 213 0266
Fax: 0191 284 5069

NRA North West Region
PO Box 12,
Richard Fairclough House,
Knutsford Road,
Warrington WA14 1HG.
Tel: 01925 53999
Fax: 01925 415961

NRA Severn Trent Region
Sapphire East,
550, Streetsbrook Road,
Solihull,
West Midlands B91 1QT.
Tel: 0121 711 2324
Fax: 0121 711 5824

NRA Southern Region
4, The Meadows,
Waterbay Drive,
Waterlooville PO7 7XX.
Tel: 01903 820692
Fax: 01903 821832

NRA Southwestern Region
Rivers House,
East Quay, Bridgwater,
Somerset TA6 4YS.
Tel: 01278 457333
Fax: 01278 452985

NRA Thames Region
Kings Meadow House,
Kings Meadow Road,
Reading RG1 8DQ.
Tel: 01734 535000
Fax: 01734 500388

NRA Welsh Region
Rivers House/Las-y-Afon,
St Mellons Business Park,
St Mellons, Cardiff CF3 0FT.
Tel: 01222 770088
Fax: 01222 798555

THE RIVER PURIFICATION BOARDS – SCOTLAND
Highlands RPB
Graesser House,
Fodderty Way,
Dingwall Business Park,
Dingwall IV15 9QY.
Tel: 01349 862021

North East RPB
Greyhope House,

Greyhope Road,
Torry, Aberdeen AB1 3RD.
Tel: 01224 248338

Forth RPB
Heriot Watt Research Park,
Avenue North,
Riccarton, Edinburgh.
Tel: 0131 449 7296

Clyde RPB
Rivers House,
Murray Road,
East Kilbride,
Glasgow G75 0LA.
Tel: 013552 38181

Tweed RPB
Burnbrae,
Mossilee Road,
Galashiels TD1 1NF.
Tel: 01896 2425

Solway RPB
Rivers House,
Irongray Road,
Dumfries DG2 0JE.
Tel: 01387 720502

Tay RPB
1 South Street, Perth PH2 8NJ.
Tel: 01738 27989

Department of the Environment for Northern Ireland (DoE – NI) Environmental Protection Division
Calvert House,
23 Castle Place,
Belfast BT1 1FY.
Tel: 01232 230560

The Water Service Companies (WSCs)
England and Wales
South West Water
Peninsula House,
Rydon Lane,
Exeter EX2 7HR.
Tel: 01392 219666

Wessex Water
Wessex House,
Passage Street,
Bristol BS2 0JQ.
Tel: 01179 290611

Southern Water
Southern House,
Yeoman Road,
Worthing BN13 3NX.
Tel: 01903 64444

Thames Water
Nugent House,
Vastern Road,
Reading RG1 8DB.
Tel: 01734 591159

Anglian Water
Ambury Road,
Huntingdon PE18 6NZ.
Tel: 01480 433433

Yorkshire Water
Broadacre House,
Vicar Lane,
Bradford BD1 5PZ.
Tel: 01274 306063

Northumbrian Water
Abbey Road,
Pity Me,
Durham DH1 5FJ.
Tel: 0191 384 4222

North West Water
Dawson House,
Great Sankey,
Warrington WA5 3LW.
Tel: 01925 234000

Severn-Trent Water
2297 Coventry Road,
Sheldon,
Birmingham B26 3PU.
Tel: 0121 722 4000

Welsh Water
Plas-y-Ffynnon,
Cambrian Way,
Brecon,
Powys LD3 7HP.
Tel: 01874 3181

The Scottish Regional Councils

Borders Regional Council
Water and Sewerage Dept,
Regional Headquarters,
Newtown St Boswells,
Melros,
Roxburghshire TD6 0SA.
Tel: 01835 23301

Central Regional Council
Water and Sewerage Dept,
Viewforth,
Stirling FK8 2ET.
Tel: 01786 442000

Dumfries and Galloway Regional Council
Water and Sewerage Dept,
Regional Council Offices,
English Street,
Dumfries DG1 2DD.
Tel: 01387 61234

Fife Regional Council
Water and Sewerage Dept,
Regional Headquarters,
Fife House,
North Street,
Glenrothes,
Fife KY7 5LT.
Tel: 01592 754411

Grampian Regional Council
Water and Sewerage Dept,
Woodhill House,
Westburn Road,
Aberdeen AB9 2LU.
Tel: 01224 682222

Highland Regional Council
Water and Sewerage Dept,
Regional Buildings,
Glenurquhart Road,
Inverness IV3 5NX.
Tel: 01463 702000

Lothian Regional Council
Water and Sewerage Dept,
Regional Headquarters,
George IV Bridge,
Edinburgh EH1 1UG.
Tel: 0131 229 9292

Strathclyde Regional Council
Water and Sewerage Dept,
20 India Street,
Glasgow G2 4PF.
Tel: 0141 204 2900

Tayside Regional Council
Water and Sewerage Dept,
Bullion House,
Invergowrie,
Dundee DD2 5BB.
Tel: 01382 23281

Orkney Island Authority
Council Offices,
School Place, Kirkwall,
Orkney KW15 1NY.
Tel: 01856 3535

Shetland Islands Authority
Council Offices,
Town Hall, Lerwick,
Shetland ZE1 0HB.
Tel: 01595 3535

Western Isles Authority
Council Offices,
Sandwick Road,
Stornoway,
Isle of Lewis PA87 2BW.
Tel: 01851 703773

Leisure and Recreation Contacts

The National Trust
36, Queen Annes Gate,
London SW1H OAS.

The National Trust For Scotland
5, Charlotte Square,Edinburgh
EH2 4DU.

The Manx National Trust
The Manx Museum,
Douglas, Isle of Man.

The Isles of Scilly Environmental Trust
Hamewith,
The Parade, St Mary's,
Isles of Scilly TR21 OLP.

The Heritage Coast Forum
Manchester Polytechnic,
Bellhouse Building,
Lower Ormond Street,
Manchester M15 6BX.

Central Council for British Naturism
Assurance House,
35-41 Hazelwood Road,
Northampton NN1 1LL.

The Royal Yachting Association
RYA House,
Romsey House,
Eastleigh,
Hampshire S05 4YA.

British Sub Aqua Club,
Telford's Quay,
Ellesmere Port,
South Wirral,
Cheshire.
L65 4FY.

INDEX